US Medium Bomber Units of World War 2

Northwest Europe

Jerry Scutts

Ian Allan
PUBLISHING

Front cover:
Lt-Col Robert McLeod's 'Dee Feater' (alias B-26B 42-96142) of the 596th BS, 397th Bomb Group, in post D-Day guise. McLeod named the aircraft after his wife, Dee. *Author's collection*

Back cover (upper):
The three-man crews of the A-20s did sterling work in Europe, although not everyone thought the Havoc an ideal type for the theatre. The gunner in the centre of this 416th Group crew carries the single machine gun operated from the Havoc's ventral position. *Imperial War Museum*

Back cover (lower):
A 554th BS B-26B taking-off from Boxted, the Essex base of the 386th Bomb Group. The fuselage insignia has the new (June 1943) red-outlined 'bars to the star' which gave unit painters a job to find room for the code letters on Marauders.
Imperial War Museum

Title page:
The early-morning sun dramatically catches a pair of B-26s coming off a V1 launching-site target in the Pas de Calais on 25 April 1944.
Imperial War Museum

First published 2001

ISBN 0 7110 2876 1

Published by Ian Allan Publishing

an imprint of Ian Allan Publishing Ltd, Hersham, Surrey, KT12 4RG.
Printed by Ian Allan Printing Ltd, Hersham, Surrey, KT12 4RG.

Code: 0109/B2

Acknowledgements

As ever, my thanks to a number of individuals and organisations that helped make this project happen, mainly on the photographic side: Jim Bivens, Ian Carter, Jim Crow, Richard Denison, Rene Francillon, John Hamlin, Imperial War Museum, Norman Malayney, Merle Olmsted, Jochen Prien Frank F. Smith, United States Air Force and Richard L. Ward.

Worldwide distribution (except North America):
Ian Allan Publishing Ltd
Riverdene Business Park
Hersham
Surrey
KT12 4RG
Tel: 01932 266600   Fax: 01932 266601
e-mail: info@ianallanpub.co.uk

North American trade distribution:
Specialty Press Publishers & Wholesalers Inc
11605 Kost Dam Road, North Branch, MN55056
Tel: 651 583 3239   Fax: 651 583 2023
Toll free telephone: 800 895 4585

Contents

Introduction

Of all the air elements that contributed to the Allied victory in World War 2, that of tactical airpower was the most decisive. To counter any argument that this was not the case, one has only to imagine D-Day taking place without close battlefield support from the air. The armies would have been very hard-put to break the deadlock in Normandy, perhaps to the point where defeat would have been a very real possibility.

The USAAF's Ninth Air Force and the RAF's 2nd Tactical Air Force were primarily responsible for the magnificent air cover that Allied troops enjoyed, from Normany to the Rhine and beyond. The race across France all but ended in the winter of 1944, when the German counter-attack in the Ardennes provided a clear illustration of what could actually happen when the Allied armies were denied the air support they had come to rely upon so heavily.

It was, of course, the appalling winter of 1944/5 that largely enabled the German counter-offensive — the Battle of the Bulge — to be as successful as it was in the early stages. And, as happened surprisingly frequently during the latter half of the war in Europe, the elements appeared to Allied airmen to side very definitely with the Germans — on numerous occasions they felt they were fighting two adversaries!

This book is a record of the part that American tactical airpower — in terms of medium bombers — played in that great conflict in the area known to the participating crews as the European Theatre of Operations (ETO). It re-tells some of the stories of the Marauder, Havoc and Invader medium and light bomber groups that made up part of the Ninth, against a background of the operations they flew and the ground operations they supported. The Ninth was far from alone; able support was provided by several tactical air arms based in southern Europe, three strategic air forces in England and the Mediterranean Theatre of Operations (MTO) — and the ultra-important fighter bombers of its own tactical air commands. All of them contributed to the victory that then really required (and still does require) the 'taking of real estate' by foot soldiers to make it complete. But those same soldiers will do their job that much more easily if they know they don't have to hit the dirt every time an aircraft appears, and if they can rest assured that the guy up there is on their own side. For many a GI slogging his weary way across Europe, Allied air superiority guaranteed him a marginally easier task.

That tactical airpower's contribution was indeed decisive might be further shown by the composition of most air forces since 1945. In the USA, from helping to win the political war to free the air force from the purse strings of the army, US first-line airpower gradually became almost totally tactical in nature. That doctrine survives to the present day — in fact it has all but outlived the much-vaunted (and feared) long-range strategic bomber, the 'big stick' of the Cold War.

A final note about this narrative is to not lose sight of the fact that the US medium-bomber force in Europe constituted 11 bomb groups comprising 44 squadrons plus the Pathfinders and PR units. Covering them all in equal depth is a daunting task, so my apologies for any perceived oversights. Some units have published group and squadron histories, but by no means all, and a really balanced picture will have to await the day when every unit has a history in print. But I hope the following sheds a little more light on medium bomber operations in the European theatre, particularly the poorly-documented record of the units equipped with the Douglas A-20.

Jerry Scutts
London 2001

1 Build-up

Although the Martin B-26 Marauder was no stranger to combat by the time the 322nd Bombardment Group arrived in England in the spring of 1943, this unit was to be the first to operate the aircraft as part of an Eighth Air Force medium-bomber element. There was some kudos in being chosen to open a tactical offensive in company with B-17s and B-24s, and the group, led by Glenn C. Nye, awaited its first combat missions with considerable anticipation. For their part, the aircrews flew one of the 'hot ships' of the Army Air Force — an elegant bomber graced with a very good turn of speed. If anything could get them out of trouble over European targets, it was the B-26. Despite some adverse comments about its high landing speed, and the group's having suffered the loss of six aircraft in the US during training, the Marauder had already been used successfully in combat in the Pacific and North Africa.

Carrying a crew of six or seven comprising pilot, co-pilot, navigator/bombardier, turret gunner, tail gunner and two waist gunners (the number of gunners varied through 'doubling up' by other crew members), the early B-26B production models were fitted with a 'short' wing, spanning 65ft, which contributed to a maximum speed of 315mph — at the time, very good for a 27,200lb medium bomber. Power was derived from two R-2800 Pratt & Whitney Twin Wasp engines, and progressive improvements had given the aircraft more firepower than a contemporary fighter. A 4,000lb bomb load was carried internally, and normal range was 1,000 miles; in its class the Marauder had few equals.

In planning for a US strategic bomber force that would attack Germany from the United Kingdom, it was assumed that a number of groups equipped with shorter-range, twin-engined mediums would be a useful adjunct to raids by the longer-ranged heavies. Having thus planned for two heavy bombardment wings, the Eighth was directed to create a third wing organisation to deploy medium bombers. Without too many proven AAF operational options

open to it, the Eighth chose to follow a low-altitude attack plan for its B-26s, such having been used by the type with some success in the southwest Pacific. As the RAF had also attacked targets in Europe at 'zero feet' with some good results, both with British aircraft and the American Douglas A-20 (the Boston in the RAF), the omens looked good, and the die was cast. It was Glenn Nye who had written a paper stating that such bombing was feasible in Europe, and he was given command of the 322nd Group soon after it arrived in England lacking a regular CO.

The pioneers

As is well enough known, the 322nd's B-26 crews were not the first Americans to fly combat missions from England in medium bombers. That honour fell to selected individuals attached to 2 Group RAF, which then had several Boston squadrons; it was agreed in the spring of 1942 that the British would make room for a number of AAF crews on future operations.

These American airmen, among the first assigned to the Eighth Air Force, were individual members of the 15th Bomb Squadron (Light) who had been seconded to No 226 Sqn at Swanton Morley in Norfolk to gain experience. Becoming part of the Eighth Air Force on 14 May, this AAF unit — an original component of the 27th Bomb Group (L) — had been activated at Barksdale, Louisiana, on 11 February 1940.

Commanded by Maj J. L. Griffith, the squadron had been split from its parent group to become a more-or-less independent unit, and, with hindsight, it could deem itself lucky when the rest of the 27th Group was decimated by the Japanese attack on the Philippines.

Reflecting the hurried actions taken after the US found itself at war, the 15th Squadron had on 26 March 1942 been redesignated (over the telephone!) as the 1st Pursuit Squadron (Night Fighter). It was to go to England without aircraft and fly British Havocs in the night interception rôle, using the Turbinlite system. The American flyers arrived at Grafton

Underwood in Northamptonshire anticipating that they would soon be illuminating German bombers with searchlights for fighters to destroy — a somewhat risky-sounding venture and one that was completely new to the USAAF, which at that time had no night-fighters. After the completion of specialist training, the RAF had agreed to pass on enough Havocs to equip the 15th.

The Americans were then sent to Molesworth in Huntingdonshire, the RAF having in the meantime abandoned the Turbinlite method of interception in favour of airborne radar. This latter, even more interesting rôle was also denied to the American crews, at least in terms of operational flying, although some ground training in the operation of radar and its function was provided. By late May 1942 politics intervened to the effect that AAF Chief Henry H. 'Hap' Arnold, in discussion with Winston Churchill, sanctioned an early entry into combat for this nomadic group of American flyers. It was felt that positive intent would accompany this milestone if it were achieved as soon as possible, before the initial echelons of Eighth Air Force heavy bomber groups arrived in England. The official intention was now that the 1st PS (NF) should revert to its original designation and gain combat experience by flying standard day-bomber sorties with an RAF Boston squadron.

As the 27th Bomb Group had taken delivery of its first A-20s at Fort Benning, Georgia, in 1941, the crews of the 15th Squadron were not inexperienced at flying the Douglas attack bomber, but being exposed to war conditions in Europe would be something new. While the bulk of the AAF men went to No 226 Squadron at Swanton Morley in Norfolk, some were attached to No 107 Sqn, which also flew Bostons, from a second Norfolk airfield at Great Massingham.

After a few weeks' working-up period, which involved learning RAF operational methods, the Americans were deemed ready for their baptism of fire. This was undertaken gradually, with individuals making up crew rosters on RAF operations for a few weeks before the

15th's debut mission with a full US crew. This took place on 29 June 1942, when 12 Bostons attacked railway yards at Hazebrouck, one machine (AL743/MQ-L) being flown by Capt Charles Kegelman and his American crew. All the Bostons returned safely.

A number of British-contract Boston Mk IIIs had meanwhile been made available to the 15th BS, and on 1 July the American contingent suffered two fatalities — Capt S. F. Strachen and Lt C. R. Mente — when Z2200 crashed on approach to Molesworth. At the time this aircraft was technically part of No 107 Squadron and still bore that unit's RAF code 'OM'.

Independence Day raid

A broadening of the American medium-bombing effort took place a few days later, six crews of the 15th joining No 226 for a 4 July attack on German-held aerodromes in the Netherlands: De Kooy, Bergen, Haamstede and Valkenburg. The American-manned Bostons carried four-man crews, the force being completed by six RAF aircraft with three-man crews for the mimimum-altitude operation. Charles Kegelman's crew were briefed to attack De Kooy, and they experienced a hair-raising mission; well used to Allied air attack, these important Luftwaffe bases (around 200 in total) were skilfully defended. Kegelman's Boston was hit and the right engine caught fire after the propeller was shot away, flak bursts also damaging the right wing. As Kegelman was trying to keep control, his Boston actually struck the ground, but it bounced back up again and flew on. Noticing a flak-tower crew swinging their weapons around, Kegelman let fly with his nose guns. No fire came from the tower.

De Kooy ground fire meanwhile claimed the Boston III (AL677/MQ-P) flown by Lt F. A. Loehrl and his AAF crew, which went down on fire in the target area from a flak hit. Only one member of the crew, Lt M. Draper, survived to become a PoW. Even worse was the fate of Lt W. G. Lynn's crew, briefed to attack Bergen. The Boston (AL741/MQ-V) reportedly broke up after being hit by flak north of the target, all of Lt Lynn's crew perishing as a result. In addition, No 226's Z2213/MQ-U was lost to enemy fighter attack when Uffz Hans Rathenhow of 10./JG 1 caught and shot it down over the sea. Crews of No 226 reported the flak as the worst they had ever encountered, and it was suspected at the time that coastal craft known as 'squealers' had used their radio sets to forewarn the German airfield commanders of the impending raid.

While this symbolic Independence Day mission achieved little in military terms, it underscored US commitment to the 'Germany first' policy agreed by the Allied high command. The positive publicity generated by this gesture enforced the pledge that the USAAF would remain in Europe for as long as it took to defeat Nazi Germany. More positive publicity stemmed from the ceremony at Molesworth on 11 July, when Gen Ira C. Eaker, Eighth Air Force commanding general, presented the Distinguished Service Cross to Charles Kegelman and his crew — Lt Dorton and Sergeants Cunningham and Golay. The 'Independence Day raid' went into the

Above: The first aircraft used by the Eighth Air Force for medium-bomber operations were borrowed RAF Bostons. Maj Charles C. Kegelman (second from right) won the DFC for his part in the 'Independence Day raid' in 1942. Boston III AL750/G, with 14 operations completed, was 'Keg' Kegelman's personal aircraft. *Imperial War Museum*

records as the first by the Eighth Air Force in World War 2.

The Dutch airfield raid had stressed the deadly opposition to low-level raids represented by the German flak crews, and for a time the 15th continued its rather lonely war as the only USAAF bomber squadron flying missions from England — although crews had plenty of company in the form of their British allies flying the same type of aircraft.

A theatre transfer of Boston IIIs from RAF stocks saw 23 machines re-marked with the white star of the USAAF, the American crews flying three further combat missions during the summer and autumn of 1942. Abbeville/Drucat airfield was attacked on 12 July, again using British-marked Bostons. On that occasion the Bostons made their target approach at 8,500ft in deference to the deadly low-altitude flak they had encountered before. All aircraft returned safely.

Above: Transferred from RAF stocks, this Boston III (AL452) was taken over by the 15th BS (Light) for several Eighth Air Force operations from England before the unit departed for North Africa in late 1942. *R. L. Ward collection*

Above: American groundcrews of the 15th Bomb Squadron (L) working on a Boston III at an airfield in England. *Imperial War Museum*

Between the July raid and the next one to Le Havre on 5 September, the 15th BS prepared 17 of the ex-British Bostons, and the Eighth Air Force began combat operations in earnest. By the latter date, missions had been flown by B-17s, P-38s and two AAF groups of Spitfires.

On an unspecified date towards the end of their service, the Bostons apparently acquired the only identity marking they were to carry — a single aircraft letter on the vertical tail surfaces; otherwise they retained standard RAF camouflage and serial numbers.

The Bostons, identified as DB-7Bs in American records, dropped 44 500-pounders on the Le Havre port area without loss or incident, and returned to Abbeville aerodrome on 6 September to release another 48 500lb bombs, again with no noticeable reaction by the Germans. And that was almost that.

On 13 September the 15th Squadron had moved from Molesworth to Podington, Bedfordshire, and after flying another 12-ship mission (11 sorties were effective) to Le Havre on 2 October, the unit stood down to prepare for further overseas movement, destination Tebessa, Algeria. It duly shipped out, to continue operating DB-7s (later A-36s) as an independent unit in time for Operation 'Torch' that November. The 15th was assigned to the Twelfth Air Force and existed until 1 October 1943, when it was deactivated.

This was not to be the end of operational sorties by US-marked DB-7s/ A-20s from the UK, as the 10 DB-7B aircraft left behind when the 15th BS departed were used on second-line duties. In addition, 13 Havoc Mk Is and six Mk IIs (DB-7 and -7A sub-types in US records) were passed to the Eighth in February 1943 for reconnaissance duties. Converted to carry cameras, these aircraft were deployed by the 153rd Squadron of the 67th Observation Group (redesignated a Reconnaissance Group after May) and based at Keevil, Wiltshire. A number of A-20Bs which had arrived in the county during late 1942 were similarly converted for the PR rôle, and these were issued to the 153rd OS beginning in April 1943. They largely replaced the obsolete ex-RAF Havocs, which were passed on to B-26 groups to tow targets for gunnery practice.

The 67th RG was itself short lived in the ETO, being redesignated and then disbanded late in 1943, Eighth Air Force

Gunnery and Tow Target Flights taking over the A-20Bs for crew training, mainly from Goxhill, Lincolnshire. There they joined the surviving DB-7Bs on similar duties. Others found their way to combat units and headquarters organisations for various second-line communications and liaison flying duties, and not until the spring of 1944, when the 416th Bomb Group arrived, would another AAF unit fly regular A-20 combat missions from the UK.

Long wait

No further expansion of the Eighth Air Force medium-bomber force would actually materialise for nearly a year, despite the fact that by late October 1942 England was playing host to the 47th BG at Horham with A-20s, plus one B-25 and three B-26 groups, the latter awaiting their aircraft. While the 15th BS 'pioneers' became part of the build-up for Operation 'Torch', these other units remained only briefly in England before similarly departing for North African bases to join the Ninth or Twelfth Air Forces.

Such were the demands of the USAAF in the Mediterranean during and after 'Torch' that the Eighth Air Force was, for the time being, denied any trained groups to constitute a medium-bomber force, even one of modest size. The winter of 1942/3 came and went while new B-26 units trained in the US to reach the point where they could be effective in combat. A delaying factor to them doing so any earlier was the protracted training programme necessitated by the high performance of the Marauder, which was rumoured to be proving quite a handful for student pilots used to more sedate aircraft.

The beautifully-streamlined B-26 had a landing speed of 130mph, which was about 20mph higher than average for a bomber; it cruised at fighter speeds and appealed more to the 'snappy, alert flyer', as one informed source put it. It could be quite unforgiving of inattention, sloppiness or indeed a US training régime that was hardly very sophisticated. It was further stated by those in a position to know that the B-26 appealed to pilots who understood what 'seat of the pants' flying was all about. Small wonder that it took little to upset some of the ultra-conservative elements who held sway in the Air Corps at the time it first appeared. Fortunately it was the men who flew the B-26 in combat who were to prove its undoubted capabilities.

It was ultimately decided that groups equipped with the B-26 (and subsequently the A-20) would be attached to the Eighth's Third Wing, and, although the strength that would be despatched to England remained to be finally decided, the 322nd Group was the first of four Marauder units selected to operate in the European Theatre. When Brig-Gen Fred Anderson, Third Wing CO, visited Bury and realised that the 322nd Group had no authorised CO, he charged Glenn Nye with that responsibility, as acting group CO. Brig-Gen Francis Brady took over command of the Third Wing in April.

Multiple targets

Notwithstanding the gallant effort by 2 Group RAF, which had striven to give the German tactical targets little peace since the first weeks of the war, there were numerous other targets in occupied Europe, particularly factories, ports, power generating plants and airfields, that lay within range of mediums such as the B-26. While some of them had been repeatedly bombed by the British and occasionally by US heavies, the RAF had few tactical bombers that could survive enemy defences without prohibitive losses, and American Fortresses and Liberators were needed for the more distant targets in Germany.

Less important though the potential targets in French, Belgian and Dutch territory undoubtedly were compared to Germany's aircraft factories, shipyards, seaports and industrial areas, the Allies could hardly afford to ignore them. A great many manufacturing plants had fallen into enemy hands virtually undamaged during the invasion of France and the Low Countries in May-June 1940, and the majority, by coercion or commercial necessity, were working directly for the German war effort. And, of course, the Luftwaffe had occupied most of the captured continental aerodromes. Fighter Gruppen of JG 1, 2 and 26 were based in France for lengthy periods, these units, along with elements of others, often changing their location as the tactical situation demanded.

The geographical spread of these targets covered a huge area, from Belgium, down through Holland, to the south of France. Those that lay within a rough arc out to a maximum distance of about 400 miles from the nearest British airfield could ostensibly be attacked by medium bombers.

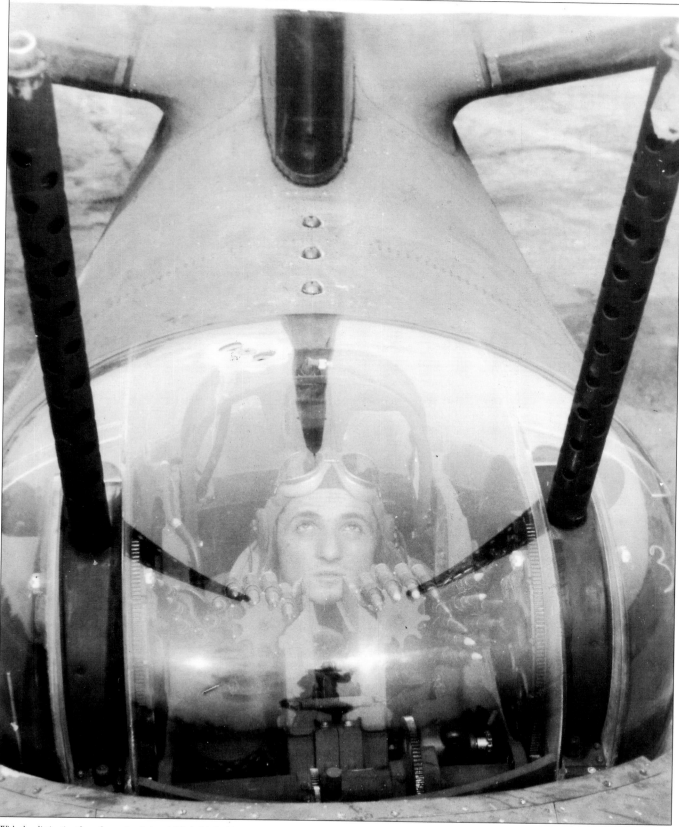

With the distinctive three formation lights visible behind, this view of the virtually frameless Martin turret of the B-26 shows to advantage its near-perfect visibility. *N. Malayney*

Groundcrew's-eye view of the left landing-gear well of a B-26 parked on a section of steel-plate matting. The shape of the fuselage package guns can be seen to advantage. *J. Hamlin*

Apart from deploying the de Havilland Mosquito (itself in short supply as a bomber at that time), the RAF was hard-put to attack them all because it had too few suitable aircraft. Destruction or severe damage to even a percentage of the targets was therefore very difficult — in fact, until 2 Group had almost fully re-equipped with modern American medium bombers, the majority of the potential targets would remain untouched. It would have been ideal if a major effort to destroy or cripple them could have come from USAAF units which had potentially better aircraft with the required range and capability. Such an offensive would also have brought closer the day when an Allied invasion of northwest Europe could have taken place — a goal uppermost in the minds of American air chiefs when formulating the 'Germany first' war policy.

There remained the question of the most effective altitude the bombers should adopt against targets that always had to be assumed to be well defended by flak and fighters, as most were. By their very configuration, the US medium bombers of World War 2 were limited to carrying bombs of up to 2,000lb in weight, or a maximum of 4,000lb in the case of the B-26 (in some instances the maximum load carried was a good deal less), which in turn meant that only multiple formations of as many bombers as could be practically deployed could cause damage severe enough to make the Eighth Air Force's Third Wing a potent force. Those bombers would be made available, but, until the early operations in the Western Desert had helped defeat Rommel's Afrika Korps, most types of aircraft were in short supply.

Low-level choice

When it was decided that the B-26 would be the mainstay of AAF tactical squadrons based in England, with the B-25 undertaking a similar rôle in the MTO, and the A-20 divided between both theatres, the planners made an assumption. Based on combat reports showing how well the Marauder had done in the Pacific by flying at low level to avoid the worst attentions of Japanese fighters, it appeared to have a good chance of repeating that success in Europe. There were precedents: a number of low-level attacks by RAF aircraft far less able than the Marauder (particularly the Blenheim) had been fairly successful under the right conditions.

Lacking a viable alternative operational plan, the 322nd Group would follow suit. If the fast and well-armed B-26 could indeed survive at 'zero feet', it was optimistically anticipated that it could probably do so even without a fighter escort, which would be doubly welcome.

At that stage of the European air war, the US heavies were continuing to take punishment on most daylight missions, and fighters with the range to escort them across Holland and France and a short distance into Germany were worth their weight in gold. P-47s and P-38s were too few in number for many to be spared for medium-bomber escort until the Eighth could be substantially strengthened by new groups.

Good as the B-26 was, its crews were occasionally experiencing a tough time against Axis opposition in North Africa, where low-level attacks had not proven to be much of a guarantee of survival or of accurate bombing of small targets. In addition, during accelerated training at home, the Marauder had picked up an unfortunate and ill-founded reputation as a dangerous aircraft, bringing it under the scrutiny of an independent committee chaired by one Harry S. Truman. This Senate Special Committee was a watchdog body set up to investigate the national defence programme and to report honestly on problems and/or malpractice of any description and at any level in regard to the industrial and technical support of the US war effort.

As far back as 1941 the committee had interviewed Glenn Martin himself and asked specifically why the Marauder had been built with wings that were 'not wide enough'. Martin replied that by then the design had been set and the current contract was too far along to make significant changes. According to one source, Truman replied that if the B-26 were not given a bigger wing, he would have the contract terminated — which he certainly had in his power to recommend, if not carry out. Martin extended the Marauder's wingspan without delay — a modification that certainly improved the aircraft. Having already come down hard on the manufacturer in respect of the Marauder's perceived poor safety record during its early crew-training period, Truman would continue gunning for the aircraft for some time to come.

This was the situation as the 322nd Group prepared to fly its debut mission against the power-station complex at

Ijmuiden in Holland: it had a potentially excellent aircraft which was nevertheless picking up some adverse criticism even before it had had a chance to prove itself. There were almost bound to be some doubts that only a successful combat record in Europe would dispel.

Comprising the 449th, 450th, 451st and 452nd Bomb Squadrons, the 322nd had existed since 17 July 1942 and had thereafter trained on the B-26 at MacDill Field in Florida, before the first movement overseas was made in the spring of 1943. The first aircraft arrived in England on 7 March. As ever, the 322nd crews were confident that they and their new bomber could make the grade in combat. In performance terms there was little to touch it, certainly not in the AAF or even in the combat-hardened RAF at that time.

When a low-level combat deployment of the B-26 was decided upon, the 322nd indulged itself in further hours of flying training, this time at 'zero feet' over England, much to the consternation and/or excitement of the local population around the group's airfield at Bury St Edmunds in Suffolk. A satellite airfield for use by the group was established at nearby Rattlesden, where advanced ground echelons had arrived late in 1942.

When the Marauders began their theatre training, local reaction to the sight and sound of hedge-hopping bombers ranged from positive to very negative, depending very much on the age of the observer! For their part, most of the aircrews enjoyed the experience, although one or two had reservations about the inherent danger of such a practice, and some crewmen were shaken to the point of vomiting after a particularly 'hairy' flight. Much depended on which seat an individual occupied in a Marauder, for few had ever flown in a medium bomber at altitudes quite like this.

Before the first raid took place, the 322nd, which had arrived in the UK with the B-26B-2, had received the B-26B-4. Still configured with the 'short wing and short tail' which identified the early models of the Marauder, this version had four forward-fuselage package guns, which were operated by the pilot, and a 6in extension of the nosewheel leg, which improved the aircraft's ground angle. A bulge had to be made in the forward part of the nosewheel doors to clear the repositioned retracting mechanism.

As with most US aircraft operating in the ETO, the Marauder had to have

Above: Armourers trundle the bomb-load under the bay of a Marauder during a bright day in 1943. Sunshine was often a rare commodity on medium-bomber missions in Europe. *Imperial War Museum*

some equipment changes. These included the fitting of radio sets compatible with those used by their British hosts, an important requirement being to provide IFF (Identification Friend or Foe) capability. In addition, to bomb effectively from low level, the 322nd's aircraft required the replacement of the Estoppy D-8 bombsight with a modified N-6 or N-6A reflector gunsight. This enabled the co-pilot to drop the bombs via a release button on the end of a cable, an *ad hoc* arrangement which nevertheless worked well enough. Each B-26 navigator, who normally occupied a compartment behind the flightdeck, used a newly-installed compass from a seat in the nose.

Encouraging debut

Nearly one year on from the day 15th BS personnel made their initial foray over Europe in Bostons, the 322nd Group undertook its first raid on a European target, on 14 May 1943. Twelve crews,

Above: This may show the same base as that in the previous photo, but exact details are unknown. The B-26 had flown six bombing and two decoy missions, as the bomb log and tiny duck symbols indicate. *Imperial War Museum*

drawn from the 450th and 452nd Squadrons, would fly the mission without fighter escort, although a larger force of Liberators operating elsewhere was expected to occupy enemy fighters. Take-off for the B-26s was at 09.50hrs, with group commander Lt-Col Robert M. 'Moose' Stillman acting as deputy lead, flying a B-26B-4 (41-17995/DR-T) named 'Tondelayo' on the right wing of the lead Marauder. This, Capt Othel D. Turner's B-26B 'Lorraine' (41-18099/ER-V) was being flown on the mission by Capt Roland Scott. Leading the flights from the 452nd Squadron was Capt F. F. Rezabeck, whose aircraft, 'Chickasaw Chief' (41-17999/DR-W) carried Brig-Gen Brady as an observer.

The target for the 322nd was the PEN electricity-generating station at Velsen, which adjoined Ijmuiden; its importance lay in the fact that the plant supplied power to much of northern Holland — power that was now additionally harnessed to the German war effort.

All 12 participating aircraft had taken off by 09.56 hours, and climbed out to maintain 250ft over England. The formation dropped to 50ft over the sea, the leading Marauder crews soon looking out for their first reference point — the hotel at Noordwijk on the Dutch coast. By 10.52 they had crossed into Holland and were racing above the dunes and fields, picking up some light flak and small-arms fire as they went.

Several of the Marauders were damaged by shrapnel from bursting shells, with the result that seven crewmen sustained wounds. Among the worst-hit was the aircraft flown by Lt Robert C. Fry of the 452nd Squadron. Its port engine and rudder having taken 20mm fire, 41-19785/DR-Q (named 'Too Much of Texas') wallowed. Luckily used to flying a Marauder on one engine, Fry held it steady, but, realising he would be hard-put to maintain speed and altitude on one engine, decided to abort the mission before the target run-in. He turned for home, jettisoned the bombs into the sea and flew back to England, aiming to put down at the first available airfield. This turned out to be Great Ashfield, which had only recently been completed.

Meanwhile 11 B-26s sped onto the target and climbed to 250ft to clear the plant's tall chimneys. As the lead flight dropped their load and exited over the

target, the flak grew heavier and far too close for comfort: Capt Roland Scott was badly wounded by a shell which struck the top of his windscreen and showered the cockpit with fragments. The second flight also took hits, although this formation was more widely spread to make sighting more difficult for the enemy gunners. The B-26 flown by Lt John Howell (41-17988/DR-R) was also badly damaged during the course of the operation, which resulted in 43 500lb bombs being dropped without any explosions, due to the delayed-action (DA) fusing.

Howell nursed the crippled Marauder back to England and ordered his five-man crew to bail out. He then attempted either to make a landing at Bury St Edmunds or to bail out himself, but the Marauder crashed with him still aboard. Examination of the wreckage suggested that it probably went out of control as the pilot left the cockpit in an attempt to abandon it — a not unusual occurrence in the B-26.

Despite this sobering incident, the crew casualties and the obvious results of AA fire on the airframes of the B-26s, there was a great sense of achievement at Bury, as the raid appeared, from initial crew reports, to have been a success. It was only when the subsequent RAF reconnaissance photographs were studied that doubt set in. The photographs were very sobering: no material damage appeared to have been done to the power station, and the Marauder crews were both surprised and annoyed. Bombardiers of the 322nd were not the first (nor would they by any means be the last) to swallow the bitter pill of implication that they had simply missed. But, despite the fact that some official latitude was built into bombing performance on a debut mission, there was no denying the stark evidence seen by the PR camera lens. What the crews saw in this case was an industrial plant barely scratched by any of the bombs aimed at it.

At the time it was felt that using British Mk VIII bombs with 30min delayed-action fusing was the root cause of the apparent lack of damage, it being assumed that the Germans had had a chance to remove them — that and the fact that the Dutch had been forewarned that, if any Allied bombers appeared over targets in their country, the delay would give them time to get clear.

Harsh reality

What the crews of the 322nd could not know or see on the PR photos was that, for a new group on its first mission, the bombing results had actually been fairly good. Some of the bombardiers who swore they had bombed accurately were correct, while others had indeed missed. The suspicion that some of the bombs were duds was also true, as was the fact that British DA fuses could take even longer than 30 minutes to detonate individual bombs. Half the force — four and possibly five crews — had dropped their bombs on the power-station complex.

In view of the visible results, however, there was little alternative — the 322nd would have to return to Ijmuiden and attempt to finish the job. Eighth Air Force target lists were drawn up in accordance with comprehensive war plans with the help of much intelligence data, and to ignore the first and go onto the next one, as might have seemed prudent in this case, was not the way things were done: if numerous targets were missed, the list could not be modified and extended. And the bombs that had hit Ijmuiden had not actually caused widespread damage, as correctly indicated by the aerial photographs.

When he heard the news that the group would return to the same Dutch target, Robert Stillman protested to the point of insubordination to Gen Brady. All officers present, including Brady, appeared to agree that a return to Ijmuiden was an acute risk to the B-26 crews, although no-one seemed to realise that the low-level approach was flawed, Stillman included. He had earlier been warned off such tactics by Gen Joseph Cannon, who had experienced low-level operations by B-26s in North Africa and found them to be too costly.

Although the Marauder crews were disappointed at the results of 'first Ijmuiden', there was some satisfaction throughout the group that a unit and aircraft new to the theatre had been able to penetrate Europe's defences without losses, the low altitude seemingly taking the Germans by surprise.

Three days later, the 322nd was briefed for a return to Ijmuiden. It was decided that crews from the 450th and 452nd Squadrons, those who had not generally participated in the first mission, would go this time. Able to field only 12 aircraft on 17 May, the 322nd was not alone in heading for a European target at low level that day, for Eighth AF headquarters concurrently sent a wing of B-24s to the U-boat base at Bordeaux at an altitude of 2,500ft. A slight change in the Marauders' target schedule was that six aircraft would bomb the Ijmuiden powerplant, whilst six would attack a second plant at Haarlem. The duration of the raid would be about two hours.

TABLE 1

B-26B-4 Marauders on the second Ijmuiden raid, 17 May 1943:
452nd Bomb Squadron: callsign 'Blueroad'
41-17979/DR-O (Purinton)
41-17982/DR-P (Stillman)
41-17991/DR-S (Wolfe)
41-17998/DR-V (Matthew)
41-17999/DR-W 'Chickasaw Chief'(Wurst)
41-18052/DR-N (Garrambone)
41-18080/DR-K (Converse)
41-18090/DR-L (Norton)
450th Bomb Squadron: callsign 'Snellgrove'
41-18058/ER-S (Stephens)
41-18086/ER-U (Jones)
41-18099/ER-V 'Lorraine' (Crane)

Briefing completed, the men of the 322nd piled into their aircraft. Lt-Col Stillman, who had had a premonition of disaster and was convinced that he would not be coming back, rode with Lt E. J. Resweber, taking the place of the latter's co-pilot. The Marauders took off, adopted a two-element 'javelin' formation, and dropped down to low (about 50ft) altitude. Over the North Sea, the B-26s skirted some fishing boats right in their flight path just in case they may have been German-manned and armed, and possibly equipped with radios. This turn away from a potential source of danger helped seal the fate of the 322nd for it put the bombers 18 miles southwest of their intended landfall.

As the Marauders approached the coast of Holland, one B-26, piloted by Capt Stephens, experienced engine trouble followed by power loss to the turret and was forced to abort. Unfortunately, as per standard procedure to get some altitude whenever there was any malfunction, Stephens initiated a gradual climb to around 1,000ft, thereby warning — or so it was believed at the time — the ever-alert

German radar that some further enemy-bomber activity was building. Luftwaffe airfields within range of the incoming raid were alerted, and, although the low altitude adopted by the 322nd's formation had thus far resulted in its being hidden from radar detection, when Stephens climbed away his B-26 was rapidly left behind, and few of the other crews saw it go.

Unaware that their cover had been blown, the B-26 skippers boosted their engine manifold pressure to 40in and charged into Holland at just over 230mph. Stillman saw columns of water in front of him as the enemy gunners tried to pick off the bombers before all of them made a landfall. Anxious eyes searched for the railway track and canal that would lead them into Ijmuiden after a turn. That they could not be seen was due to the fact that the Noordwijk area over which the group should have passed lay miles off to their left. Instead, the 322nd had run in over the mouth of the River Maas, where the shoreline was well protected by light AA and machine guns.

Immediately the crews saw the winking lights of the flak, the formation was spread out to make aiming more difficult for the enemy gunners. As it was, the Marauders were very low, some of them barely scraping the ground, with just 15-20ft under their bellies. There was no margin for error.

Flying at the head of his group, Stillman noted machine-gun fire from the coastal sand dunes. Using his package guns, the 322nd's commander strafed the dunes as he raced inland, his fire appearing to silence two emplacements, but then a third stream of fire went into the Marauder. Stillman felt himself losing control as the bomber went into a snap roll. One wing down, the aircraft turned over seconds before ploughing into the ground, inverted, at 200mph.

Stillman's next conscious memory was of being carried on a stretcher by two German medical orderlies. Seconds after Stillman's aircraft crashed, the flak systematically chopped down the B-26 flown by Lt Garrambone, which plunged into the Maas.

A collision between Converse and Wolfe brought down no fewer than three Marauders, two in the initial contact and one (Wurst's 'Chickasaw Chief') as a result of exploding bombs and flying debris. The low altitude gave the crews

little chance of avoiding such a disaster, but all of Wurst's crew survived when the pilot brought off a belly-landing in a field at Meije, north of Bodegraven. The Ijmuiden return mission was becoming more of a *débâcle* with every passing minute.

Over Holland, things were going from bad to worse. An air-raid alarm received four minutes after the Marauders were seen over Rozenburg was responded to by the FW190As of II./JG 1 based at Woensdrecht. Twenty-six fighters lifted off at 11.55, and, although their controller estimated the bombers' altitude as 3,500ft, the American aircraft were soon seen below the formation. Two '190s' from each flight were despatched to deal with what were understandably identified as 'Havocs'. Attacks by the fighters flown by Fw Kurt Niedereichholtz of the II. Gruppe Stab accounted for Crane's Marauder, from which two survivors emerged to clamber into a liferaft. No such luck attended the Matthew crew, all of whom perished after Oberfw Ernst Winkler shot their B-26 down into the North Sea west of Zandvoort at 12.30hrs.

Stillman, undergoing hospital treatment before being moved to a prison camp, learned later that, by some miracle, 10 officers and 12 enlisted men had survived the *débâcle*. All 11 Marauders, with a total of 60 men aboard, had been shot down. Stillman marvelled that anyone had survived.

Back at Bury, the groundcrews sweated out the mission long past its intended two-hour duration. Only when no B-26 appeared and no news was received of diversions to other airfields was the awful truth realised.

Gradually the salient facts of the 'second Ijmuiden' emerged: two survivors able to offer first-hand details of the fighter attack a few days after the raid were Staff Sergeants Jessie Lewis (tail gunner) and George Williams (engineer) from the Crane crew. Manning a waist gun and having tried in vain to help Lewis deter the Germans, Williams realised the aircraft had taken mortal damage from cannon fire. Both men had ridden the bomber down to ditch and taken to their liferaft. After drifting in the North Sea for several days, they were rescued by a Royal Navy destroyer. But the stark, overriding fact was that, apart from the early return, none of the B-26s on the mission had come home — a disaster in anyone's view.

Taking over what was understandably a very despondent group of men, the new 322nd Group commander — soon confirmed as Glenn Nye — waited while higher authority considered what to do next. A thorough investigation was promised into why the 322nd had been decimated on 17 May, but it was clear that the policy of sending medium bombers out at low level had fundamental flaws. The risks of losing the vital element of surprise were high and the consequences could obviously be disastrous.

When the results of the second Ijmuiden mission became known in Washington, the powers that be were understandably appalled, and there were those eager to hammer a final nail into the coffin of the Martin B-26. Truman's zealous committee deliberated and recommended that production of the B-26 should be cancelled forthwith. Perhaps not realising the full implication of this drastic action, the committee's collective hand was stayed. But in England the morale among B-26 crewmen at Bury St Edmunds was at rock bottom; few of the air or groundcrew personnel on the base would have been surprised if orders for their immediate transfer had arrived without further delay. That they did not was fortunate in several ways.

Chagrined that low-level attack missions appeared to be virtual suicide in the ETO, the Army planners had to come up with alternatives. Clearly the enemy defences were murderous against bombers operating at less than 5,000ft: the Germans had developed a range of light- and medium-calibre guns to defend every variety of target. And used *en masse*, these could be lethal to aircraft, whatever their speed. Swift reaction to Allied air raids from the Luftwaffe fighter force had added to the danger on the low-level mission to Ijmuiden.

It was finally decided to deploy medium bombers such as the B-26 in the rôle for which they had been designed — bombing from 12,000 to 15,000ft altitude. Other than in bad weather, which could often obscure an industrial target completely, making the bombing run from a much higher altitude seemed a sounder practice in

Above: Flak was more deadly to B-26s than were enemy fighters, and 'flak suits' and GI-issue helmets helped protect the crews from splinters. Wearing the suits here are Sgt William F. Vermillion (left) and Lt Ralph M. Phillips (with seven mission bombs painted on his helmet), of the 455th BS, members of the crew of the B-26C (41-34692) 'Mr Fala', named after Roosevelt's dog. *Imperial War Museum*

Above: Along with the B-26, the medium-bomber crews based in England relied heavily on bicycles to get about. The aircraft is named 'U.S.O.', after the well-known American entertainment organisation. *USAF*

Europe. The operating conditions in the theatre, as many airmen soon appreciated, were not comparable to those anywhere else.

To ensure that combat flying over Europe was made as safe as it could be, the 322nd practised not only new, close formations but also evasive action. This was essential if the enemy gunners could be kept guessing for a few vital seconds, and it became standard procedure for the Marauders to alter course or change their altitude every 20 seconds, but doing so demanded skill and observation. It was obviously necessary to ensure that the formation did not stray too far off course and to get back on track before the Initial Point (IP) on the bombing run. Routes into the targets were planned to avoid known concentrations of flak, and the 'big wing' B-26B had an armoured panel under the cockpit windows to protect the pilot. The Eighth Air Force fashioned a similar plate for the co-pilot's side, and crew members were issued with body armour. Each man was also supplied with a standard GI steel helmet which was worn over enemy territory.

After much experimentation and discussion on formations and numbers, it was decided that each group should operate 36 aircraft in two elements (or 'boxes') of 18. Each box adopted a different height and flew as the 'high' or 'low' formation; the latter ('trailing') box was usually lower than the first. In time a highly-concentrated bomb pattern could be achieved, provided that each aircraft in the boxes maintained station with its neighbour.

Bombs and sights

To improve bomb patterns, the groups tried a number of methods; a shortage of Norden sights led to a standard procedure whereby only the lead and deputy lead in a three-ship element carried a sight, the others in each following flight or the rest of the box dropping on the lead's signal. The bombs were usually dropped in salvo by using the intervalometer — a device which, as its name implies, could time the interval between the release of each bomb from its rack in the internal bay. All Ninth Air Force medium bombers relied on a single internal fuselage bay, only the A-20 being capable of boosting the load with bombs carried on underwing racks.

Early-model Marauders actually had two bomb bays, but the aft one was rarely used for anything other than a ferry tank or a storage bin for ammunition for the tail guns, particularly when the shorter Bell tail turret was fitted, starting with the B-26B-20. The aft bay was eliminated from the B-26B-35 and subsequent models.

Marauders generally carried a maximum bomb load of 4,000lb, this being made up by the armourers according to the mission field order, which detailed the type of target to be attacked and its distance from base. The latter factor was very important, as an extreme-range mission would dictate the load accordingly — although it is true to say that this was never so critical a factor with mediums as it was with heavy bombers.

The first operational B-26s in the Eighth Air Force had their loads made up with the bombs originally supplied for use by the heavies — the M30 100lb, M31 300lb, M43 500lb or M44 1,000lb, or a combination of two or more types. In late

Armourers checking the rear guns of a 452nd Squadron B-26 fitted with the much-improved Bell tail position, which shortened the fuselage by some two feet.
N. Malayney

1943, American bomb designations were changed, with the M57 250lb being added and the M64, M65 and M66 identifying 500lb, 1,000lb and 2,000lb bombs respectively. Whereas the most commonly-used small bomb was the 250-pounder, the 300lb size was used by the B-26 for certain missions, as was the 100lb variety.

Most USAAF aircraft, the B-26 included, could also accommodate British bombs in the above weights, with adaptors attached to the integral suspension lugs, if required. The bombs most commonly used were of the high-explosive, all-purpose (general) type, although variations with special-purpose warheads, including semi-armour piercing (SAO) and fragmentation (FRAG) in the same general weights as the HE type, were used by American mediums. Two 2,000lb bombs could be accommodated by the B-26 as a maximum load; the weight could also be made up by incendiaries, which were produced in standard weights and sizes and were often carried in streamlined containers shaped like conventional bombs.

Dodging the flak

Despite being able to detect a force of US bombers from some distance by radar, the German flak crews had accurately to calculate their range and speed, and try to follow any evasive action, which served to foil even radar prediction and proximity-fused shells on numerous occasions. The difference between shell avoidance or impact was measured in mere seconds, and, when committed to their bomb runs, the crews of the mediums knew their options were limited. But by alternately executing shallow turns, climbing or diving, there was a good probability — indeed it happened on numerous occasions — of the shells missing whole boxes of aircraft when they combined timely evasive action with a pass over the target at a good turn of speed.

Barrage firing, where the bombers had no choice but to pass through a dense belt of shell detonations, often caused peripheral damage and crew casualties but rarely destroyed an aircraft unless it took an unlucky direct hit which knocked out an engine, exploded in the bomb bay or punctured the fuel tanks. Even when any of these disasters overtook individual aircraft, the bail-out and overall survival rate among crews flying the American mediums was gratifyingly high, if total losses of aircraft and personnel are considered. In percentage terms the cost in human lives was significantly lower than comparable figures for other wartime air operations.

Checking the results

To assess bomb damage with as much accuracy as was possible from the air, the AAF drew up a list of categories. Using post-mission PR photographs, photos from strike cameras in the bombers and combat reports, the results were analysed in terms of bomb pattern and classified. The categories 'good', 'excellent' or 'superior' appeared at the top end of the scale, but the planners were forced to concede that some early medium-bomber missions returned some 'poor' to 'fair' results while the crews gradually gained the necessary experience. Even as they did so, some bombing continued to be classified as 'gross' — the worst possible rating. This usually meant that a crew, flight or entire box of aircraft had missed the target completely, sometimes by a very wide margin.

To check the bombing results, plots were made up to indicate all impact points and detonations, these radiating out from the aiming point (AP) and mean point of impact (MPI). The MPI was centred on the target and was the undisputed evidence of where bombs had actually fallen. Ideally, it should have had most of the bursts grouped together on or in close proximity to it, provided that the aiming had been good. This was not always the case; some bombs invariably fell wide of the target for a variety of reasons, and for some time the difficulty lay in correcting such errors. Crews may have released on the signal of the lead or deputy lead bombardier as they

Below: Considering how often fighters escorted the early Marauder raids, little photographic evidence seems to have survived showing both types of aircraft in the same frame, but a turning Spitfire is just visible in this view from a B-26 cockpit in 1943. *Imperial War Museum*

had been briefed to do, but had failed to allow for wind conditions (ie the degree of drift), or had not come exactly back on track after evasive action (however brief). Aircraft damage, leading to bomb-release malfunction, and numerous other factors could also adversely affect accurate aiming. These ranged from the loss of the pathfinder aircraft, or that carrying the lead navigator and sometimes the deputy lead as well, to simple navigational error. Missing an important turning point over unfamiliar territory could compound the problem, the classic mistake being wrongly identifying a town on the flight into the target. All these events connived to throw an operation badly out of kilter.

When Air Support Command, under Brig-Gen Robert C. Candee, returned to the business in hand in the summer of 1943, it was stronger in several respects than the 3rd Wing of VIII Bomber Command had been: it had more Marauder groups, improved aircraft, a much sounder operational plan, and crews who had a better appreciation of how demanding a theatre of the war the ETO could be. And these groups would not venture far beyond England's shores without protection; in order for the B-26s to be effective, they were to be assured of a fighter escort so strong that the Luftwaffe would think twice before taking it on. In consequence the American bombers were covered by multiple squadrons of RAF fighters, the majority of them Spitfires.

Escort tactics

To provide adequate protection for their American charges, it was agreed that 11 Group, which commanded scores of Spitfire squadrons based mainly in southeast England, would shoulder the main responsibility of escorting the American B-26s. RAF pilots (flying mainly Spitfire Mk Vs and IXs during the main period of Marauder-escort operations) operated in full squadron strength of 12 to 18 aircraft, adopting a rough 'V' formation composed of three flights of four to six machines. In line-astern formation, they were stepped down from front to rear. Visible (and comforting) to the bomber crews was the close support — a squadron of Spitfires stationed about 1,000yd on each side of and about the same altitude as the bomber boxes, which usually maintained a height of 11,000 to 12,000ft. An escort cover composed of another squadron of fighters patrolled at

3,000 to 6,000ft above the bombers to guard against any attack on the bombers or their close support. Finally, a high cover was maintained 2,000 to 5,000ft above the escort and out of sight of the bombers.

Such precise positions were naturally subject to revision and change, particularly as the Spitfire pilots were obliged (depending on their escort position) to weave, to avoid out-running their charges. In the event of combat, the fighters tried their best to regain their basic escort positions and, as always, to fly as pairs for mutual protection. Although the fighters were faster than the B-26, the escort position from the former's viewpoint was more comfortable than it was when covering slower bombers. Pilots confirmed that the Marauder was a better aircraft in this respect than most other Allied types, and pilots of Typhoons, which later supplemented the Spitfire squadrons, were quite complimentary on the ease with which they could maintain station with the American mediums.

Bomber crews were naturally reassured by their highly-visible fighter escort — few things boosted morale more than seeing their 'little friends' on patrol. For its part, the RAF decreed that the fighter leaders could, at their own descretion, turn the bombers back if they felt that conditions were too bad. Low visibility risked separation of fighters and bombers, with consequent increased danger to the latter.

The aftermath of the Ijmuiden raid had led Washington and the Eighth Air Force high command seriously to reconsider the merits of having a medium-bomber force based in England, although there was certainly a need for it. By mid-1943 the RAF's tactical bomber force was only beginning to re-flex its muscles with new aircraft. The majority of these were the US light and medium bombers obtained under Lend-Lease arrangements.

In the meantime, 2 Group Bomber Command, with the able assistance of Fighter and Army Co-operation Commands, continued to take the air war into occupied Europe during the hours of daylight. The Boston had become a dependable and well-liked type, the command anticipated the operational debut of the Ventura and Mitchell, and there were several squadrons equipped with the Mosquito. As desirable as it might have been to re-equip the entire group with Mosquitos, this did not prove to be possible, so help in the form of an American light and medium force would

therefore be very welcome. There were no plans as such to integrate AAF and RAF medium-bomber operations, but an American contribution to the Allied tactical bombing offensive would continue the process of whittling down Germany's industrial base in occupied Europe.

Fortunately for the Allied war effort, the AAF realised that it could ill afford to strike aircraft such as the B-26 from the inventory, as there was little to replace it. And while the American 'arsenal of democracy' would eventually build all types of combat aircraft in unprecedented numbers, much of the industry was still building up to that pitch in mid-1943. Had the B-26 indeed been cast aside, the Eighth would probably have received the B-25 and A-20 to fill the gap, although both types were heavily committed to the MTO and the Pacific. Retention of the Marauder was therefore little short of essential.

For the time being the 'short wing' B-26B and C models intended to equip the four groups originally assigned to the Eighth Air Force continued to be delivered to home-based units and be readied for movement overseas. Advanced echelons of the 323rd — the second of these groups — were ferried over the South Atlantic route to begin arriving in England on 27 May, when the Ijmuiden raid was still a potent talking point. Men of the 323rd Group's squadrons — the 453rd, 454th, 455th and 456th — naturally wondered how they and their aircraft would fare in combat. The responsibility resting on the shoulders of group commander Col Herbert Thatcher was not exactly a source of great envy!

June '43

Part of the 386th Bomb Group was also in England by June, and on the 12th the Marauder force was formally transferred from Eighth Bomber Command to Eighth Air Support Command, the existing Third Wing administrative organisation being retained. Air Support Command, which had originally been intended to direct a force of dive bombers in the ETO, had not been officially activated up to that time, and an intensive theatre re-training programme was initiated for the attached B-26 units in order for these groups to make a fresh start over Europe as soon as possible. The final echelon of the 387th Group, with its component 556th, 557th, 558th and 559th Bomb Squadrons, had also arrived in England by 25 June.

Above: One of the most striking tail markings of Ninth Air Force B-26s was the yellow and black 'tiger stripes' applied by the 387th Group to its Marauders. *J. Hamlin*

It was fortunate that, in July, command of the Third Wing would pass to a very able and respected officer, Col Samuel E. Anderson. When he moved into wing headquarters at Mark's Hall, near Braintree, Anderson learned that the USAAF had decided to postpone the movement of further B-26s to England, and, in response to criticism by the Truman Committee, had implimented moves to terminate production of the B-26. A Marauder pilot himself, Anderson was appalled at the lack of foresight and the implication that the Martin bomber was little more than a failure. He knew otherwise.

The Eighth Air Force's Air Support Command groups were transferred to airfields in Essex for further training (the so-called 'Doughnut' sorties) in medium-altitude bombing — a move that put them about only 300 miles from continental targets. The groups were distributed thus: the 322nd went to Andrews Field, the 323rd moved to Earls Colne, and the 386th occupied Boxted. Chipping Ongar was the allocation for the 387th.

Andrews Field, the new home to the group that had (perhaps in defiance of any further portents following the Ijmuiden disaster) adopted the nickname 'Nye's Annihilators', had formerly been known as Great Saling. The base had been renamed on 21 May, shortly after it had opened. The reason for this unique 'Americanisation' of a British aerodrome was to honour General Frank M. Andrews, one of the nation's most

Above: A 554th BS B-26 taking-off from Boxted, the Essex base of the 386th Bomb Group. The fuselage insignia has the new (June 1943) red outlined 'bars to the star', which gave unit painters a job to find room for the code letters on Marauders. *Imperial War Museum*

respected airmen. Lost in a B-24 crash on 3 May 1943, Andrews was greatly missed. His shoes were hard to fill, particularly as he had been named eventual successor to Dwight D. Eisenhower as commander of all US forces in the European theatre.

Before they began combat operations from England, all B-26s — and other American aircraft — had to have their radio communications changed to comply with the British system, particularly so that the emergency channels could be used to obtain headings to home or diversionary airfields, and to make contact with the air-sea rescue services. Specialist ground engineering teams had consequently to install VHF radios to replace the US HF sets. Fitting armour-plate protection for Marauder co-pilots was a large-scale 'field modification', as was the installation of a more operationally-suitable compass. Such labour-intensive work was necessary on all aircraft in a bomb group. And the work had to be completed without delay if the B-26 force was to return to combat within a matter of weeks, as was required. The list of modifications was lengthy, and only those absolutely necessary could be carried out in the time available.

For the revised ETO rôle of medium-altitude bombing, the Marauder required a better sight than the D-8 which Martin continued, for the time being, to fit in production aircraft. There was little question that the M-series Norden sight was the key to achieving accuracy, but delays in delivery of these sights was one factor that put back the reappearance of the B-26 in the AAF order of battle for the ETO.

Switching the bombing requirement from below 2,000ft to 12,000ft-plus was one thing; having the crews become proficient in the revised rôle was something that could not be achieved overnight. As far as the crews were concerned, the B-26 was a low-level bomber; pilots had to be re-trained to use the Pilot Direction Indicator (PDI), which enabled the bombardier to 'fly' the aircraft for the duration of the bombing run, reading directions off the Norden.

To compound the Third Wing's problems, two squadrons of the 323rd Group had brought with them Omaha-built B-26C-6s configured for single-pilot operation. While lightening the Marauder was a welcome move, taking out the co-pilot's seat, all his controls, some of the armour plate and a radio set was not a modification that was greatly appreciated by front-line commanders, to say the least!

The reason for the changes to the B-26C-6 could be traced to the flawed 'low level' deployment doctrine, which put much of the attack responsibility onto the pilot, whereas the European theatre demanded a full team effort. Although they disliked the 'one man' Marauders, the flight crews of the 323rd had little choice but to fly them in combat and try to minimise their drawbacks. A solution was partially achieved by ensuring that standard 'two pilot' B-26s always occupied the lead position in all flights participating in a combat mission, with the B-26C-6s tucked further back and bombing on signals.

Fortunately, the other Marauder squadrons that had recently arrived in England had been equipped with B-26B-10s and later-production B-26Cs, both of which had the larger vertical tail surfaces and increased, 71ft wingspan. Both these features bestowed much-improved directional stability and 'lift'

compared to the early B-26Bs — but new models of American aircraft, however much they had been improved, still needed modifications to tailor them to Europe's operating conditions. This in turn increased the workload of the groundcrews and caused delays, but, to their credit, the ground maintenance teams were outstanding. They were as eager as anyone to see their flyers prove themselves.

Work was particularly feverish in the hangars and workshops of the 323rd Group at Earls Colne, for it was this unit that was slated to initiate the B-26's medium-bombing phase of operations. At last everything was as ready as it would ever be; a mission to the marshalling yards at Abbeville was scheduled for 16 July.

Sixteen aircraft took off at around 18.00hrs and climbed to rendezvous with their Spitfire escort at 10,000ft. Fourteen Marauders found and bombed the target, releasing 16.75 tons of bombs. The flak responded to wound two American crewmen and damage 10 aircraft, but none was shot down. The jubilation at Earls Colne when all 16 aircraft appeared in the landing pattern can be imagined.

For some AAF individuals there remained one more symbolic milestone to be reached: the successful return to combat of the 322nd Bomb Group. This was not long postponed, and on 17 July the group was officially put back on combat status. There followed a busy period before the group made its second ETO 'debut'.

This mission, a run to the coke ovens at Ghent on 25 July, was flown by the 323rd, which despatched 18 B-26s. These dropped 16 tons of bombs, and, although six aircraft were damaged by flak, there were no crew casualties. The 323rd flew mission number three on the morning of the 26th, but only 15 out of the 18 aircraft involved managed to locate St Omer/Fort Rouge aerodrome, the briefed target. The B-26s dropped nearly 15 tons on the airfield at 11.15hrs. Occasionally the mediums were escorted by USAAF fighters rather than the RAF, and on 27 July 119 P-47 Thunderbolts shepherded the crews of the 323rd. Those who took part in the mission at least felt confident that, with a huge fighter escort, the Luftwaffe would once again all but ignore their incursions into occupied Europe. Seventeen aircraft bombed Triqueville aerodrome, 18 tons of bombs being released by the Marauders at 18.25hrs.

There was another run to knock out coke ovens for the 323rd on the 28th, 17 aircraft flying to Zeebrugge to drop 33,000lb of HE bombs at 11.05hrs. In an attempted second mission for that day, the group set out but failed to rendezvous with the P-47 escort, and the 18 B-26s intending to make a repeat visit to Triqueville were recalled. Missions in the morning and afternoon were quite feasible in the longer summer days, providing that the weather remained fine.

On 29 July a double airfield strike was planned for the 323rd, while the 386th flew its first shakedown mission. In the morning, 18 of the 323rd's B-26s brought their bombs back without attacking Amsterdam/Schiphol, which was found to be cloud-covered. The B-26s headed out a second time, late in the afternoon, to strike St Omer/Fort Rouge aerodrome. The bombers arrived at 18.30hrs to drop more than 18 tons of bombs, flak resulting in damage to eight aircraft. It was for this later raid that the freshman 386th was briefed. Dragging their collective coats not too dangerously, as they were covered by 128 P-47s, the group's 20 B-26s made a feint towards the St Omer region in an attempt to dissuade the Luftwaffe from intercepting the 323rd. One FW190 pilot unwise enough to pick up the gauntlet had his aircraft damaged in the single fighter action reported by the escort.

Following three shakedown missions in co-operation with the 323rd, the 386th at Boxted was alerted for its first bombing mission. The target was Woensdrecht aerodrome in Holland. The moment could not have come soon enough for Lt-Col Lester Maitland, CO of the group which was later to take the name 'Crusaders'. An old campaigner himself, Maitland had gained his wings in 1916, and, at 45, he was twice the age of most of his crews. Despite that, he 'led from the front', and was on the flying roster for many of the group's early missions.

At 05.25hrs, the 24 Marauders, six from each squadron, began their take-off roll. As the group was new to combat, the briefing had been somewhat chaotic, with men leaping to their feet to quiz the intelligence officers about every detail of the mission. Flak and fighters were naturally hot subjects.

As the aircraft took-off in a steady stream at half-minute intervals, everything seemed in order. Pilot 1st Lt Ray Williamson thought so too as he fed in the

Above: Early-morning preparation of Marauders for a mission involved removing protective covers from turrets to prevent damp from playing havoc with delicate mechanisms. This typical morning scene shows aircraft of the 323rd Group. *J. Hamlin*

power to get 'Two-way Ticket' off. The B-26 cleared the perimeter and its gear had come up — but at less than 100ft one engine suddenly died. Williamson had few options and he crashed back down, flying straight ahead, into a field across the road from the aerodrome. Very shaken, all his crew emerged with cuts and bruises. Few could believe their luck; the B-26 lay engineless, broken beyond repair. Above their heads roared a Marauder that would serve the 386th appreciably longer. This was 'Rat Poison', a group stalwart that would ultimately brave the wrath of 'Fortress Europe' more than 100 times.

Over the Channel, the 386th's crews tried to anticipate what lay in store for them. They soon found out. Rendezvousing with their Spitfire escort, the bombers raced into Holland, puffs of flak coming close enough to rip the skin of several aircraft. Watching for the element leader's red nacelle light to come on to signal the point of bomb release, the pilots made the bomb run, but haze intervened and only half the force were able to release their loads.

As they turned away from Woensdrecht, the Marauders came under attack from FW190s of JG 26. The day had already been a sobering introduction to combat in the ETO — and now the appearance of enemy fighters provided another rush of adrenalin. Telling the inexperienced crews that this sort of thing would happen only infrequently from then on would hardly have

convinced anyone, for the phrase 'flak and fighters' had become synonymous with combat in Europe for many American flyers. As the fighters came in, the bomber gunners blazed away at them for all they were worth. This hot reception did not prevent Lt Karl 'Charlie' Willius of 3. Staffel from making short work of 1st Lt Glenn F. Zimmerman's B-26, which spun into the Scheldt with no sign of survivors. One of the gunners was picked up by Dutch fishermen, only to be taken prisoner later.

In an action which the B-26 crews swore lasted three minutes but which was actually over in a few seconds, one FW190, piloted by Lt Heinrich Sprinz, went down as he came in on what the Jagdflieger identified as Bostons. Only eight Focke-Wulfs were involved, but in the confusion the Americans 'saw' 15 or more plus Bf109s, and the gunners were credited with six destroyed and five probables. That even a single German fighter actually succumbed to the bombers' fire was quite an achievement considering the relative experience of the combatants, which must have been well loaded in favour of the fighter pilots.

On 31 July the 322nd made its second combat 'debut' in the ETO; to the great relief of everyone involved, from the group commander down to the lowliest clerk, this was not a repeat of the Ijmuiden disaster, as some doom merchants might have predicted. Bad news travelled fast in the service, and many people were convinced

that the 322nd was a 'hard luck' group equipped with a dangerous aircraft. By successfully sending out a mission to Triqueville aerodrome with 18 aircraft, the unit laid a ghost to rest. Thirteen aircraft managed to drop 16 tons of bombs. Hero of the hour was Lt-Col Robert C. Fry, who had gained some early fame by landing a B-26 on one engine. This time he also lost an engine during the course of the mission. Forced to shut it down completely, Fry headed for home, where he again made a successful emergency landing. In the days when such a feat was still thought to be well-nigh impossible (mainly, it must be said, by those who did not fly Marauders), Fry was heartily congratulated. And, just to show that such flying skill was not the proverbial 'flash in the pan', Fry went on to make more 'engine out' landings, his total of six being rumoured to be higher than that of any other B-26 pilot. Robert Fry flew combat with the 322nd until the ill-fated night mission of 7/8 July 1944, when he was shot down and became a PoW.

Four separate missions were flown by the Marauders on 31 July — the largest-scale effort to date. The 323rd flew a double in the morning, 18 Marauders appearing over Merville aerdrome and 19 over Poix/Nord at 11.20hrs, to drop a total of 44 tons of bombs. One B-26 from the force attacking Poix was lost along with its seven-man crew, and seven other aircraft sustained flak damage. Apart from the 322nd, the 386th was also out, its second-mission target that day being Abbeville/Drucat aerodrome. Flak response there was aggressive enough to cause damage to five of the B-26s.

The foregoing week of operations showed that the B-26 crews had quickly put the ill-advised low-level doctrine behind them. It was perhaps not very surprising that a medium bomber designed as such was doing well on missions at those altitudes best suited to its capabilities.

Diversionary raids to draw enemy fighters away from actual targets became standard procedure for AAF units based in England. Such sorties were valuable in that they did sometimes divide the defences, and they gave new crews a taste of the operating conditions, a view of the European terrain within their range, and perhaps a sight of the opposition. They invariably drew a little flak, to highlight the main hazard the medium bombers would continue to face.

August '43

Despite the fact that it was supposed to be summer, the weather over the UK and the Continent now began its tricks to disrupt a number of air operations in late July-early August. On 30 July the 323rd Group had been forced to return due to fog covering its airfield target, and on 2 August the 322nd's mission to Woensdrecht was cancelled while a combined total of 49 Marauders were sent by the 323rd and 386th to the enemy aerodromes at Merville and St Omer/ Fort Rouge respectively. The flak reacted, to put holes in 28 of the bombers; one B-26 was so badly damaged that it had to make a forced landing in England. Six crewmen were wounded.

Opening with scrubbed missions on the 2nd and no flying on the 3rd, August would bring more indicators that German flak was potentially far more damaging to medium bombers than any other form of defence, including fighters, few of which ventured to penetrate the RAF fighter screen and the massed fire from the dozen or so 'fifty calibre' machine-gun positions on each Marauder. In reality only six or seven guns (nose, turret, waist and tail) per aircraft would usually be brought to bear on fighters diving from above, or making beam or tail intercept passes. Lucky indeed was the B-26 pilot able to loose off a broadside from his package guns plus the fixed gun positioned in the plexiglass nose and hit a fighter coming in from straight ahead — and unlucky the Jagdflieger who lingered long enough directly in front of a Marauder formation to be shot down. It did happen, but rarely.

The shipyards at Le Trait, near Rouen, gave the 322nd Group bombardiers a different target viewpoint as they hunched over their Norden sights on 4 August. The 33 Marauders that reached the target area dropped 60 500lb GP bombs from 11,000ft and hit a power station, boiler rooms and manufacturing areas plus several vessels dry-docked and on slipways. The raid, which left the entire waterfront area wreathed in smoke, was an outstanding example of precision bombing, with no resulting crew casualties or aircraft damage, despite reaction from the flak defences.

After a quiet 48 hours, another mission was aborted on 8 August when cloud covered Poix airfield, and it was not until the 12th that a successful B-26 mission could again be carried out. On the 9th, the 322nd and 386th had flown to St Omer

only to find the target airfield obscured by cloud. Injury was added to insult when radar-predicted flak nevertheless found the bombers' altitude, put holes in 11 Marauders and wounded six men.

Further recalls marked the early-August period, the Marauder force continuing to draw enemy airfields as its main targets on the days when attacks were possible. Often requiring repeat visits to keep them closed, airfields were relatively easy to locate and hit. For its part, the Luftwaffe fighter force became adept at moving its units around to circumvent damage at its forward bases. Many such locations had already became 'bomb magnets', obliged to absorb many hundreds of tons of high-explosive before they were eventually abandoned. That was one reason Marauder groups tended to aim their bombs not at the runways but at the taxiways, hardstands, hangars and adjacent buildings. It was rightly reckoned that more lasting damage could thus be inflicted, particularly amongst dispersed aircraft and storage and repair facilities.

There was a maximum effort by the Eighth Air Force on 12 August, with the First and Fourth Bomb Wings sending out their B-17s in force, supported by four groups of P-47s. The 322nd and 323rd Groups meanwhile attacked Poix/Nord airfield, 71 B-26s dropping 161 tons of high-explosive in the process. On this and other missions during the summer, the B-26s of ASC served in an indirect support rôle to the heavies by concurrently bombing Luftwaffe aerodromes when long-range strategic missions were flown. If the mediums could wreck enemy aircraft on the ground, destroy facilities and burn fuel stocks, then there would be slightly fewer German fighters to challenge the B-17s and B-24s on their way home to England.

Quartet of groups

On 15 August the 387th Bomb Group finally got into action after a frustrating and protracted training period for all personnel involved.

When this, the fourth unit in the Third Bomb Wing, achieved this milestone, it gave the command a nominal strength of 256 B-26s, assuming that the basic AAF establishment of 64 aircraft per group remained constant. This total (which was later increased) obviously fluctuated as a result of repair of combat damage or unserviceability, as did the authorised 16 aircraft per squadron laid down for a medium-bomber group. The optimum-

sized group formation of 36 aircraft on combat missions made due allowances for attrition, and, with a total of upwards of 250 B-26s in the four groups, a sizeable enough force was available, and one increasingly capable of inflicting severe damage on a range of enemy targets, notwithstanding the weather and strong defences.

Other raids on tactical targets in August continued the encouraging pattern of low crew casualties in the B-26 force. Although flying shrapnel from close-proximity flak bursts put numerous holes in some of the aircraft that flew these missions, no crew fatalities had occurred for some weeks.

On 18 August, ASC missions (Nos 25A and 25B in Eighth Air Force records) saw the 322nd and 386th Groups briefed to bomb Ypres and Woensdrecht airfields in Belgium while P-47 fighter sweeps were flown in support of the mediums. For the bombers these were secondary targets, as the primary — Lille/Vendeville aerodrome — could not be reached due to bad weather. No American aircraft were lost from either force, although 31 B-26s returned with varying degrees of battle damage. The day also recorded the first mission by the 67th Reconnaissance Group flying the A-20 — a type familiar enough in England but as yet relatively rare on combat missions with American units. Two aircraft flew PR sorties to the Lannion/Brest and Penn areas, the Havocs being escorted by Spitfires of No 610 Squadron.

On 19 August unseasonal weather brought about a smaller-than-planned attack on enemy aerodromes: the 323rd sent 36 B-26s to Amiens/Glisy, while the 387th despatched 35 of its Marauders to Poix. The 322nd's target was to have been Bryas Sud, but thick cloud cover caused the mission to be abandoned.

As the weather showed little sign of improving, Headquarters ordered no further operations by the mediums until the 22nd, and even then only the 386th managed to carry out the mission as briefed. The group put 35 B-26s over Beaumont-le-Roger at 21.10hrs. Intending to take another crack at Poix, the 322nd was again frustrated; the mission was abandoned when its RAF fighter escort failed to materialise. Poix was spared another visit from the Marauders on the 23rd, both the 322nd and 386th being obliged to forgo their bombing due to cloud cover.

The mediums left the French airfields to the heavies on 24 August, B-17s from the First and Fourth Wings doing what they could in less-than-ideal weather. As the heavies also needed visual conditions for bombing, they did little better than their smaller counterparts.

Apart from several crewmen wounded in operations towards the end of the month, the rest of August passed with but three B-26s lost, one of them in a landing accident. Taking-off late in the somewhat brighter afternoon of 25 August, crews of 21 B-26s from the 387th Group attacked a power station at Rouen at 18.32hrs, dropping 63 1,000lb bombs in the process. Two minutes after the last of the 387th's B-26s headed out, 36 322nd Group aircraft were above Triqueville in the third attack on this aerodrome within a month. At least 65 craters were made by the bombs going down across the airfield from west to east at 18.34. Crews observed a large hangar in the western

dispersal destroyed by a direct hit and another severely damaged, also by a direct hit, and several near misses. In what was identified as an oil-storage area, a workshop was swept by fire, and there were observable craters in roadways and taxiways in the northern dispersal area. Other buildings were also damaged. The Germans did not take all this passively, and the flak made holes in two Marauders but without causing any crew injuries.

PR overflights and crew observation determined that damage done at Bernay/St Martin aerodrome was accumulative, the base having been attacked by 36 Marauders on 16 August and again on the 25th. To the 42 craters made by bombs in the earlier raid were added some 63 more on the runways and aircraft taxiing areas, with bombs having fallen on the dispersal area.

Caen/Carpiquet was bombed by 36 B-26s without loss on 26 August, and at least 30 bomb bursts from the 47 tons

dropped were observed in the area of the former aircraft assembly plant of SNCA du Nord. Three hits and some near misses were scored on the main building occupying this site. Twenty bursts were seen on the main runway, and a small hangar in the southern dispersal area was also seen to receive a direct hit.

From the other side

If they were undeniably making life on the ground difficult at numerous aerodomes under Luftwaffe occupancy, the planners of the US medium bombing campaign had their own problems. For example, accurately determining the degree of damage to airfields in northern and western France and the Low Countries was rendered more difficult for Allied photo interpreters by the flexible system used by the Luftwaffe. This was on the lines established before the war whereby one operational unit was normally dispersed on a number of permanent bases

Above: On 17 August 1943 the 322nd Bomb Group blasted Bryas-Sud aerodrome. B-26B 41-34949 was snapped as it began to turn away from the target. *Imperial War Museum*

Left:
Left:
A B-26B-30 being readied
for eventual combat on
18 August 1943 after its
transatlantic ferry flight.
Imperial War Museum

Above: Crews from the famous Dam Busters of No 617 Sqn RAF, including American Joe McCarthy (fourth from right), visited a crew of the 452nd BS on 18 August 1943. A 'long tail' B-26B (41-17750) provided the backdrop, with a Marauder of the 323rd Group's 456th BS in the right background. *Imperial War Museum*

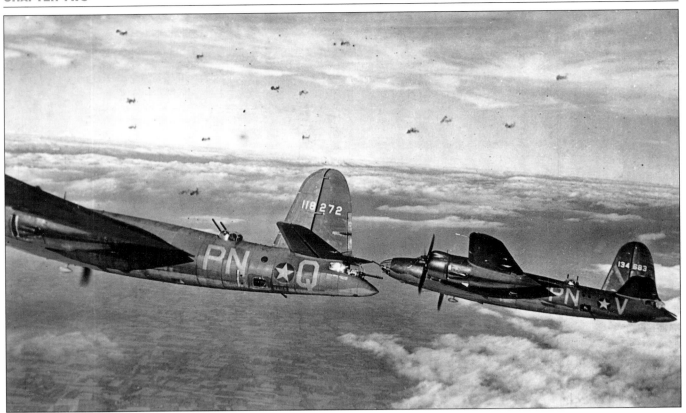

Above: In August 1943 the British Ministry of Information released some of the first of many thousands of photographs of USAAF medium bombers in action from England. That month Pfc Ben Rosenblatt of the 322nd BG took a series of frames during his first operational mission. *Imperial War Museum*

Above: Another famous Rosenblatt picture, showing B-26B 41-34683 of the 449th BS in typical early 322nd Group markings. The diagonal tail stripes seem to have been an early attempt at formation markings, which were not apparently very effective, as they were soon removed. *Imperial War Museum*

and used a network of forward bases, as required. Maintained by a skeleton staff which performed the basic duties needed to keep them open in the event of the flying unit coming in, usually for a short period, the system worked well enough in Germany and elsewhere. Much the same arrangements were made with captured airfields.

By late 1943 the above areas of France contained the most aerodromes, although there were considerably fewer than the 400-plus which had existed in 1940. Those that remained were more than the enemy could possibly have used even by deploying a manyfold increase in the number of flying units on the Western front — indeed, it was said that the entire Luftwaffe could have been accommodated, had there been such a need!

Many major operational bases were developed by the Germans during 1940/1 and these invariably covered a very large area, often with lengthy supplementary runways laid well outside the normal boundary of the landing ground itself and with many dispersals sprawling over miles of adjacent countryside. One of the original reasons for spreading everything out had been to make airfields almost impossible to disable in night bombing attacks. Furthermore, it was intended that all Luftwaffe units using these bases could do so in a degree of comfort. Most locations had two or three dispersal areas, and each was a self-contained unit with a repair hangar, fuel and ammunition stores, usually widely separated and well camouflaged against detection from the air.

When the Allied tactical bomber offensive did result in damage, some of it considerable, the flexible system of using alternative aerodromes more than paid off. It meant, for example, that there was seldom any need to implement repair work with great urgency, particularly when there was every likelihood of the bombers' returning. It very much depended on where the airfield was: reconnaissance photos showed little evidence that some heavily-cratered landing grounds were being repaired immediately, while others were cleared up in 12 to 48 hours. At some locations, work dragged on for weeks. At still more, no effort to put things right was in evidence at all.

With unlimited land areas available, the Germans tended to bulldoze a new operational strip rather than to keep repairing runways that had already been

heavily bombed, and where there would be added risk to personnel if more raids were mounted.

Emergency landing strips could be completed quickly, and, of course, the Germans usually had pools of labour upon which to draw for such work, although an assortment of workers was actually used, from Luftwaffe personnel to local inhabitants, political prisoners and PoWs. Airfield construction gangs could not easily be formed at every location, however, and a shortage of transport became acute in some areas. Another factor contributing to an uneven programme of runway repair was the psychological effect of air attacks. These often demoralised everyone, particularly the flak crews, as the base would rapidly be evacuated by almost all other personnel as soon as an alert sounded, leaving them stranded at their lonely posts. Flak duty in remote areas became intensely disliked, as did the staffing of an unoccupied aerodrome — particularly if those in charge were obliged to maintain a lonely state of readiness for weeks on end.

On 27 August the 386th Group flew an early-morning, 35-sortie mission against Poix/Nord aerodrome; 542 tons of bombs were unloaded by the B-26s at 08.26hrs, no enemy reaction being reported. The Germans did, however, respond to an incursion by the 322nd, fighters intercepting and shooting down one B-26. Six others were damaged before the group withdrew, the crews feeling disgusted at the turn of events considering that the target — another power station at Rouen — could not be bombed due to heavy cloud cover.

More flak damage was sustained by Marauders of the 323rd Group, which despatched 33 aircraft to an ammunition dump at Eperlecques on 30 August. 'Bombs away' was at almost exactly 19.00hrs, 49 tons being dropped. Fourteen aircraft were damaged and three crewmen wounded.

It was the turn of the power station and chemical plant at Mazingarbe to be visited by the Marauders on 31 August, the 322nd Group fielding 33 aircraft. Bombing at 07.18hrs, the force dropped 48 tons in return for damage to a single B-26. Less lucky in terms of losses was the 387th, which had a single B-26 shot down by the flak defending its aerodrome target, Lille/Vendeville. Thirty-six aircraft had set out fom England and 31 of these dropped nearly 54 tons of GP bombs with

reportedly good results, a closely-grouped concentration showing up clearly on the strike photos. A spectacular explosion in the dispersal area touched off what was believed to be an underground store of fuel or ammunition; crews witnessed a column of smoke reaching to at least 400ft, this later being observed to be even higher by oblique photo reconnaissance. Two crewmen were wounded in addition to the six in the downed Marauder, all of whom were listed as Missing in Action (MIA). Also out over France that day, the 322nd and 386th Groups failed to bomb through a solid overcast which completely obscured their targets.

Invaluable combat experience, both in bombing and bad-weather flying, was gained by the Marauder force during this period; it was achieved in return for a very low loss rate at a time of peak Luftwaffe strength in northwestern Europe, which was a huge boost to morale. Targets were, in the main, being hit hard despite the formidable flak defences. The record, which spoke for itself, would stand the B-26-equipped groups in good stead and help towards the creation of an overall bombing record that was very encouraging indeed. While Marauders handled the bombing missions, further A-20 PR sorties were flown by the 67th RG, which was equipped with a mixed force of combat aircraft and was, in common with the B-26s, transferred to the Ninth Air Force in October.

September '43

During its penultimate month as a constituent part of the Eighth Air Force, the Third Bomb Wing's B-26 force maintained the pressure on German targets in the face of indifferent weather. The elements intervened on 2 September to oblige a force of 216 Marauders to reduce its effective sorties to 104 bombers, which dropped just short of 150 tons of bombs on fuel dumps and airfields located in the Rouen-Hesdin-Lille areas. The 386th and 387th Groups each split their strength into two, ostensibly to attack targets simultaneously, but dense cloud cover prevented the latter unit from bombing anything. The 386th's 'half force' of 36 aircraft (less one) did, however, manage to unload over Mazingarbe, with fair results. In return for its disappointing effort, the 387th lost an aircraft and had 13 damaged, which in human terms totalled five men wounded and six MIA.

Third Wing medium bombers flew missions on consecutive days between 3 and 6 September, the targets including airfields and marshalling yards at Courtrai, Hazebrouck and Ghent. With just over 30 Marauders each attacking the airfields at Beaumont-le-Roger, Beauvais/Tille and Lille/Nord, the results appeared to be fair to good, all participating aircraft returning safely. Escorting Spitfires saw action, seven enemy aircraft being claimed for the loss of three British fighters.

The 322nd Group achieved a well-concentrated bomb pattern on the La Déliverance marshalling yards at Lille on the 4th, 33 aircraft releasing their loads at between 9,500 and 11,000ft. Engine sheds, sidings and adjacent industrial areas were badly damaged, the overall results of the bombing being officially classified as 'good'.

On the 5th, 72 B-26s were despatched against the marshalling yards at Ghent — a mission that also produced good bombing results. Accumulated combat hazards turned back a force of 36 Marauders from another mission when haze obscured the target. Enemy fighters also put in an appearance, and the bomber gunners claimed three downed.

On 7 September a not totally unknown confusion over the rendezvous point resulted in the 386th Group's abandoning any attempt to reach the marshalling yards at Lille, while only a third of the 387th's 36 Marauders managed to attack the yards at St Pol-sur-Mer.

As with airfields, railway targets demanded repeat raids to keep lines closed or to create new breaks to disrupt military traffic. Junctions with a high traffic density, such as that at Lille, were frequent targets, as large marshalling yards were rarely out of action for long as a result of a single raid.

The Germans had at their disposal an abundance of locomotives and a massive amount of rolling stock with which to move supplies. And, in a country the size of France, which was well served by a nationwide rail network, there were numerous repair facilities. In addition, the occupying power developed contingency plans to re-route trains around the most heavily-bombed parts of the network.

The medium bomber missions of 8 September, to Lille's Vendeville and Nord aerodromes as well as coastal defences around Boulogne, brought some drama to the crew of a 386th BG Marauder. Being obliged to ditch on return off the Goodwin Sands, the crew

made the first call on Air Sea Rescue by a B-26 in distress. Five men were rescued and one was lost. Meeting the day's Field Order (ASC missions No 53 and No 54) had required the despatch of 215 B-26s. Of these, 204 managed to release their bombs on the various targets, the ditched 386th aircraft being the sole loss of the day. As a result of action by the flak batteries defending the target areas, 50 Marauders required attention by the airframe-repair specialists when they arrived back at their bases. Such work became commonplace and much was achieved at unit level, which saved time and ensured that aircraft rosters were maintained at more-or-less stable levels.

More-heavily-damaged airframes were despatched to depots such as that at Burtonwood in Lancashire, which had the facilities to rebuild complete aircraft if necessary. As the strength of the Eighth Air Force built up in England, these depots stored vast quantities of spares for all types of combat aircraft. In terms of meeting day-to-day mission quotas, it was gratifying to the groups and higher echelons that the number of serviceable Marauders remained reasonably constant. Being a particularly-well-built aircraft, designer Payton Magruder's brainchild gained a reputation as a very able warplane, capable of absorbing quite extensive battle damage.

Bad day

More airframe damage from close-proximity flak bursts was in evidence on 9 September, when 202 Third BW Marauders streamed back across the Channel after another short-range bombing of coastal defences around Boulogne — and the day was marred by the highest number of fatal casualties suffered by the mediums for many weeks. The force (217-strong when despatched) had dropped 334.65 tons on various targets for the loss of one aircraft, but 11 men perished in a combination of enemy action and poor weather conditions. A Marauder was lost from each of the 322nd, 386th and 387th Groups. One aircraft crashed on take-off in early-morning fog, a second was listed as MIA, and a third had to crash-land on return, with one crew injury.

The fact that seven men were posted missing in the 322nd BG aircraft was not that unusual, as the normal complement did vary. Occasionally aircraft carried an

additional specialist navigator or observer trained to use new electronic aids, to assist accurate bombing even in overcast conditions. Whether or not the ill-fated 322nd aircraft was carrying a specially-trained navigator that day is unknown, but an embryo Pathfinder Force (PFF) of Marauders, using the British 'Oboe' radio navigational equipment, made its combat debut in September. While this device had initially been intended to aid the American heavies, the poor weather had demanded that medium bombers be similarly assisted in blind bombing. Turning (as was often the case) to its ally, the AAF obtained British agreement to use 'Oboe' and 'Gee' (later 'Gee-H'), and the necessary receiver/transmitter sets began to be installed in a percentage of the Marauders based in England. To obtain the best results from this equipment, navigators attended specialised ground schools.

With an increasing number of UK-based American bombers attacking tactical targets in France, several more B-26 crewmen were killed during the latter half of September; statistically, the hectic pace was almost bound to prove fatal in some instances. Overall, however, serious casualties remained remarkably low, considering the weight of steel the Germans put up virtually every time the medium bombers appeared over a target.

The heavy fighter escort the American bombers enjoyed undoubtedly deterred many Luftwaffe fighter attacks on the tight, well-armed formations, but few Marauder crew members expected their group to remain completely immune from the attentions of enemy fighters. Even so, escorts could be relaxed on some missions, as the Luftwaffe opposition had rarely materialised in the kind of strength regularly seen by the Fortress and Liberator crews.

The Germans perceived that the greatest threat posed by Allied bombing was in the homeland, and a gradual increase in fighter defence had begun as soon as the Eighth Air Force heavies had begun penetrating Reich airspace on a regular basis. August had, however, recorded aerial combat against the mediums on a small scale, and the threat posed by the Jagdwaffe was never taken lightly. As if to underscore the point, a 387th Group B-26, flown by Lt George Snyder, was damaged by FW190s on 27 September. On fire in the fuselage and right engine, things looked bad for the Marauder, which

Crouched in the gunner's seat in the 'stepped' tail position of an early B-26 on 8 September 1943 is T/Sgt Lacher, a full-blooded Chickasaw Indian who received credit for an FW190 on a mission earlier that month. Note the 'flak curtain' and ammunition tracks on both sides. *Imperial War Museum*

dropped out of formation. Believing the ship to be doomed, one of the waist gunners bailed out — and inadvertently dragged open the parachute of a second man, S/Sgt Laverne Stein, who was just behind. With his 'chute billowing from the waist hatch, Stein lost his boots in the slipstream which threatened to pull him out of the aircraft. Quick thinking by turret gunner Sgt Ed Kovalchik, in cutting away the harness, saved Stein. In the meantime the fires had been extinguished, and Snyder had the Marauder under sufficient control to fly it back to England. Reaching Chipping Ongar, it was smoothly bellied in, the gear having refused to lower due to a loss of hydraulic pressure.

October '43

A small-scale B-26 mission on 2 October was followed on 3 October by a much more ambitious, multiple-airfield strike involving 252 aircraft from all four 3rd Wing groups. With Lille, Schiphol, Woensdrecht, Haamstede and Beauvais aerodromes as their targets, the Marauder force was again partially split, the 386th and 387th Groups bombing Beauvais as well as the Dutch airfields. One of the 386th's aircraft was deemed to be a Category E (write-off) on return, and no fewer than 74 machines suffered varying degrees of battle damage, although there were no crew casualties.

A modest 25-sortie mission on 4 October was recalled to be followed by weather-related stand-downs until the 8th, when Eighth Air Support Command authorised Mission 80. This 'all groups' run to Lille and Chièvres airfields — the penultimate mission for the 322nd and 386th Groups as part of that higher echelon — had to be abandoned in deference to bad weather. This left the 323rd and 387th Groups to fly 72 combined sorties to Woensdrecht airfield the following day. Sixty-six B-26s reached the target to drop just under 100 tons of bombs and return home with battle damage to 26 aircraft.

Thus on 9 October 1943 the four B-26 groups bowed out of the Eighth Air Force; before their next mission they would come under the operational control of the 'new' Ninth Air Force. On that day, the 323rd and 387th Groups flew 66 effective sorties to Woensdrecht aerodrome to drop 98.15 tons of 300 and 500lb GP bombs between 15.16 and 15.26hrs. In the 10-minute pasting of the aerodrome, the B-26s 'took it' from the flak batteries, 26 bombers returning home with varying degrees of damage. That the Marauder could protect its crews was again shown in a casualty list of zero.

With the completion of that mission, control of the medium bombers in the ETO passed from the strategic Eighth to the tactical Ninth Air Force. For the crews, the job in hand would be much the same as before in terms of daylight bombing, which they had, through dedication and faith in the aircraft they flew, brought to an acceptable standard of accuracy. Although the Eighth Air Force had relinquished its Marauder combat groups, a handful of B-26s would remain under its direct control, to fly special missions.

3 Planning the Great Endeavour

As the war in Europe entered the last quarter of its fourth full year, the planning for a full-scale invasion of northwestern Europe moved into a higher gear. While the actual date was still unconfirmed by October 1943, the Allies were fairly certain that an assault could be launched early in 1944. Among the myriad challenges to such an undertaking were the composition of the various armies which would be the spearhead of the long-awaited 'second front', the objectives they would aim to secure once a beach-head had been established, and the air support they would require.

A cornerstone of Allied tactical airpower had long been 'support of armies in the field', still only vaguely defined when the wartime American bombers were under testing pending actual combat experience; war service would adapt and alter a concept which nevertheless remained essentially sound. As regards the ground forces that airpower would support, the US, British and Commonwealth armies had gained the necessary experience manyfold by late 1943. The Mediterranean theatre had supplied the bulk of this, the amphibious operations to secure French Morocco (Operation 'Torch') and Sicily ('Husky') having highlighted the vital need for good air support. What the southern front actions had also indicated was how much larger a task an invasion of France would be.

It was to meet this challenge while maintaining the strategic pressure on Germany that Hap Arnold and his air chiefs implemented a significant reorganisation of USAAF tactical airpower assets in the European and Mediterranean theatres. Strength had built up in both areas since mid-1942, and the US training programme was producing crews well enough able to man the new groups now urgently required for overseas duty. The successful completion of operations in North Africa and the relatively static nature of the war in western Europe in 1943 was such that time could be taken to consolidate and build up the very strong forces that would be needed to bring about a decisive defeat of the Axis. Any invasion of Europe had to succeed, and there was nothing to be gained by rushing things; opening the assault with any numerical deficiency in troops, material and aircraft could be disastrous. It had to be assumed that the Germans would oppose any landings in northwestern Europe with every means at their disposal.

Proven aircraft

In determining the composition of a new tactical air force to support the invasion, the AAF planners had some encouraging combat statistics to hand. There was little possibility that entirely-new aircraft would be deployed, and a combination of existing light/attack and medium bombers would be used. The A-20 had been well tried in

Above: When the Eighth/Ninth Air Force bombers switched to medium-altitude attacks, a heavy fighter escort was deemed vital. It turned out to be not so necessary, but many fighter units undertook the task, including P-47s of the 48th FG, one of which is seen here with 41-34976, a B-26C of the 323rd Group. *Imperial War Museum*

action in the MTO with the 47th Bomb Group, while Allied operations in North Africa with the similar Boston had more than proven the capabilities of the type.

The Marauder had found a new lease of life in the medium-altitude bombing rôle with the Eighth and Twelfth Air Forces, and it was clear that, with more groups, the light-to-medium attack element of invasion air support would be safe enough in the hands of these two types. It was fortunate that the new IX Bomber Command was headed by Sam Anderson, as continuity was retained and the experience gained while the mediums were part of the Eighth could be built upon.

To date, AAF operations had reflected some of the rapid changes brought about by the pace and nature of the air campaigns against the Axis. Single-seat types such as the P-40, P-47 and P-38 had become capable ground-support aircraft, thereby increasing the 'precision' nature of bombing tactical targets in direct assistance of ground forces, with far less personnel risk than deploying bombers with multiple crews. But bombers were still required for the physically larger targets, and, if fighters were combined with groups of mediums able to bring a far greater weight of bombs onto these more substantial targets, then a truly flexible tactical force should result. With the advantage of being more-or-less able to select the ideal aircraft type to carry out a given mission, the AAF had the potential to bring close air support to a greater effectiveness than ever before. And, having been obliged to loan its P-47s for long-range escort to Eighth Air Force heavy bombers, the Ninth's commanders awaited the arrival of P-51 Mustangs, which would shoulder this task brilliantly. There would follow, as is well known, a degree of 'horse trading' between the commands to ensure that the P-51s were transferred to the Eighth to escort bombers while the Ninth got P-47s, primarily to fly close-support missions by attacking ground targets.

New blood

Little of this wrangling over fighters would directly affect Ninth Bomber Command, which was promised a welcome boost to its strength in the form of four more Marauder groups and three equipped with the Douglas A-20.

In Europe, the 'attack' mission for which the A-20 had been designed was not to be

entirely abandoned, but the essential low-level nature of such sorties had been proven to be risky if opposed by intense ground fire. The A-20/Boston, either in AAF or RAF hands, had tried this tactic both in Europe and in the Pacific, where machines converted into strafers had been highly successful. But it had already been shown with the Marauder that it could be folly to assume that tactics that were sound in one theatre of war would be duplicated in another, and, in regard to the invasion of Europe, the Americans wisely preferred to await developments.

It was envisaged that A-20s could still fly attack sorties, but much would bear on the strength of the defences, the type of target and the effectiveness of low-level bombing and strafing in direct support of troops. In the meantime, standard Havocs carrying a bombardier were issued to those groups designated to serve in Europe, although these units also had a number of 'solid nose' A-20G and H models equipped only with six machine guns. It was a mix that would work out well enough in combat, the one drawback with the A-20 being the fact that it was a relatively small aircraft and each member of the crew was isolated from the other. That fact rarely troubled crews assigned to Havoc units; pilots found it docile and easy to handle, and, as with numerous other aircraft types, crew loyalty to it was fierce.

New Ninth

Deliberations of 16 October 1943 officially brought an end to the old Ninth Air Force in the Mediterranean and activation of the new one in England. Lt-Gen Lewis H. Brereton remained in command in what was in most respects a relocation rather than a completely new organisation. He had at the outset four subordinate commands to direct bomber, fighter, tactical air and troop-carrier operations; these would expand significantly in 1944 with various necessary subdivisions being created as dictated by the requirements of the invasion.

In the meantime, events on the other side of the English Channel were moving swiftly. German technical ingenuity had developed a range of entirely new weapons with incredible speed, and one of the first of these was about to be deployed in occupied France. Actions there would ensure that the US tactical aircrews had

ample chance to prove the 'precision' nature of their bombing, months before a single GI had set foot on French soil. Operation 'Crossbow' was about to begin.

Improved Marauders

Mainstay of the tactical bomber force based in England had been and would continue to be centred on the B-26. By late 1943 Martin had progressively improved the design, greatly encouraged by a loss rate of just 0.3% from 6,700 Marauder sorties flown in Europe between July and December 1943. In engineering terms there was a requirement to improve take-off safety and induce an improved level-cruising attitude. A 3.5° increase in wing incidence brought about the so-called 'twisted' wing, introduced on the Baltimore assembly line late in the year. The change was reflected in a new sub-type, the B-26F. Followed into service by the similarly-configured B-26G, the new Marauder replaced worn-out B and C models in front-line units, as required. Many older Marauders soldiered on, to complete a record of combat flying rarely equalled by any other US aircraft type anywhere in the world.

A-26 progress

Although, as stated above, there would not be a new US twin-engined bomber in the European front line by D-Day, it was certainly intended that the A-26 Invader would enter combat months before it actually did so. By the date of the reorganisation of the Ninth Air Force in England, the Douglas plant at El Segundo had completed a lengthy series of tests on the XA-26, and the AAF had narrowed down the official requirement.

The prototype had flown on 10 July 1942 and what emerged was an elegant, twin-engined attack bomber, less portly than the A-20 it would replace and including a flightdeck with side-by-side seats for the pilot and co-pilot/ bombardier. Basically a three-man aircraft (an additional crewman could be accommodated if required), the A-26 included a small 'crawlway' which gave access to the bombardier's position in the nose and the navigator's position/ radio room area behind the flightdeck. A single gunner sighted and fired the dorsal and ventral barbette guns via a periscopic remote contol. Externally, this latter was the most innovative feature of the Invader, which also had a laminar-flow wing

Above: The intended replacement for the B-26 and A-20, the A-26B Invader had six guns in the nose, eight in underwing packs and four in the turrets, representing a formidable firepower — which it was often unable to exploit fully in Europe, where low-level strafing was extremely dangerous. This is the same 671st BS aircraft seen on page 109. *J. V. Crow*

incorporating double-slotted flaps. Reportedly this wing proved something of a challenge to build quickly in the large quantities required, and was one reason for the delay in deliveries.

Apart from the barbettes, the A-26 was conventionally armed with the well-proven Colt-Browning 0.50in machine guns, the four turret guns being complemented by two optional guns in the forward nose of the bombardier version, or six in a solid nose.

Having considered installing a variety of heavy cannon on operational aircraft in an attempt to broaden the rôle of the A-26, the Army had finally realised that batteries of Brownings, supplemented by standard-size bombs, were adequate to deal with most types of wartime target. In addition, the Invader's wings were stressed and wired to accept four detachable packages each containing a pair of Brownings, a total of eight additional guns providing a grand total of 18 in the strafer version.

Invaders were built with both an attack nose (A-26B) and in full medium-bomber configuration (A-26C), the clear nose containing a bombardier's position and all essential equipment for that rôle. Production began in 1943 and picked up only gradually — far from fast enough for Hap Arnold, who gave vent to his feelings about the delay by stating acidly that 'We want the A-26 for this war, not the next.'

Understandable though Hap Arnold's frustration was, the A-26 programme had been subject to a considerable amount of change. The AAF had attempted to combine a number of conflicting functions in one airframe, which might have led to a compromise had the Invader gone to war as a ground-attack aircraft armed with heavy cannon, the need for which generally passed while it was under development. Another suggestion was that the A-26 could fill a category of aircraft almost totally lacking in the Army's inventory: that of night-fighter. Again, the Invader probably would have proved to be too heavy and insufficiently manœuvrable to fulfil this rôle well. The confirmation that Northrop would meet this requirement with the P-61 Black Widow had the effect of returning the A-26 to its original design concept — that of a modern combination of medium and attack bomber.

The AAF chief's concern about modernising the Ninth's tactical bomber force was understandable in the light of decisions taken behind the scenes. The mud thrown at the Marauder in its early days had stuck; however unfair this was, moves

were being made to close down the Martin production line prematurely to increase B-29 production. As few could predict how long the war would last, curtailing deliveries of the B-26 could lead to a reduction in the tactical bombing effort in Europe — hence the urgent need for the A-26.

October was a dismal month as regards tactical bombing operations; the weather, perhaps best described as seasonally typical, prevented hundreds of sorties from being completed. Weather prevented any of the 228 B-26s scheduled to fly the first Ninth Air Force mission on the 18th from taking off. This cancellation postponed the milestone mission until the 22nd, when only part of a force of some 200 Marauders was able to get through. Enjoying a huge escort in the form of 349 P-47s from seven groups and 42 P-38s of the 55th Fighter Group in their first outing as an escort to the mediums, about 40 bombers from the 322nd attacked Evreux and Cambrai aerodromes. The day brought some excitement when one box of B-26s was jumped by 36 Bf109s over Cambrai; the clash resulted in the loss of two P-47s, although no bombers went down and the

Above: Among the many airfields bombed by mediums during the German occupation of France was Cambrai. A 322nd Group B-26 turns away as bombs straddle the runway. *Imperial War Museum*

gunners fired back and claimed three probables.

A big operation with an Eighth Air Force fighter escort was laid on for 24 October and this resulted in the bombers getting through to Beauvais, Mondidier and St André-de-L'Eure aerodomes. The 200 participating B-26s had a more than one-to-one escort, there being 205 P-47s and 48 P-38s aloft that day — the kind of ratio that all bomber men dreamed of! It was the second time that Lightnings had escorted the mediums, and their presence was appreciated when

40 enemy fighters made a reported 54 passes on the formations. No bombers were lost and their gunners claimed three shot down, three probably destroyed and six damaged. The American fighters claimed one German fighter destroyed.

There were no B-26 missions through to the end of October, although five A-20s apparently braved the elements to fly a mission to Cherbourg/Maupertus aerodrome on 30 October. It is interesting

to speculate on the identity of these aircraft, for the three light bombardment groups equipped with this type were not assigned to the Ninth until the following year.

November '43

On 1 November the Ninth Air Force was placed under the operational control of the Allied Expeditionary Air Force (AEAF), which was to oversee operations of US and

Allied tactical air forces for Operation 'Overlord'. As was standard AAF practice, the Ninth Air Force was given subordinate commands within which were combat wings, each with a number of operational groups. To direct the medium and light bombers, IX Bomber Command, which had existed under that title since November 1942, was transferred to England from the Mediterranean.

On the 3rd the command sent B-26s to attack a well-battered Triqueville aerodrome and that at St André-de-L'Eure. One B-26 was lost over the latter target, while a further force of 65 Marauders pounded Amsterdam's Schiphol Airport. A period of dismal autumn weather caused numerous aborts by individual B-26 crews but on the 5th, IX BC sent 150 bombers to Mimoyecques, site of extensive earthworks for the so-called 'V3'. This weapon, consisting of massive long-range guns designed to bombard London from huge underground firing sites, was to attract a significant quantity of Allied high-explosive

before it was neutralised. Little data on exactly what was at Mimoyecques was then available, this and other targets associated with Hitler's 'V' (*Vergeltungswaffe*, or vengeance) programme being identified merely as 'secret military construction sites'.

During this early pre-invasion period the Marauder force began to be more regularly escorted by US rather than British fighters, the new groups of P-38s and P-47s arriving in England thus gaining valuable combat experience. Such an escort was provided on 7 November for another airfield strike, but the 200 B-26s despatched were obliged to return early and only the fighters sought any action. None was actually forthcoming, but two P-38s failed to return.

Weather continued to 'side with the enemy', but on 11 November 162 B-26s again bombed the V3 site and targets of opportunity in the Cherbourg Peninsula. The following day the 97th Combat Bombardment Wing headquarters was activated to direct operations by three

A-20 groups, and the old Third Bomb Wing was redesignated as the 98th Medium Combat Bombardment Wing; in addition, the Eighth Air Force transferred the headquarters of the 44th Bomb Wing to the Ninth and redesignated it as the 99th MCBW, all being assigned to IX Bomber Command.

Assignments of the four existing B-26 units to the new wing organisation placed the 323rd and 387th Groups in the 98th Wing, while the 322nd and 386th came under the direction of the 99th Wing.

The AAF subsequently attempted to plug another gap in the tactical order of battle by reorganising the 67th Reconnaissance Group, transferring it from Eighth ASC to the Ninth Air Force and re-equipping it with P-51As. US aerial reconnaissance and photography in Europe was largely undertaken by the F-4/F-5 and F-6 PR versions of the P-38 Lightning and P-51 Mustang respectively, but, as far as the Ninth was concerned, a small number of medium bombers were

Above: The crew of B-26B 'Loretta Young', one of the best-known Marauders in the 386th Group. It was part of the 553rd Bomb Squadron. *USAF*

Above: Showing the WACs the waist guns of a B-26 was a pleasant duty for Lt Paul P. Phillips in December 1943. *Imperial War Museum*

also used for similar specialised tasks. Douglas had produced a camera-equipped version of the A-20, known as the F-3, and several examples of these were shipped to the ETO. They were, however, compromised by the ever-increasing defences, and their original rôle — that of daylight photography — was abandoned. Standard A-20Js (otherwise F-3As) were flown by the 155th Photo Squadron (Night) for nocturnal illumination of potential targets with flares. Such deployment proved to be well within the capabilities of the aircraft, which had the advantage of being large enough to accommodate a bulky wartime aircraft camera (a K-17, K-22 or a K-19B night model) and 10 photoflash bulbs in the bomb bay. This latter area was provided with increased armour protection to ensure that the bulbs came to no harm during a combat mission, for without these no photography could be carried out. Brilliant illumination was provided by the Edgerton Lamp, a powerful flash unit that was

synchronised with the camera and which fitted into the A-20's fuselage forward of the bomb bay. Tail-warning radar was also fitted to guard against a sneak attack by enemy-night fighters from behind.

As mentioned elsewhere, the A-20 was regularly to be seen around Ninth Air Force bases on second-line duties. One of the liaison squadrons attached to the Ninth's 67th Reconnaissance Group, the 153rd LS, is listed in references as also flying A-20s along with the L-4 'Grasshopper'. The night-flare mission was also the rôle of several Havocs attached to the P-61-equipped 422nd and 425th Night Fighter Squadrons.

New targets

For a short period in mid-November the Ninth stood down the medium-bomber force from operations, although training flights were undertaken when the weather

allowed. It remained bad over continental targets and further missions were aborted, sometimes when the aircraft were *en route*, so quickly could the conditions change. Build-up of cloud was often extremely rapid, and in a matter of minutes the ground would be all but invisible. It was not until 23 November that 88 B-26s found conditions clear enough to be able to bomb Berck-sur-Mer and St Omer/ Longuenesse aerodromes. These targets were also attacked by the Marauders the following day.

Further missions were undertaken before November ended, that on the morning of the 26th resulting in the 322nd and 386th bombing Roye/Amy aerodrome instead of the briefed target at Rosières-en-Santerre. A target at Audinghen was attacked by the 323rd, 386th and 387th Groups, the B-26 crews being informed that this was another military construction site. It was in fact a

The third raid by B-26s on Schiphol airport took place on 13 December 1943 and, although the place gained a reputation as a very well-defended target, the 323rd maintained a good formation to bomb on that occasion. *Imperial War Museum*

On 28 December 1943 press coverage of the B-26 units included a portrait of 1st Lt Arnold C. Swain, kitted-up in the nose of his aircraft. As is obvious, this position got very crowded in a Marauder! *Imperial War Museum*

V1 flying bomb launch site — the type of target that would soon become familiar to US airmen under the codename 'Noball'.

Birth of the bomb

Set up under the operational control of the Luftwaffe, the programme to establish the pilotless Fieseler FZG 76 as a viable front-line strategic weapon had involved a lengthy test period, primarily to perfect the flight characteristics of the small aircraft which came to be known as the flying bomb. Initially mystified as to the exact nature of the new German weapons, the Allies closely studied photo-reconnaissance coverage of the test establishment at Peenemünde. Finally, on 28 November, the photo interpreters confirmed the link between the ski-shaped bomb-storage buildings and the launching ramps being built along the coast of France.

The Luftwaffe had planned to initiate a flying bomb assault on England by December 1943, and the unit that would direct it, Flak Regiment 155 (W), had meanwhile been posted to France as early as 21 October. Allied bombing of the first series of completed launching ramps (56 of which were planned in the Pas de Calais, with eight in Cherbourg) foiled this plan, which was originally intended to be a dual assault on England in conjunction with the conventional bombers of Fliegerkorps IX. The V1 programme was revised and the firing date postponed, pending the erection of new launching sites.

As new construction proceeded, Allied 'Noball' missions attempted to destroy the sites; the bombing codeword, borrowed from an English cricketing term, represented a major part of the overall campaign waged against the V-weapons as Operation 'Crossbow'. Detecting the well-camouflaged sites was far from easy, but there were various visual clues that well-trained photo interpreters could identify, including evidence of vehicle traffic, construction work in progress — and shadows. While disturbed ground could be smoothed over and buildings hidden under foliage, it was often impossible to hide such activity completely; from the air, details showed up that were not visible at ground level. The Germans made every effort to camouflage the sites, which on average covered an area of approximately one square mile. Buildings were set 100 to 200yd apart and were dispersed around the site, which was invariably served by a spur railway. And, as bomber crews soon realised, the protection of the launching areas had a high priority and the AA gun defence began to multiply.

Chièvres aerodrome in Belgium was hit by the B-26s on 29 November, the medium-bomber force also attacking Cambrai/Epinoy aerodrome in France to round out a difficult operational month.

December '43

After sending 176 B-26s against enemy aerodromes on 1 December, IX Bomber Command was notified that the Combined Chiefs of Staff had authorised the AEAF to give top priority to 'Crossbow' targets. Reconnaissance was discovering more of the ski-shaped buildings at new sites in France, virtually with every passing day. By December about 100 had been detected by a combination of aerial reconnaissance, Enigma code decrypts and reports from Allied agents.

The 'ski sites', as they became known (more familiarly to the RAF than the AAF, which usually referred to all V-weapons sites as 'Noball' targets), were mainly located in a corridor 200 miles long by 30 miles wide. The Pas de Calais area held the most launching sites, which were set a few miles back from the Channel coast and ranged on London. In and around Caen the sites were aligned on Southampton and Portsmouth; those grouped separately on the Cherbourg Peninsula were aligned on the cities of Bristol and Plymouth. When it was confirmed that the structures adjacent to the ski-shaped storage buildings were indeed inclined launching ramps for pilotless bombs, the Allied leaders realised that the V1 could pose a significant threat to the build-up for 'Overlord' in southeast England, although London and a number of English provincial cities and towns were to be the main targets. In the light of the worrying developments in France, the 3 December Sextant Conference confirmed that the earliest date an invasion could be launched was 1 May 1944.

4 Vengeance Postponed

As a massive aerial reconnaissance campaign now opened, with the object of confirming the location of as many V1 launching sites as possible, the IX BC Marauders were briefed for one more attack on enemy aerodromes on 4 December. The weather remained obstinately bad and the mission was recalled.

On the 5th, the Ninth opened its part of the 'Crossbow' campaign, and, although the initial medium-bomber sorties were all but neutralised by the weather, 52 B-26s did attack V1 sites at three different locations.

A ski site in Florida

As soon as Allied intelligence had sufficient data to determine the details — composition, size, number of buildings and so forth — of a V1 launching site, these were supplied to the AAF Proving Ground at Eglin Army Air Base in Florida. Work was quickly put in hand to construct an exact, full-scale replica of the typical 'ski site' then being built by the Germans in France. The object was to determine the most effective method of destroying the sites by air attack. To make things even more realistic, the Florida range brought in camouflage units to duplicate the dense foliage so typical of the real flying-bomb locations in rural France.

Having completed the dummy site in 12 days, the Army flew more than 1,200 practice sorties over the Eglin range, using heavy, medium and light bombers which dropped from all altitudes, from a very low 30ft to 20,000ft. Fighter-bombers also made glide and dive bombing attacks.

The tests concluded that the surest method of destruction was a single 1,000lb bomb dropped from low level by a P-47 or P-38; a subsequent combat mission by Thunderbolts apparently confirmed this, to the satisfaction of three proving-ground observers sent to England to test their theories. No aircraft were lost on the mission, which succeeded in crippling a V1 site.

Despite these results, many 'Noball' sites were actually destroyed by a deluge of high-explosive dropped by medium and heavy bombers. The reason is not hard to find: risking valuable fighters against tiny, well-defended targets, mere months before they would be needed to spearhead the air support for the invasion, was impractical. If heavy losses had resulted, replacements could not have been guaranteed — which meant that vast tracts of the French countryside were about to be disfigured by thousands of overlapping craters.

While not being unduly troubled by attacks on its bases by bombers of the Luftwaffe, the Ninth Air Force could hardly hide the new airfields being constructed for its tactical bomber and fighter groups in East Anglia during the winter of 1943/4. It should not be assumed that enemy air reconnaissance correctly identified these airfields, or had any inkling of their intended purpose — they were simply legitimate military targets. Accordingly, on 11 December, Dornier Do217s (almost certainly of Kampfgeschwader 2) dropped several bombs on Gosfield, killing and wounding several US construction personnel. At the same time the Dorniers also scattered a few bombs on Andrews Field, without causing any damage.

Three days after the Luftwaffe carried out an ineffectual raid on airfields in East Anglia, the Ninth Air Force demonstrated once again how it should be done. On 13 December 199 B-26s bombed Schiphol. The force dropped 78 1,000lb bombs on the German-occupied airfield from 15,900 to 23,000ft. A heavy concentration was achieved on hangars, dispersals and an ammunition-storage area.

January '44

Poor bombing weather in the early days of January nevertheless did not prevent the heavies attacking 'Noball' sites, but it was the 7th before the Ninth's B-26 groups could make another contribution to the war effort. The target was again an airfield, that at Cherbourg/Maupertus; 35 aircraft attacked the target, but all other medium-bomber operations were cancelled due to the weather.

Ferry flight

By that time the 391st Bomb Group was well on its way to England. Ahead lay a ferry route that took the crews over various sea and land masses representing a large slice of the world; each waypoint had been selected to ensure that US aircraft with the necessary range could reach each location in safety, with adequate fuel reserves. Having departed Hunter Field, Georgia, on 3 January, the group's Marauders headed for Morrison Field in Florida, then Borinquen in Puerto Rico, Atkinson in British Guyana and Belém and Natal in Brazil. Following a two-day stopover, the B-26s took-off for Ascension Island. The next leg took them to Roberts Field in Liberia, where they arrived on 21 January. As a precautionary measure, each aircraft was given a thorough overhaul before the crews embarked on their next leg, which took them to Marrakesh, Morocco. Arriving there on the 22nd, the Marauders encountered bad weather (an ominous portent!), and after one day's delay they departed for St Mawgan in Cornwall. On 30 January the first B-26s appeared in the circuit at Matching aerodrome in Essex. Others came in over the next few days, but the group's full complement of B-26s did not finally arrive until 24 February.

The January weather provided some respite to the heavy-bomber crews, who, finding their primary targets in Germany 'socked in', bombed some of the V1 launching areas in France. Little other tactical activity was possible until the weather cleared up. Poor flying conditions could be expected for that time of year, at least by the natives, but it is fair to say that a proportion of the Americans who had joined the USAAF to fight had never had to contend

Above: Conditions described as 'rugged' helped make many Marauders take on a weathered look, none more so than 'Idiot's Delight' of the 391st Group. *J. Hamlin*

with the kind of weather they found in Europe. The demands this made on them were not to be minimised, for they often compounded the inherent dangers of combat flying, at times proving far more hazardous than enemy action. The European theatre was otherwise rated as one of the best as regards living conditions and amenities.

V-weapons sites in France were attacked by 193 B-26s on 13 January, and they met, not unusually, the kind of opposition described by one Marauder pilot as '10/10ths flak'! This mission was the last for a week, as the weather clamped down again, and not before the 21st could the B-26s sortie against the V1 construction sites. That day 119 aircraft were despatched. Little activity was possible on the 22nd, but on 23 January some 200 B-26s were again able to bomb 'Noball' sites on the Channel coast. A repeat attack was made the following day, involving slightly fewer Marauder sorties.

New group
On 25 January IX Bomber Command could formally announce the arrival in the ETO of its fifth Marauder group, the 391st. Based at Matching and joining the 98th Wing, the group had the 572nd, 573rd, 574th and 575th Squadrons assigned to it. Col Gerald E. Williams was group commander.

Elsewhere on the 25th, the bulk of the B-26 force was again assigned to V-weapons targets, although all 150 aircraft involved had to abort due to bad weather. A second attempt was made the next day, with yet another recall resulting.

The war news was dominated by the Allied invasion of Italy at Anzio, and January was all but over before the B-26s were able to bomb 'Noball' sites again, fewer than 100 aircraft hitting locations along the Channel coast on the 29th. During the month, Eisenhower directed that Carl Spaatz assume administrative responsibility for all United States Strategic Air Forces Europe (USSAFE) commands and units in the UK, which he did on the 20th. There must have been some protest over this acronym, as it was changed to USSTAF on 4 February, the introduced 'T' standing for 'tactical'.

February '44
Behind-the-scenes planning for the invasion proceeded, and on 1 February details of the air/ground/naval operation known as 'Neptune' were circulated. Triqueville aerodrome was bombed on the 2nd, just 36 B-26s reaching the target. Next day the B-26s were despatched in

force, with 152 aircraft taking-off, but only 52 were actually able to bomb V-sites on the west coast of France. Air activity was again significantly reduced, as the weather continued to be less than conducive to air operations over England, the front extending across most of the Continent. It was hardly any better in the south, with a familiar pattern of bomber missons being recalled or abandoned as the Allied armies became stalled at Anzio.

In France, the respite from Allied air attack had given the Germans a chance to strengthen the defences around their V-weapons sites and ensure that bomber crews got a hot reception on most missions to destroy them. On 5 February, 226 B-26s sought to obliterate six launching sites around St Omer. The typically heavy flak now concentrated around these targets greeted the 180 or so aircraft that located them, and the Germans brought down six aircraft — the worst single-day loss for the Marauder force for some time.

On the 6th, as well as attacking the familiar 'Noball' targets, the Marauder crews bombed Amiens/Glisy aerodrome and a factory in the Amiens area.

With D-Day provisionally set for early May, Ninth Air Force planners began to

Above: The famous 'Rat Poison', long-lived 164-mission ship of the 322nd Group, had hardly got going when this photo was taken at the B-17 base at Ridgewell on 27 November 1943. An A-26 became 'Rat Poison Jr'. *USAF*

examine important targets other than airfields and those connected with V-weapons; they felt that the time left to them to implement a wide-ranging offensive, aimed at isolating the planned beach-head areas as completely as was possible by aerial bombardment, was running short, and, while 'Noball' targets would remain top priority (after the destruction of the Luftwaffe under the Pointblank plan) within the aims of the Combined Bomber Offensive, other targets would be attacked concurrently. While the parameters set by the CBO/Pointblank directives were primarily strategic, the tactical side could not be allowed to slip any further as a result of the preoccupation with 'Noball' targets.

Consequently, the mission schedule for 8 February reflected an acceleration of operations in line with Headquarters' directives, the most immediate result of which were the first consecutive missions to be launched by IX Bomber Command in

one day. In the morning 200 B-26s attacked V-weapons sites and targets of opportunity, while the afternoon mission had a similar choice of target, 100 B-26s participating. In the event, most of the bombs fell on 'military installations' at Berck-sur-Mer.

By 9 February the B-26-equipped 344th Bomb Group had settled into Stansted, Essex, with its 494th, 495th, 496th and 497th Squadrons, to prepare for its combat debut under group commander Col Reginald F. C. Vance. Across the Channel, the Ninth's other medium groups were setting their sights on Tergnier's marshalling yards. A relatively small force of 54 aircraft from the 322nd and 386th Groups bombed this rail junction, with reportedly excellent results, while 79 other Marauders sought out targets of opportunity and V-weapons sites.

A great weight of bombs was being aimed at the locations supporting the

German pilotless-bomb programme — so much so that no V1s had yet been launched. Heavy bombers were also regularly pounding the areas identified by aerial PR and intelligence sources, enabling the tactical bombers to broaden their curriculum, although, in line with the late-1943 directives, there could be no let-up until the 'vengeance weapons' were utterly destroyed. 'Noball' targets would therefore continue to occupy the medium-bomber groups, but the impressive strength of the Allied air forces at that point of the war meant that some diversification to equally-important locations could be made without any lessening of the effort to block the V1. For the invasion to succeed, the enemy had to be denied flexibility of movement, which meant bombing and interdiction of the transport system on a gigantic scale.

War of the rails

Although the railways in occupied Europe had been attacked sporadically by Allied aircraft from the earliest days of the war, many hundreds of miles of the huge and comprehensive French, Belgian and Dutch

Above: 'Willie the Wolf' graces the nose of the nearest of these 344th Group B-26s, an aircraft of the 494th BS coded K9-D. Behind is Y5-N, a 495th BS machine. *Imperial War Museum*

systems remained functional by early 1944. Northwest Europe then had a more complete rail network than any other part of the world. In density terms it meant that 12.6% of France was served by the railways, of which 47.2% was double-track. For Belgium the figures were respectively 27.5% and 58.3%, and for Holland 15.3% and 50.8%. In Germany itself, 20.8% was accessible by rail, 35.3% of this being double-track.

The Germans were known to have been using only 30% of the captured European system prior to the invasion, although they had appreciated its vulnerability to air attack. Accordingly they had augmented the regular emergency crews with gangs of extra workmen whose job was to stand by in all the important yards, ready to carry out urgent repairs as and where necessary. For this purpose, large stocks of extra rail sections, points and sleepers had been stacked alongside the lines at frequent intervals. It had been found in earlier air attacks that, on average, a well-placed load of, say, 500 tons of HE/GP bombs would block a line for a day or so.

Repairs would be put in hand immediately, after which one or more lines could be in operation, depending on their importance.

In terms of locomotives and rolling stock, Germany enjoyed an abundance of both, its invading forces having captured and systematically collected train sets from all over the Continent. At numerous crossing-points, railways connected all the occupied territories with Germany. Thus, until the invasion proper, Allied airpower would have an uphill task in keeping lines closed; not until air units were based on the Continent and a programme of continual interdiction could be implemented would the Germans be seriously hampered in terms of loss of rail traffic.

A further urgent requirement by IX Bomber Command was to do something about reducing the disruption caused to operations by bad weather, and to that end it anticipated a very important mission taking place in a week or so. A more immediate problem was that, with the plethora of targets open to massive air attack, the Ninth was running a little short of bombs.

On 10 February the Marauders bombed Poix and Beauvais/Tille aerodromes, plus a bridge and a coastal battery as well as V1 sites on the Channel coast. The following day saw the weather close in, the result being that only 35 of 139 B-26s despatched — mainly against V-weapons sites — were able to locate the marshalling yards at Amiens, while the balance of this force had to be recalled.

In December 1943 US-built examples of 'Oboe' navigation equipment had begun to arrive in the UK. These sets were installed in B-26s intended for a new unit, the 1st Pathfinder Squadron (Provisional). The Eighth Air Force was already using 'Gee-H', but the Ninth clearly needed its own electronic aids in its own medium bombers in order to penetrate the troublesome cloud cover.

In terms of new groups sent from the States to swell the tactical offensive in Europe, the first A-20 unit — the 416th Bombardment Group (Light) —was in receipt of its aircraft by February. Initially Havocs were not being flown to Europe, the group's aircraft having instead been crated and shipped across the Atlantic. Each one then had to be assembled and inspected before theatre training could begin. This was a time-consuming process and one where minute checks were advisable; a sea voyage under wartime conditions could occasionally be detrimental to aircraft, and minor damage occurred despite care in loading and stowage.

Pathfinder debut

The 1st Pathfinder Squadron (P), equipped with B-26s, was formally activated at Andrews Field on 13 February. Its first 15 crews, including the CO — Capt Robert Porter — were drawn from the five Marauder groups in the ETO. Porter was a veteran of the first Ijmuiden mission with the 322nd Group and had been instrumental in forming the special squadron which would have a far-reaching influence on future medium-bomber operations. The Pathfinders' primary duty would be to defeat the weather, but the B-26 force faced other challenges. For months, radar-predicted flak had boosted the accuracy of the German AA fire, and any measure that would spoil the aim of the gunners by neutralising their electronic eyes had to be tried. The answer was 'Window', the bundles of tiny aluminium strips cut to the wavelength of German radars. Dropped *en masse*, 'Window' would swamp radar scopes with millions of false returns, making it all but impossible to distinguish the real target. Marauder groups now began to include a screening force of aircraft to precede the main attack. Releasing 'Window', these bombers achieved a fair degree of success against gun-laying radars, and they remained an integral part of missions in the future. The effectiveness of 'Window' was not always easy to judge — but crews reported that, on those occasions when this anti-radar measure was not taken, the flak did indeed appear to be heavier.

As the 1st PS anticipated its first combat mission, the Ninth sent another 182 B-26 sorties to bomb V-weapons sites on the French coast.

By the 14th, arrangements had been made to overcome the recent bomb shortage by acquiring fresh stocks from the Middle East and Iceland, pending further deliveries to the UK. This was a temporary situation that did not apparently curtail tactical missions to any appreciable degree. Most of the munitions for the Ninth and other US air forces in the UK came, of course, by sea, and the dangers and difficulties that could still beset such voyages, even at that stage of the war, were obvious. There had been a fair degree of drawing on British bombs by the Ninth (and, on occasion, by the RAF on American stocks) and this co-operation continued, albeit on a relatively small scale.

On the morning of 15 February, 247 B-26s bombed Cherbourg/Maupertus aerodrome and V-weapons sites; in the afternoon a second mission by 141 aircraft disrupted construction work on additional flying-bomb launch areas.

Aborted missions shredded everyone's nerves, none more so than when the weather ruined a first mission. That happened to the 391st Group, which had arrived in England mere weeks before the first scheduled combat mission on 16 February. Having flown a few practice missions over the Midlands and the North Sea, the group was suddenly alerted to ready 36 aircraft for an attack on Beaumont-le-Roger aerodrome, and all personnel rushed to comply fully with the requirements of Field Order 202. Taking-off on time, the Marauders set their course to rendezvous with their RAF fighter escort before entering enemy airspace. Then the cloud began to build, to the point that the chances of bombing accurately would have been almost nil. The flak opened up half-heartedly as the Marauders turned for home, but, having penetrated as far as France, the crews were at least allowed a mission credit. That this was not, however, the 'real thing' hardly needed stressing to the crews involved.

The acute need for the Pathfinder unit that entered combat the next day was again demonstrated on 20 February, with the start of the Eighth Air Force's 'Big Week' heavy-bomber attacks on German industry. Only 35 B-26s were able to bomb Haamstede aerodrome, while 100 other Marauders gave up attempting to locate their targets and turned for home.

Taking-off from Andrews Field on 21 February to rendezvous with 200-plus B-26s, the aircraft of the 1st PS (P)

gathered up 18 of them and led the way to Coxyde/Furnes aerodrome. It was a mark of the successful debut of the Pathfinder unit that this small force was the only element that was able to bomb, while the rest were forced to return early. The use of 'Gee' and 'Oboe' blind-bombing equipment to locate hidden targets was henceforth to become an integral part of Ninth Air Force operations. While this could not entirely overcome the weather problem, even small-scale success was welcome, if only to justify the huge effort that went into getting a mission on its way. To have scores of aircraft return without reaching the target at all was highly frustrating for everyone involved.

There were only 66 successful B-26 sorties on the 22nd, and a similar ratio of 'actual' bombing attacks as against 'despatched' numbers was recorded on other missions for the remainder of February. It was rare for all the bombers that set out on a given mission to reach the target area and bomb the designated target; numerous factors (weather apart) came into play almost as soon as a formation took-off, and a few aircraft were invariably forced to turn back. A whole series of technical malfunctions could cause a bomber to return to base, pilots understandably not wishing to risk the lives of the crew and a valuable aircraft by ignoring whatever problem had arisen. An emergency landing in enemy territory or a ditching in the sea achieved nothing.

Flying its postponed debut mission on the 24th, the 391st Group did well to deliver a damaging attack on Gilze-Rijen aerodrome. With 36 of its own aircraft and three spares that joined up with it, the group bombed in two box formations, the first releasing from 12,000ft and the second from 11,500ft. Later, the Ninth BC summary of the day's operations stated that the 391st had scored direct hits on four or five aircraft shelters and several other buildings and made holes in the south/north runway. Category A (ie slight) battle damage was sustained by two aircraft, the flak being described as 'moderate and accurate'.

On average, the best results achieved by the mediums during periods of inclement weather were sorties against V-weapons sites, the clear delineation of sea and land areas a short distance in from the French coast assisting bomb-aiming. And, although 'Noball' launching sites were among the shortest-range targets the bombers attacked, they were hardly ever 'milk runs', the defending flak seeing to that.

The airfields at Deelen and Leeuwarden — as well as Gilze-Rijen — were successfully attacked on 25 February, as was Rosières on the 28th, but, overall, the bombing results obtained in the last week of February were disappointing.

That bad weather could indirectly create dangerous situations was brought home to the crews of the 391st Group on its intended debut on the 23rd. Two missions were scheduled and the group complied, sending B-26s out in the morning and afternoon. The earlier mission resulted in the fighter escort being forced to head for home low on fuel, probably after trying to skirt around the overcast. Now on their own, the Marauders made (as the unit's history later put it) 'a 40-minute tour of France', quite exposed to enemy fighter attack. None came, fortunately. Neither mission could be completed due to 10/10 cloud coverage, and, as was usual, most crews brought their bombs back, although others chose the option of reducing any risk there might be on landing by jettisoning them over the sea.

March '44
Further organisational moves towards the tactical air component for 'Overlord' were made during March. In regard to the Ninth's mediums, the fine support provided by the predominantly Spitfire-equipped squadrons of 11 Group RAF was formally relinquished in favour of USAAF fighter squadrons. Gratifyingly, the Luftwaffe interceptors had often ignored incursions into their airspace by the tactical bombers, leading to the conclusion that the heavy fighter escort the mediums had hitherto enjoyed could safely be relaxed or (at the very least) reduced. This had already been done on several occasions, as the tight bomber boxes had proved capable of putting up a formidable pattern of gunfire. Indeed, it was well known that US machine-gun fire was more than capable of destroying opposing fighters. It was not that escort was to be denied the bombers, but, from March, on those occasions when one would be required, the Ninth Air Force's own units would undertake more of the task. In reality, medium-bomber escort was shared between the Ninth and Eighth Air Forces and RAF fighter squadrons; much depended on other operational commitments and factors such as weather

conditions, aircraft serviceability, the type of target and its distance from the bomber airfields in England.

In line with the pre-invasion campaign to paralyse the French railway system, the marshalling yards at Amiens were blitzed by 126 Marauders on 2 March in the initial direct assault on such a target by IX Bomber Command. The same day the Marauders struck V-weapons sites at various locations, the bombing involving 353 sorties. The day's work, which also recorded numerous sorties by the RAF, represented an enormous operational effort typical of this intense period in the European air war.

For the morning mission the 386th Group sent 54 B-26s divided into three boxes whch took off from Great Dunmow at 08.20hrs and set course for the coast of France. 'Oboe' was used to assist navigation and confirm target location. En route, one crew reported a technical malfunction serious enough to abort the mission, and this aircraft returned. As was common practice, the 386th had included two spare aircraft on the mission schedule to allow for such an eventuality. Fighter escort to the 386th's bombers was vested in two squadrons of Typhoon 1bs — No 181 based at Merston and No 245 at Westhampnett.

The 323rd contingent also consisted of 54 Marauders, again divided into three boxes. These Marauders also had two Typhoon squadrons as escort. The 'third wave' of bombers was 36 aircraft from the 322nd Group with escort provided by a single squadron of Typhoons, while the fourth element of the force comprised 36 Marauders from the 387th Group, which were also covered by the strength of two Typhoon squadrons.

The primary targets for the bombers were V1 launching sites located in the Ardes, Lumbres, Hazebrouck, Hucqueliers and Aire-sur-la-Lys regions. Specifically, the sites were at Lostebarne, south of Ardes; in the Forêt Nationale De Tournehem, northwest of Lumbres; at Lottinghem, north of Fruges; in the Bois des Huit Rues, south of Hazebrouck; and at Linghem, lying north/northeast of Saint Pol.

The mission, identified by the RAF as 'Ramrod 609', was to involve a strafing attack on the sites by the Typhoons as well as bombing by the Marauders.

Most of the sites had been attacked previously by both the AAF and RAF,

the spiralling bomb tonnage being quite typical of the effort put into utterly destroying the V1 sites. Many of them could be spotted from a considerable distance by the numerous bomb craters. As was also not untypical, the reports from these earlier raids had rated the damage achieved as 'Category B' — rather less than complete destruction, hence the necessary repeat visits.

In their distinctive arrowhead flights, the 386th B-26s met no problems in forming up into three separate attack waves: the leading box of 18 B-26s headed for the site at Lostebarne, the second (17 aircraft) aiming for the target in the trees of the forest at Tournehem and the third (also 17 aircraft) going to Lottinghem. The bombers had rendezvoused with their escort at 09.29hrs and nine minutes later had crossed the coast south of Le Touquet, heading for the IP at Fruges. The objective was picked up visually by the bombardiers at 09.45 and 'bombs away' was at 09.49hrs.

The crews observed evidence of excavations around the Lostebarne site as well as one of the familiar ski-shaped buildings used for storage of flying bombs. In total the 386th dropped 102 500lb GP bombs, the results by the lead and low flights being rated as 'good', although the crews in the low flight were off-target, with 30 of their bombs falling southwest of the objective. Adopting a dogleg flightpath out of the target area, the bombers crossed the coast between Calais and Dunkirk and arrived back over Great Dunmow at 10.35hrs.

In the meantime, the second wave had bombed the V1 site hidden in the forest at Tournehem, again with good results, although the third wave encountered overcast and completely missed the site at Lottinghem, all bombs falling to the northeast. Other morning bombing results by other participating groups were varied: the 323rd's visual bombing of Tournehem was 'good', while the same group's effort at Lostebarne was only rated as 'poor'.

That HE bombs could not demolish the 'Noball' sites unless a good concentration was achieved is evidenced by the fact that a considerable number of the concrete supports for the inclined launching ramps, ski-shaped buildings and various examples of blockhouse can still be seen today in parts of rural France. Reconnaissance photographs of the areas in which the Germans positioned the flying-bomb assembly and launching sites show just how small they were — a fact appreciated only too well by the Ninth's bombardiers.

Having been briefed to attack the V1 site at Linghem, the 387th at Chipping Ongar readied 35 B-26s. Take-off was at 10.10hrs, the group including two Marauders that would act as spares. The formation was met by a single aircraft from the 1st PFF Squadron, but one B-26 from the first box and two from the second were obliged to turn back with technical trouble. Choosing to cross into Belgium between Ostend and Nieuwpoort, the Marauders attracted flak. The deadly 88mm shells soon found the range, and aircraft in the first box bore the brunt. Despite taking the usual evasive action, B-26B-25 41-31868/TQ-L 'Do It II' of the 559th Squadron took a bad hit in its left engine and dropped away. Far more serious was the fate of B-26B-20 41-31698/TQ-N 'Hot Garters', which had its right wing blown off, probably as a result of a direct hit in the fuel tanks. The pilot, F/O Oliver Jopling, could do nothing to save the aircraft, but incredibly three men, including Jopling, survived. They managed to bail out of the doomed B-26, as did the bombardier, 1st Lt Irving Lerman, but his parachute caught fire. At the controls of '868', meanwhile, the pilot, Lt Lyster, nursed his charge out of the target area.

Despite this early setback, the B-26s came through the flak belt and, led by the pathfinder ship using 'Oboe', reached Linghem. Bombing was only poor to fair, resulting in Category B damage. Typhoons of Nos 1 and 3 Squadrons escorted the bombers home, the latter's ETA being 12.30hrs.

The day was far from over as the morning missions returned; a separate bombing and strafing attack on 'Noball' sites was carried out by Typhoons before the late-afternoon USAAF tactical bomber missions got underway. This time the Marauders were ordered to bomb the marshalling yards at Tergnier and Amiens/Longueau. Five boxes totalling 91 B-26s (53 from the 322nd Group and 38 from the 386th) went to the former target, covered by four Typhoon squadrons, with three more as back-up. Tergnier was an important rail junction as it carried traffic serving Paris and numerous points throughout northwestern France; it also contained extensive locomotive-repair facilities.

Take-off for the bombers was at 14.55hrs. The formation formed up well, the 322nd making up the lead boxes with the 386th following. Almost inevitably there were early returns as a result of malfunctions, and two aircraft left the 322nd's formation before the others crossed into French territory at Le Tréport at 16.15hrs. Then things started to go wrong. Whether compounded by navigational error or other contributary cause, the Marauders encountered heavy cloud and this clearly confused the bombardiers, who identified not Tergnier but the town of St Quentin, about 13 miles to the north. There was considerable confusion as the lead flights made a right turn away from the real target and headed for St Quentin, which they had apparently decided was the target. All 51 of the 322nd's Marauders passed the IP over Roye. They picked up some ineffectual flak from batteries at Montdidier, but there were no reported incidents as a result. The bombers ploughed on and some released their loads at 16.59hrs. There was clearly some doubt as to the right target and only 23 crews bombed — but this represented a shower of 184 500-pounders which in the event killed 65 people in the town and damaged 300 dwellings. Headlines in the St Quentin press understandably asked why the town had been bombed at all.

Meanwhile, the 386th had located the correct target, Tergnier being the group's primary target with Amiens/Longueau airfield as the 'last resort'. Providing the bombers with a choice of targets had worked well, as the option usually ensured that, if one of two boxes could not (for one reason or another) hit the primary, the bombs were not wasted but dropped on the alternatives. The 38 B-26s of the 386th bombed the rail yard, while four boxes (19 aircraft) attacked the (secondary) aerodrome at Rosières-en-Santerre, which was occupied by the Luftwaffe at that time. A number of enemy aircraft were observed by the crews as their bombs were released, the bursts appearing to be right on target. The raid was judged to have achieved excellent results, with a number of buildings and dispersal areas having received direct hits.

Four more boxes of the 386th had also gone to the aerodrome at Amiens/Glisy. Once again, the bomb pattern was satisfactory, all bombs impacting within the confines of the base, along the runways and the dispersal areas.

RAF Typhoon pilots later reported in no uncertain terms that some of the B-26s on the 2 March missions had not followed the arranged course, and implied that this was not uncommon! It may perhaps have been that some pilots did not fully appreciate the desire by the American bomber crews to take constant evasive action, although the fighter pilots could see little reason for this if the flak was not firing and there was no threat from enemy aircraft. Eight Typhoons each from Nos 181 and 245 Squadrons had been charged with close escort to the bombers briefed to attack Tergnier, and some of the fighter pilots reported that they had observed no bombing in that area. This was possibly a reference to the 322nd turning the wrong way and missing the rail yards.

At 15.16hrs on the afternoon of 2 March a further two waves of respectively 54 and 72 Marauders set out from England, bound for the rail yard at Amiens; these formations were from the 391st BG at Matching. Shortly afterwards the 387th despatched 39 aircraft and the 323rd 36, these latter two groups forming up as a joint force. Covering the first wave of the Amiens attack were two squadrons of Spitfire Vs (Nos 306 and 315 from Heston), with three of Typhoons as back-up. The second wave of bombers enjoyed the protection of two squadrons of Mk IX 'Spits' (Nos 401 and 412 from Biggin Hill), with two more (also flying Mk IXs) as back-up.

At 16.51hrs the 391st arrived at the IP at Poix, followed by the 323rd. In clear conditions the Marauders had thus far encountered few difficulties, and the first bombs were dropped at 16.58. Despite having to plunge through the flak, the bombing by the two formations was observed to be well concentrated, the bombardiers having had a useful landmark in the shape of a prominent roundhouse adjacent to the tracks, which made a long curve around Longueau town. Bombs from the following boxes of B-26s fell a little haphazardly on the outskirts of the built-up area, part of which extended almost to Glisy aerodrome. The entire formation of Marauders chose to fly directly over the air base on their exit from the marshalling yards. Further sticks of bombs went down on Glisy.

There were plenty more targets at Amiens/Longueau for the 387th Group, which carried out a follow-up attack. Two boxes, of 21 (leading) and 17, went across the yards and bombed the tracks well to the north of the previous attack. Avoiding overflying Glisy and instead arrowing out over the Somme in the direction of Arras, the Marauders were picked up by the Spitfire IXs of No 308 Sqn over Le Tréport, and these and other Spitfire squadrons provided strong withdrawal support for the American mediums.

The fighter and bomber formations headed for home, leaving much devastation at the targets. A considerable weight of HE had torn up the tracks and adjacent buildings of the marshalling yards, and bombs were evenly distributed across Glisy to good effect. A total of 855 bombs had fallen on Longueau and 288 on Glisy. The misfortunes of war visited Longueau town, as many bombs overshot the long, curved track on the south side of the yards and took 24 more civilian lives. As the American mediums and British fighters headed home, the airspace around Amiens was still full of aircraft; large formations wheeled around the city, setting off on their briefed routes out over the coast.

More air activity had taken place in mid-afternoon, with RAF Bostons and Mitchells attacking 'Noball' sites in the same general area as the Ninth Air Force; a great many more sorties would be flown over this particular area of France well into

Above: One of the most able leaders of the Havoc force was Col Harold L. Mace, seen here clambering into an A-20G (43-9701) coded 5H-H of the 668th BS. *Imperial War Museum*

Above: Boosting the B-26 force in the spring of 1944 were three groups of A-20 Havocs. One of the solid-nosed A-20G models is seen here in the colours of the 668th BS, 416th BG. *Imperial War Museum*

the night of 2/3 March. B-17s had carried out 'Noball' strikes early in the day, and these were repeated before darkness fell. Then it was the turn of the RAF heavies, the Pathfinders and the USAAF Carpetbaggers. Last (but far from least) were the reconnaissance flights to photograph the day's results, so that analysts could determine whether the entire process needed to be begun again.

Havoc's debut

A similar massive scale of constant air operations took place over much of France in the days and weeks before the invasion. The size and scope of the Allied missions varied, particularly with the onset of inclement weather, but heavy flak defences did not prevent the vital job from being carried out. A number of German Army installations were attacked on 3 March, the mediums also leaving their calling-cards on several enemy airfields.

Having shouldered the lion's share of AAF tactical bombing in the ETO for the best part of a year, the B-26 force was about to be joined by the 416th Group. Assigned to the 97th Combat Bomb Wing, the unit was based at Wethersfield, Essex, equipped with a range of Havoc production models from the solid-nose G and H batches and the J and K versions with bombardier provision; the group was commanded by Col Harold L. Mace. Placed on operational status on 3 March, personnel geared up for their combat debut the following day.

As was to be more-or-less standard practice, the 416th would generally operate much like the Marauder groups by bombing from medium altitudes, those aircraft not configured to carry a bombardier flying 'in trail' with lead ships that did. The component squadrons of the 416th were in common with the other ETO A-20 and B-26 groups, in

numerical sequence: the 668th, 669th, 670th and 671st.

It has been said that the way in which the A-20 was used in the ETO tended to nullify some of the aircraft's undoubted qualities, and that the decision was a compromise. A fast, well-armed and reliable aircraft, the Douglas light bomber arguably found most success in the Pacific, where its speed, coupled with increased armament, made it the first of the famed strafers that became the very scourge of the Japanese. The early negative results of the Ijmuiden raids, plus some similar problems in the Mediterranean, led IX Bomber Command to deploy its Havocs in much the same way as the Marauders, although, despite an external similarity, the two types were actually very different in detail.

To overcome any perceived drawbacks in operating solid-nosed A-20s, the light-bomber groups had to adopt formation or 'trail' bombing on bombardier signal. This

Left:
The three-man crews of the A-20s did sterling work in Europe, although not everyone thought the Havoc an ideal type for the theatre. The gunner in the centre of this 416th Group crew carries the single machine gun operated from the ventral position.
Imperial War Museum

Below:
Tails twitching to keep everything in an orderly line, 671st Bomb Squadron A-20s prepare to take-off from Wethersfield on another post D-Day mission.
Merle Olmsted collection

Above: The single-seat fighter-like cockpit of the solid-nosed A-20Gs and Hs used by the Ninth included a thumb button on the control column for the fixed nose guns. *Imperial War Museum*

much-enhanced danger of being shot down by the defences, compared with other theatres), numerous A-20 crews flying aircraft with gun-noses did so. There was an understandable temptation to let fly with the concentrated firepower which was better than that of some fighters, but the vicious flak was an effective disincentive.

An additional bonus to A-20 crews was that the turret gunner, who rarely had cause to trade shots with enemy fighters, came to be the 'eyes' of the crew. With the excellent visibility afforded by the almost frameless turret, the occupant could maintain a running commentary on what went on in the vicinity of the aircraft and, particularly, on the ground. A ventral hatch in the aft fuselage also enabled a crew member to see what was going on behind and below the aircraft, although this was 'the worst seat in the house' due to the fact that, when in use, it was open to the elements. The hatch was provided with two folding doors so that a brave soul was also able to help defend the A-20 from fighter attack, as the position had a single 'fifty' complete with bolt-on armour plate.

The type of 'mixed' formation adopted by the Ninth for the A-20 helped to retain the inherent flexibility of the Havoc, which had exemplified the original AAF 'attack' concept better than any comparable aircraft. In addition, some crews were

resulted in a relatively small weight of bomb delivery: each A-20 carried a maximum of 2,000lb in the internal bay, boosted, from the later-production A-20Gs onwards, by an additional 2,000lb under the wings on four racks holding up to 500lb each.

Protected from above by an excellent Martin dorsal turret, the Ninth's Havocs usually made their target run-in at about 280mph. Although the ETO missions did not advocate strafing of targets after bombing (as, statistically, there was a

Above: The bomb-on-lead crew system used in the ETO meant that many A-20s with solid gun noses, like '"R" Shanty', could be used as bombers, but were rarely able to make ground attacks in the face of heavy flak defences. *Merle Olmsted collection*

Above: Fine view of an A-20J or K lead ship of the 410th Group, complete with flash suppressors on the turret guns and underwing bomb-racks which boosted the internal load by 1,000lb — a useful addition. *USAF*

trained to fly the A-20 at night — which few other AAF units did at that time — and in this way the Douglas attack bomber added to its laurels. Disturbing the enemy's nocturnal respite — one he had long enjoyed when the last of the day bombers turned for home — became something of a Havoc speciality, albeit on quite a small scale. The 'daylight only' mission was a recognised failing of the USAAF tactical force, as the enemy had no hesitation in exploiting it and using the hours of darkness to maximum advantage to move troops and equipment, effect repairs and establish or reinforce defensive positions.

Twenty-one A-20s were despatched to various enemy airfields on 4 March in company with 251 B-26s, but the intended combat debut of the 416th had to be postponed as far as the actual bombing of the enemy went, as a solid overcast

remained stubbornly unbroken to cloak all the intended targets.

B-26s bombed V-weapons sites at St Omer and Abbeville on the 5th, 207 aircraft participating. More sites were pounded on the 6th, and Beauvais/Tille aerodrome was also attacked, as was a marshalling yard at Hirson. This large-scale, 300-aircraft mission by the medium groups was not as effective as intended; fifty B-26s and A-20s despatched concurrently to Creil marshalling yards had to abort when they ran into bad weather. Escort to the B-26 force was again in the capable hands of RAF Typhoons, which on this occasion recorded a rare clash with Luftwaffe fighters. One Typhoon was lost and another damaged.

Among the B-26s operating that day

were those assigned to the 344th Group at Stansted, which made its operational debut. The target for 37 Marauders from Col Reginald F. C. Vance's group was Bernay/St Martin aerodrome, and, although flak welcomed the group to France, there were no crew casualties. Four aircraft received slight damage.

The last echelons of the 409th Group — the second with A-20s to join the Ninth — were established in the UK by 7 March. As with the 416th before it, groundcrews of the 409th had had to assemble aircraft that had come over from the US as deck cargo. This work was all but completed, and as the unit was about to go operational it found itself in the middle of a minor crisis not of its making.

For some time the units in IX BC had

A flight of A-20s from the 671st Bomb Squadron, which applied the code '5C' as part of the 416th Group. *USAF*

Above: Eight 671st Squadron A-20s over the English countryside. The aircraft on the left has the disruptive medium-green camouflage that was common on Havocs. *USAF*

been experiencing personnel shortages, and the arrival of a new Havoc unit threatened to make this situation worse. The reason was that the 409th had been trained as a night-bomber unit — one of the few the AAF had. While there was little doubt that further disrupting the enemy during the hours of darkness could only assist the Allied war effort, the freshman group found itself with a shortage of night-qualified bombardier-navigators. This problem was addressed by making in-theatre transfers of individual crew members from B-26 units and re-training them — a move that imposed a further strain on already-stretched resources in some quarters.

Missions for 7 March included a double effort for the Marauders, 112 of which bombed installations at Creil-sur-Mer and Greny, coastal V-weapons sites and targets of opportunity. A further force of 150 Marauders would have attacked rail targets

at Creil had they not been forced to return home on receipt of another bad-weather recall.

That the weather seemed to be, as one anonymous airman put it, 'still batting for the Germans' was a phenomenon beyond human explanation, but locals living around the medium-bomber airfields could have assured their American guests that the English spring weather would eventually improve. Such a promise would have been only half believed by the crews.

Satisfying though it was in military terms, the attack on Volkel and Soesterburg airfields in Holland on the 8th brought a weather-related disaster to the 344th on only its third mission. Taking-off and climbing to get above a low cloud ceiling, the group's 54 Marauders were suddenly reduced by two. The aircraft flown by 1st Lt John K. Eckert and Capt

Jack W. Miller had collided in the murk. So sudden had the impact been that no one had a chance to get out — in a matter of seconds, fate had claimed the lives of 12 men.

The bombing at Soesterberg was rated 'good', the 344th dropping 571 100lb and 49 500lb bombs in the face of intense flak, which hit 14 aircraft. The subsequent PR coverage of the aerodrome confirmed the crew reports that they had hit the place hard.

Inclement weather continued to interfere with air operations, plaguing crews with continual recalls, impeding accurate navigation and increasing the danger of collision. Such only added to the daily strain of operational flying, which could be bad enough even when things did go according to plan. This worried IX Bomber Command Headquarters to the extent that

Above: A-20 of the 416th Bomb Group coming off the target. It carries the '2A' code of the 669th Squadron. *USAF*

it notified all groups that, in view of crew shortages (caused mainly by battle fatigue and 'war neurosis', as it was officially termed), each A-20 and B-26 group was, until further notice, to send out no more than 36 aircraft on normal missions and a total of 54 on 'maximum efforts'.

Weather problems continued to dog the AAF tactical bombers, which were on 10 March officially ordered to concentrate almost exclusively on pre-invasion targets. This was a broad term that indicated targets other than those directly associated with the V-weapons construction programme. This latter was being well contained, but such targets continued to be attacked by the medium bombers, as the records clearly show. More 'Noball' sites were bombed the day following the 'switch of target' directive, although nearly half the 114 sorties despatched from the B-26 bases had to be aborted in deference to the weather.

In the following weeks there was little actual change of emphasis: 'Noball' sites

continued to figure prominently on the IX BC target list, as did marshalling yards, locomotive works and bridges, all of which were attacked during the remainder of March.

The war against the German robot bombs was shared with the RAF and USAAF heavies, which were able to deliver tons of HE from altitudes that put them well above the overcast that continued to frustrate the medium-bomber crews. Such a mission took place on 21 March, when B-24s did at Watten what the Marauders again failed to do because the crews could not see the ground. This location was later revealed as being associated with the second of the *Vergeltungswaffe* weapons — the Army-directed A-4 (V2) long-range rocket — rather than the flying bomb. Watten was eventually so devastated by air attack that any further work there was abandoned by the Germans.

Debut, 394th

Somewhat clearer conditions over Europe on 23 March at least allowed the B-26s of the 394th Group to complete their debut mission by bombing Beaumont-le-Roger aerodrome. It was always hoped by the crews that mission number one would be completed on schedule, and the participants returned to Boreham airfield greatly elated that things had indeed gone well enough on this occasion. With the 584th, 585th, 586th and 587th Squadrons assigned to it, the 394th was commanded by Col Thomas B. Hall.

Other B-26s had meanwhile flown the morning mission to Beaumont and followed up with a second raid, to make a mess of the marshalling yards at Haine-St-Pierre.

On 26 March 1944 Dwight D. Eisenhower, designated Supreme Allied Commander for 'Overlord', approved the plan that would aim to achieve complete

About to touch-down at its Continental base is an A-20G or H of the 409th or 416th Bomb Groups. *USAF*

Above: Unusual style of bomb log for an A-20G/K, believed to have been from the 409th or 416th Groups. The cowgirl was a popular Vargas pin-up copied onto a good many US aircraft. *Imperial War Museum*

isolation of the selected invasion beaches from the European transport system. The AAF and Allied air forces henceforth set out to do just that; the burgeoning might of the US tactical and strategic bomber forces could now, if necessary, enjoy the support of more than 950 fighters in a single day's operations — a figure contrasting sharply with the waning strength of the Luftwaffe. The likelihood of conventional airpower being able to disrupt the assault on Europe began to look quite remote — for, unless the Germans stripped all other war fronts of fighters to reinforce northern France, there would be little to stop the Allied armies from getting ashore.

Eisenhower anticipated that Allied air superiority over the invasion beaches, barring the totally unexpected, would be absolute. There remained, however, the threat from the unconventional. Many people appreciated what a rain of V1s might do to an amphibious landing force (although such was never a serious intention on the part of the Germans), and numerous launching sites on the Operation 'Crossbow' list were wiped out by bombing and never used in anger. Some sites and bomb-storage areas had by the spring of

1944 already been abandoned as totally untenable or not worth the time needed to repair them — but until every site within range of the coast was in the hands of Allied troops, the danger remained acute. Having been denied all the sites built under the first phase of the programme, the Germans had embarked on the construction of a second set which were smaller in area and better camouflaged than before. These were also found and bombed.

Return to Ijmuiden

Aircrews on the Marauder bases could have been forgiven for leaving the briefing rooms on 26 March with a steely glint in their eyes. When they knew the target, cheers went up, for they were going back to that Marauder nemesis, Ijmuiden. Etched in the minds of many a B-26 crewmen, the very name of that area of Dutch territory brought about feelings of revenge. 'Give 'em hell!' took on a whole new meaning.

In fact, the day's 'hell' was to be directed at the German Navy's E- and S-boat docking facilities and pens at

Ijmuiden, rather than the notorious generating plant itself. A substantial force of 338 B-26s and A-20s was assembled for the attack, which was a US contribution to a considerable degree of torpedo-boat combat in and around the English Channel at that time. Marauder crews had previously flown training exercises with British MTBs, so they had some idea of the speed and manoeuvrability of such craft, should their German equivalents be found at sea. But this was a far-from-ideal target for the mediums; concrete pens for naval vessels were usually very well built, and to break them really required much more destructive bombs than the Marauder could carry.

Crews expecting to score a moral if not physical victory at Ijmuiden were frustrated, for the formation leader misdropped his bombs, and enough of the other crews followed suit to result in only very slight damage to the target. Two S-boats destroyed in return for a B-26 lost to inventory was not seen as a good result!

The unfortunate statistic on the American

Above: A long-serving veteran of the ETO was 'Bar Fly' of the 554th BS, 386th BG, which survived all the rigours of combat only to crash in the US during a bond tour. *USAF*

side was Gove Celio, who had flown the first Ijmuiden mission and took much satisfaction in leading the third medium bomber strike to that area on 26 March. Having lost an engine to flak, Celio led the strike in and bombed. Heading home, he reached England but was forced to crash land, writing-off the Marauder in the process. Celio's second-element leader had been Howard M. Posson, and at the head of the third box was Louis J. Sebille — both were veterans of the Dutch power-station raid that had almost broken the B-26. In the crews were three Purple Heart recipients who had been wounded at Ijmuiden; had the mission actually been to that same location, if determination counted for anything, the 322nd would surely have wiped it off the map!

Bad weather still prevented the full weight of bombs from falling on all the targets selected by the AAF high command, despite the fact that the raids were invariably planned, the crews were briefed and the aircraft took-off. On more occasions than anyone liked, that was all that happened. 'Turn around and go back, buddy, the weather is SNAFU — again.'

Aborted missions tore at the nerves of crews almost as much as flak-filled skies over a hot target because, more often than not, they did not count on a man's record. Most individuals looked forward to going

Above: Lt Jack Logan's B-26B 'War Horse' was one of many skillfully decorated Marauders in the 394th Bomb Group. *R. M. Brown*

home at the end of their tours of duty, and, if missions were scrubbed, it took that much longer to complete the obligatory 'tour' of 65 missions, with the increased risk of injury or worse if the war situation changed and, for example, the targets got even tougher.

Not surprisingly, bomber crews already knew the worst targets by heart. Word of mouth made flyers new to the theatre well aware of what they might expect if they were briefed, for example, for Amsterdam/

Schiphol airport, which, everyone said, boasted about 120 guns of varying calibres. But, while it was undoubtedly true that the high-level German flak could be uncomfortably accurate, it still took a direct hit in a vital spot to explode a Marauder — or any other aircraft — in mid-air. Such a feat was not, mercifully, achieved by many flak batteries. It did happen, but not with the frequency that might have been expected, when one considers the high number of guns ringing specific targets directed by

Above: A typical formation of staggered flights in tight combat boxes as adopted by the Marauder formations being demonstrated by the 323rd Bomb Group on 26 March 1944. *Imperial War Museum*

radar, the well-known quality of those guns, and the experience of the people who operated them.

That does not mean that damage from flak (some of it very bad) was not an important consideration to the Army Air Forces, but, in the profit-versus-loss equation, a damaged aircraft that returned home to be repaired many times, while hauling several thousand pounds of bombs at a time to three score or more (many more, in a lot of cases, with the B-26) targets, ensured the loss fell squarely on the shoulders of the Germans.

Taken in the context of the total tactical bombing campaign, the Allied air forces carried out a relatively small number of sorties specifically aimed at silencing AA guns. Conversely, the fact that target defence with artillery was given a much higher priority by the Germans than the results ever merited — a policy that ultimately required a personnel strength equal to that of several Luftwaffe field divisions, which might otherwise have been deployed as infantry — actually came to be seen as an advantage by Allied army commanders. For the Germans, this represented a significant waste of resources; had all the flak guns defending tactical targets — targets that were mostly destroyed or badly damaged, whatever their efforts — been used instead on the battlefield, they would have proven at least as effective as they did against aircraft.

5 Light Bombers Join Up

April '44

On 1 April further administrative changes that would directly affect the Ninth Air Force before and during the invasion were made at SHAEF headquarters. On the first of the month the Allied Expeditionary Air Force came into being, commanded by AVM Trafford Leigh-Mallory. For the succeeding months he would directly command the tactical bombers of the Ninth in conjunction with Sam Anderson.

By 5 April Col Richard T. Coiner Jr had his 397th Bomb Group organised and ready to begin operations from Gosfield. The last of the B-26 groups assigned to the Ninth Air Force — the 397th and its component 596th, 597th, 598th and 599th Squadrons — became part of the 98th CBW.

With little activity taking place in the first week of April, IX BC then launched 196 B-26s against Coxyde aerodrome and marshalling yards at Hasselt in Belgium on the 8th. P-47 fighter-bombers were also active in the latter area that day — the date administrative control of the 97th, 98th and 99th Wings passed to the direct control of IX Bomber Command.

While the effort put in by every group to set a combat mission in motion was largely the same, the bombing results were not always to the high standard of accuracy that Headquarters required. Bombing results were carefully scrutinised to see where improvements might be made, particularly in view of the requirements of the forthcoming invasion. On 10 April Lt-Gen Brereton, having studied numerous reports of bombing that had fallen below the 'good' to 'excellent' categories, ordered that all groups be stood down on a rotational basis, primarily to train replacement crews to the standard required. One of his reasons for this move may have been the bombing of Namur rail junction that day. Of the 267 tons of bombs dropped, strike photos clearly showed that there were good and bad results. Aiming for engine sheds at the heart of the yard, the bombers instead

Above: Plain and simple dedication to a wife, sweetheart or daughter on an A-20J-1 (44-84) of the 410th BG. *USAF*

plastered fields with HE bombs, although, as was usually the case, crews quickly recognised the error, corrected and hit the target. Good results were observed when a later force dropped squarely on the loco sheds. If Brereton believed improvements to be necessary, there was evidence to support this; on 2 May Busigny was hit, although, again, the early strike clearly showed bombs bursting in adjoining fields as well as detonations across the railway tracks. The bombers had dropped in boxes of 18 aircraft, but one flight in the first box was clearly off-form that day. One flight from the second box also missed, although the majority of the bombs fell where they were intended. Overall results achieved by the second box were generally good, with most bombs falling across the railway tracks, apart from those aimed by one crew which, it was later established, had experienced intervalometer trouble and bombed a nearby field.

The strangest aspect of this attack was that the second box of the second wave of bombers reversed these earlier results by dropping numerous bombs in the village of Busigny. One crew recognised this gross error and corrected, to place their bombs on the railway tracks. This well illustrated how any error in the bomb-on-leader system could be compounded. If the first bombs went down in the wrong place, many would immediately follow; it took time for following boxes of bombers to recognise and correct any error. The alternative, which was to have each crew bomb individually, had obvious flaws and the AAF was forced to adopt an inevitable compromise and accept a certain degree of inaccuracy, ie that some bombs would always miss their targets. This was small comfort to the innocents living in friendly villages and hamlets who happened to live cheek-by-jowl with military installations and thus faced immediate danger. Any drive such as that initiated by Brereton to reduce bombing errors therefore had to be positive.

One of the commanding general's problems was that many veteran B-26 crews — those who had been flying combat missions in mediums since the early days — had by the spring of 1944 completed their tours and returned home. Crews new to the demands of Europe could not be expected to reach the same standard immediately. Those combat veterans who had volunteered to became instructors undoubtedly helped to make the training of new crews in the States as

realistic as possible, but there was no real substitute for front-line experience gained steadily over a period of time. In general terms, a measurable improvement in bombing accuracy was not only desirable but expected, as crew experience built up. Good performance came only through practice and attention to detail, and this was hardly a time to let standards slip.

Allied planners were all too well aware that great quantities of lethal munitions were being dropped on countries allied against the Axis, and needless loss of civilian lives as a result of poor or indiscriminate bombing was to be avoided at all costs. Peripheral casualties were never totally avoidable, however, there being too many variable factors in the execution of a highly complex air campaign involving hundreds of aircraft flying into a relatively small area on an almost daily basis.

It is to the lasting credit of French, Belgian and Dutch civilians that, rather than bear any grudge against Allied airmen who had inadvertently killed their friends and relatives, they generally rallied to their aid. If they happened to be shot down and evade immediate capture by the Germans, AAF and RAF personnel were often whisked away via a number of secret 'lifeline' networks that in many cases saw them return to England. This risked the lives of dozens (if not hundreds) of patriots forced to live under enemy occupation.

Ike in command

On 11 April, Eisenhower, Spaatz and Brereton visited the 386th Bomb Group at Great Dunmow to watch the mission take-off. This was a regular occurrence at medium-bomber stations, which also welcomed the likes of Lord Trenchard, 'father' of the RAF, and AVM Trafford Leigh-Mallory. Some of the VIPs also flew missions with the groups, among them Cornelius Ryan — well known postwar as an author but then working for the British *Daily Telegraph* newspaper. Ryan also hitched a ride with one of the 386th's crews. This too was in no way unusual. The AAF was very accommodating of reporters who would, in the main, 'tell it like it was over there' to the friends and relatives of the air and ground crews. Great numbers of the flyers had never travelled outside the United States before the war, nor had their relatives. Despite the huge mix of ethnic groups that made up the population of the USA, modern Europe remained a remote continent to many of

them; up-to-date news of their men, and a war which few had experienced at first hand, was a significant boost to morale. It became an integral part of the important process of explaining to those at home exactly what the Army Air Forces were doing overseas. Much more free from security considerations than their British hosts, US reporters were generous in the space they gave airmen who had achieved distinction in combat. AAF press coverage via regular news releases distributed by the news agencies was also voluminous, as was official photography. Prints accompanied many of the stories about individual crews, campaigns and achievements in all fields. The work of the AAF was also made more widely known by radio broadcasts, which were a regular feature of wartime life.

At midnight on 13 April, Eisenhower was confirmed as Supreme Commander for the invasion and assumed control of all Allied air operations from the United Kingdom. For the tactical bomber force, which would soon become an integral part of the AEAF, a milestone mission that day was the delayed debut of the 409th BG (L), which was (as related earlier) the second Havoc unit to join IX Bomber Command. Based at Little Walden in Essex, the unit had the 640th, 641st, 642nd and 643rd Bomb Squadrons assigned, with Col Preston P. Pender in overall command.

By deliberately spreading its targets across Belgium and France to avoid any concentration that might give away the intended invasion area to the Germans, the Ninth succeeded on two counts. It not only kept this vital fact from the enemy, but also destroyed facilities many miles from Normandy. This was far from a wasted effort, for the more disruption caused to rail junctions, road crossings and supply dumps, many miles from the intended invasion beaches, the less chance the enemy would have of quickly reinforcing the coastal area when the time came. On the 15th, plans were issued for Operation 'Neptune', the sea-air operational phase of 'Overlord'.

On 20 April, slotting their targets in effect in between those of the heavy-bomber groups (which maintained their own strategic offensive against the V-weapons sites), nearly 400 B-26s and A-20s attacked gun emplacements, V1 sites, Poix aerodrome and targets of opportunity. The day's work was also the combat debut date for the 397th Group.

Having moved from Gosfield to Rivenhall on the 15th, the unit drew a V1 launching site at Le Plouy Ferme in the Pas de Calais as its inaugural target. Led by Col Coiner, the 36 B-26s duly bombed the site, although, in common with most of the other medium-bomber groups flying 'Noball' missions, the 397th would come to find the small sites frustrating and disappointing in terms of being able to bomb them accurately. Gosfield, having been vacated by the 397th, became the new base of the 410th Group's A-20s.

On 21 April IX Bomber Command sent 236 Marauders and 36 A-20s to carry out a similar series of raids to those of the previous day. Four B-26s were lost during the day's operations.

An even greater force, nearly 500-strong, made a further assault on 'Noball' targets on the 22nd, with 307 sorties being flown on the 23rd. Bad weather on 24 April then caused a recall, better conditions on the 25th bringing the now familiar drone of American aero engines to the ears of Luftwaffe flying-bomb and coastal gun troops as the B-26s and A-20s went to work on various V-weapons sites and gun emplacements at seven different locations along the coast. P-47s, meanwhile, attacked airfields in France and Belgium.

Plattling aerodrome was the target for 26 April — the day that the Ninth Air Force issued its own tactical air plan in support of Operation Neptune. On missions during this intensive period, the medium-bomber groups invariably mounted 'maximum effort' missions, more than a third of the total available force being deployed on some days. To enable such numbers to be despatched, all groups contributed on given days, Headquarters preparing the field orders to ensure that no unit flew a disproportionately higher number of sorties compared to the rest.

The 26 April mission sent about 450 mediums across the Channel, where these bombers poured more high-explosive onto coastal gun emplacements in the continuing effort to destroy or at least neutralise the defences of the 'Atlantic Wall'. This enormous network of 1,800 blockhouses, spaced at intervals of about 100 yards, stretched along the French coast from Cap de la Hague to Honfleur. If such fortified positions were of questionable value, in view of the overpowering strength of Allied air and naval power, they were of more use on a

coastline than anywhere else. A similar fixed defence line guarding a land border had been quickly overrun by the Germans themselves in 1940 when the much-vaunted Maginot Line had simply been bypassed.

In their attempts to break the wall, the American air forces were often frustrated in terms of actual destruction, as the huge fortifications, which took 245,000 tons of concrete to build, housed mainly large-calibre guns. Although the emplacements were all but impervious to the majority of AAF bombs, the effort was not wasted, as support facilities, including roads and storage areas, were wrecked at numerous sites and many blockhouses were damaged sufficiently to reduce considerably the weight of fire they were capable of sending out into the Channel.

Waste of the worst kind occurred when 'short' or 'long' bombing resulted in damage or destruction of civilian homes in and around the potential targets. Villages and hamlets that happened to have a V1 launching site nearby had residents killed and injured by bombs that missed their target. But the most dangerous place for French civilians — many of whom remained in their homes and carried on with daily life, tolerating the irritation of the occupying Germans as best they could — was a town with a sizeable rail junction or marshalling yard adjacent to it.

While railways generally skirted town centres, prewar urbanisation increasingly encroached, and in some locations it was all but impossible for the bombardiers to avoid peripheral damage. When a large-scale raid was in progress, the close proximity of other aircraft added to the difficulties the airmen had in accurately identifying aiming-points and targets. Heavy ground fire, haze, cloud and wind were among the factors that could ruin an otherwise well-aimed bomb pattern by distracting a number of bombardiers for even a few seconds at the critical moment.

Heavy cloud cover at the end of April again resulted in recalls, but the pace was such that some of the crews began to welcome the respite. There were 300 sorties on 30 April — a fact demonstrating to the American flyers that the English description of the weather being 'changeable' (ie foul one day and — relatively — fine the next) could be utterly relied upon!

Towards the century

It may have come as a surprise to some doubters that the B-26 was continuing to turn in a good to excellent reliability and survival record in the hands of the Ninth Air Force groups. Numerous individual aircraft had reached and surpassed the 50-mission mark by the spring of 1944, and there was every likelihood that one or two machines might just complete 100 sorties over 'Fortress Europe'. At that time the leading contender for this title was the 322nd's B-26B 41-31819 'Mild and Bitter', which flew its 83rd sortie on 18 April, its 85th by the end of the following day and had put number 91 'on the board' by the 23rd of the month.

Even though the Ninth Air Force bomber force had achieved much in its short existence in the ETO, there remained the vexed question of bombing accuracy. This had constantly to be monitored to ensure that any measures to improve it were implemented. No individual worked harder to achieve a constant measure of success than Sam Anderson.

In a memorandum dated 18 April 1944 General Anderson summed up his findings *vis à vis* bombing accuracy by Ninth Bomber Command. He had visited the Mediterranean, talked with flyers and consulted a number of officers right up to Ira Eaker, then commanding general, MAAF. Anderson realised that a number of factors divorced XII Bomber Command — which then included Wings of A-20s, B-26s and B-25s — from his own, but the problems the crews faced in terms of bombing were similar. One important advantage the tactical bombers in the MTO had over those in the ETO was that they had already had to contend with the challenge of support to an amphibious landing. As IX Bomber Command would be similarly preoccupied in a few weeks' time, Anderson was very keen to understand the special requirements of such an operation. As part of a comprehensive report to the commanding general, Ninth Air Force, Anderson also stressed the degree of interference caused by the weather. This applied to both theatres to some extent, but the medium groups operating over northwest Europe had been treated marginally more roughly by the elements than had their opposite numbers in the south. Getting down to details, Anderson said:

'IX Bomber Command cannot eliminate

Above: Easter Sunday service, 1944, probably at the 322nd's base at Andrews Field. New Marauders were by then coming in unpainted, which some commanders thought were far too much of a magnet for enemy fighters. Many had a coat of olive drab applied to their top surfaces. *Imperial War Museum*

the adverse effects of weather, enemy opposition and rate of operations on its bombing efficiency. However, a determined effort is now being made to improve our bombing accuracy by increased stress on training, selection of lead crews, maintenance of lead crew integrity, de-emphasizing the defensive in our briefing in favor of increased emphasis on the bombing problem, the elimination of incompetents, solution of the bombing problem prior to pre-briefing and finally requiring lead bombardiers and navigators to check actual winds encountered *en route* to the target against their preset meteorological data. If wind direction and speeds are found to vary from pre-set meteorological data, each bombardier will have in his possession a chart showing the change in disc speed setting necessary to compensate for the variation in actual ground speed from pre-computed ground speed. Greater emphasis will also be placed on killing drift.'

To further ensure that no invasion troops would be put at risk by navigational or other errors by his bombers, Anderson recommended:

'(i) that arrangements be made for each group of this command to have at least three practice bombing missions against beach positions at Slapton Sands; (ii) that if night harassing or reconnaissance missions are contemplated for IX BC after D-Day, one A-20 group be specially trained for and used only for this purpose; (iii) that the 322nd, 323rd, 386th and 387th Bomb Groups be stood down for a period of one week for training prior to D-Day, and (iv) that IX BC be authorised to exchange 42 inexperienced A-20 crews for 21 A-20 crews of XII Air Support Command who have had experience in the support of landing operations and in the general support of ground forces.'

May '44

The last of 11 medium- and light-bomber groups to join the Ninth Air Force in England flew its first mission on 1 May — or at least some of its crews did so, by flying in aircraft of the 416th Group. The second

day of May saw the Marauders and Havocs striking marshalling yards at Valenciennes, Busigny and Balnac/Misseron, and it was on the 4th that the A-20s of the 410th BG (L) joined other Havocs and Marauders in bombing a variety of industrial targets and marshalling yards for the first time. Commanded by Col Ralph Rhudy, the group had the 644th, 645th, 646th and 647th Bomb Squadrons assigned to it and had actually been in the UK since April. On the 4th of that month the A-20s had briefly occupied Birch aerodrome in Essex before being transferred on 16 April to Gosfield (in the same county), from which 26 pre-D-Day missions would be flown.

Like the 416th before it, the 410th had expected to fly a different kind of mission from the one that actually came its way in the ETO. Trained in low-level attack, the group had to undergo a hurried theatre conversion to medium-altitude bombing before it made its combat debut. Group personnel were the first to admit that their early efforts were poor; that the bombardiers lacked full confidence in handling the Norden sight was painfully obvious on the first few missions.

All involved had to concede that this criticism certainly applied to the group's debut attack on a 'Noball' site north of Le Havre, just in from the French coast. In a demonstration that was the complete antithesis to the goals Gen Anderson wanted from his crews, the box leader made two passes — it was said everyone was suffering from 'buck fever' — and bombs were scattered all over the area, from the IP to the target. Some crews failed to find anything worthwhile to drop on, and brought their bombs back.

These early disappointing results did not prevent the 410th's Havocs from sustaining battle damage. There was gradual improvement, but on only two missions during May and one in June was the bombing officially rated as 'excellent'. But as other groups had found, combat experience in the ETO built up fast;

encouraged by Col Rhudy, the 410th crews learned in a very short time. The group commander had the additional worry that the A-20 was not viewed everywhere as the ideal bomber for the theatre. At briefings he was fond of saying: 'Keep plugging, men, for you're proving that the A-20 belongs in the ETO after all.'

The 410th had entered combat during the campaign identified by the AAF as Air Offensive, Europe. This was reckoned to have begun on 2 July 1942 and would last until 5 June 1944; units thus engaged in this and four subsequent European campaigns up to the war's end were entitled to display a distinctive streamer denoting that service on ceremonial banners and flags. This was also a way for the AAF statisticians to break down what was becoming a complex and widespread conflict which did, of course, have clearly defined phases and was fought over particular geographical areas of the continent of Europe at various times.

Severing the arteries

Improved weather conditions enabled IX Bomber Command to send out sorties on 2, 4 and 6 May. Some of the targets were now more than familiar to the participating crews, but on 7 May the command opened an intensive campaign against rail bridges. A force of more than 100 B-26s extended their reach that day by flying to targets 120 miles northeast of Paris, to rail yards and locomotive-repair shops at Mézières-Charleville. German fighters could not pass up this chance and a number of attempted interceptions were made, although no bomber losses were reported.

Any bridges that could assist the German army in moving reinforcements into the invasion area were bombed, particularly those spanning the Meuse and the Seine. Fighter bombers were also an integral part of the Ninth's deployment against these vital targets, which were to involve a high number of sorties and absorb many hundreds of tons of bombs before they were neutralised.

Above: Charleroi power station, 30 miles southwest of Brussels, was a B-26 target in the spring of 1944. The group depicted is not positively identified, although the 344th is a possibility. The urban sprawl made target identification difficult, although crews were usually shown photographs and models to familiarise them with local landmarks. *Imperial War Museum*

The early-morning sun dramatically catches a pair of B-26s coming off a V1 launching-site target in the Pas de Calais on 25 April 1944. *Imperial War Museum*

Above: Impressive bomb logs were applied to many B-26s in the ETO, and 'Barbara Ann' of the 585th Squadron had her fair share. With about 90 already chalked up, this Marauder ultimately completed at least 125 missions. *J. V. Crow*

For IX Bomber Command it was partially back to 'Noball' sites on 8 May, the day that 'Overlord' was set for 5 June. Although the bombers again went after bridges over the Meuse, crews were now briefed to destroy specific bridges; the B-26s also flew that day to sever a link across the Seine at Oissel.

Among the aircraft returning from France on 9 May was 'Mild and Bitter', the first B-26 to complete 100 missions in the European theatre. It should be stressed that it was not the first Marauder anywhere to reach this milestone, as that honour had already been claimed by the Twelfth Air Force. But, needing little excuse to celebrate, the personnel of the 322nd in general and the 452nd Squadron in particular threw a party. 'Mild and Bitter' itself was taken off operations to make a triumphant return to the US. The broad intention of the subsequent tour it and a number of Twelfth Air Force Marauders carried out was to encourage AAF recruiting and sell war bonds — but if the sight of all those mission marks on the nose made those who doubted the aircraft's capability squirm, then the pro-Marauder lobby was hardly going to complain!

Not far behind 'Mild and Bitter' were other Ninth Air Force Marauders aiming for the 100-missions mark. As the oldest serving group, the 322nd had at least half a dozen aircraft nudging the century. They included 'Lil Porkchop', 'Clark's Little Pill', 'Bluebeard II', 'Pickled-Dilly', 'Sarah E' and 'Idiot's Delight'. Applying nose art and names to combat aircraft was not a practice invented in World War 2, but that conflict raised it to an extremely popular element of *esprit de corps*. Few practitioners were as enthusiastic as USAAF crews, and the Ninth's medium bombers were as well-decorated as those anywhere, to the point that few bombers went into combat without a name and/or painted talisman. Appearing adjacent to the name and artwork, bomb logs were almost *de rigueur*, for these presented an at-a-glance record of an individual aircraft's service.

Many Marauders with an extensive record of missions also bore the scars of war and numerous traces of the effects of hard flying to some of the world's toughest targets. And every B-26 reflected the dedication of the ground crews in lavishing time, care and patience, often in less-than-ideal conditions, on their charges. These teams of specialists, many of whom had volunteered for service 'for the duration', ensured that, each time a mission was scheduled, 'their' aircraft was ready. Leave for groundcrew could be as rare as the proverbial hen's teeth, but few complained. They took pride in getting the job done, for without them the aircraft would soon have succumbed to one failure or another.

The Ninth Air Force's pre-invasion bridge-busting campaign was not, as with other types of target, limited to areas; still mindful that, if any definite pattern of attacks were to emerge, the Germans might guess the intended invasion points, the Allied high command ordered that multiple-bridge attacks be made across a wide arc of northwestern France. These, in addition to 'Noball' sites, gun emplacements, aerodromes and marshalling yards, now figured regularly at early-morning briefings for the bomber crews. By flying several missions to multiple targets in one day it became possible for the Ninth to range far and wide, giving the enemy little respite from the bombing and, indeed, scant chance to effect repairs to structures already badly damaged. With pre-invasion 'softening up' having top priority, it was usual for some tactical targets to be attacked by heavy bombers as well as mediums and fighter-bombers. All three elements of the AAF in England worked overtime to make the ground forces' job that much easier when they got ashore.

In an area of airspace that represented the most concentrated level of military traffic ever seen, the vast ground organisation that toiled behind the scenes to assist the aircrews was worthy of the highest praise. As the number of aircraft streaming back and forth across the Channel and the North Sea multiplied, there was almost a daily risk of disaster from collision. That this rarely happened was to the credit of the ground controllers who guided their charges, via radar and radio signals, as far from England as they could, after which the bomber navigators and fighter pilots took over the responsibility of making the correct landfall, of plotting the briefed route to the target, and of getting the aircraft back to England in one piece.

For the flyers, the inevitable drawback to almost any continental target was that, once it had been attacked and damaged rather than destroyed (as was invariably the case), the Germans moved in their flak batteries in force. Anti-aircraft fire remained the most deadly adversary of the medium and light bombers, the number of guns being located around bridges being particularly heavy. Well aware that an Allied invasion was imminent, the Germans fully realised the vulnerability of the vital transport links and made every attempt to protect them.

Bad weather returned on 12 May and, although it did not result in an *en masse* recall of the bombers, many individual crews opted to return rather than to fly around in dangerous, low-visibility conditions. Various tactical targets were bombed by the aircraft that managed to penetrate the thick haze that hung over large tracts of France and Belgium. On 16 May a B-26C (41-34863/RJ-P, dubbed 'Bingo Buster') belonging to the 454th Squadron became the first in the 323rd Group to complete 100 missions and only the second Marauder in the ETO to do so. Like 'Mild and Bitter', this aircraft was rotated home to show the flag for AAF recruiting. Other B-26s were fast approaching their century sorties at that time.

Through mid-month the mediums were sent to the regular variety of targets, although the weather persisted in deterring numerous individual sorties. All group records reflected the fact that the equipment available in 1944 could often be foiled by conditions that reduced visibility. That said, much had been achieved. The 'Noball' offensive had largely succeeded in its purpose, and the heavily-bombed forward continental airfields were rendered largely untenable.

Above: Most distinctive of the ETO Havoc markings were the black and white angled rudder stripes of the 410th Group, seen on an A-20K lead ship of the 645th BS with '7X' code. *USAF*

Gaps had been created in the chain of coastal guns and anti-invasion obstacles that covered the most likely landing places, and, most important of all, huge holes had been torn in the German radar network, to the point that some areas were completely blind. Railways and roads had also been cut in numerous places, and locomotives and rolling stock had been destroyed on an impressive scale.

Against the flak

Coastal flak batteries were a constant menace to Allied air operations over France; they rarely failed to open up when a mission came within range and in many cases the only casualties from a mission were caused by these guns. In an effort to deplete this troublesome enemy response to AAF operations over France, the 344th and 397th Groups attacked batteries at Marquise, northeast of Boulogne, on 19 May. The 38 B-26s from the 344th were escorted by P-47s of the 373rd Group — which encountered intense AA fire. The 397th's objective was at nearby Plage-de-Ste-Cécile, and elements of the 373rd also covered these Marauders. Concurrently, in a day of typically heavy aerial activity, the 323rd despatched 35 aircraft to targets in

the Dieppe area under Spitfire escort, while the 394th's 28 B-26s bombed Varengeville-sur-Mer, also with an escort of Spitfires. The 358th Fighter Group drew escort duty to other Marauder attacks that day, the 391st and 386th bombing flak batteries at Fécamp and Ste-Marie-au-Bosc respectively.

A similar level of activity against the same targets took place the following day when the Ninth Air Force pressed home the positive results of the previous day's work by sending the bombers to pound the lair of their main antagonists. There was something satisfying in these missions in that, if the flak ceased firing after the bombs burst, the crews knew they were right on target — anything that could reduce the volume of high-explosive that clawed at the medium bombers raiding the continent was welcome. The command ordered the bombers to hit batteries at Plage-de-Ste-Cécile, Varengeville and Fécamp, and, for good measure, sent additional sorties to Beaumont and Cormeilles aerodromes, as well as the port of Dieppe to knock out several installations within the dock area.

The 323rd hit Dieppe with 36 sorties. During the attack a B-26B (41-31950) of

Above: A-20G/H Havocs of the 410th demonstrate their technique with an impressively close formation. These 646th Squadron gun-nosed Havocs have a J/K bombardier ship in the lead position. *USAF*

the 453rd BS, flown by Major J. Heather, was hit by two flak bursts and was last seen going down in the target area. A second Marauder (B-26B 41-31818) from the 453rd was hit by a heavy burst, as was B-26B 42-107584 from the 454th Squadron, which fell out of formation to explode in mid-air near Calais — a grim reminder (if any were needed) of what the crews were usually up against. Thunderbolts of the 406th FG were powerless to stop the AA fire put up to destroy the bombers, although other missions that day went largely untouched. The 37 B-26s bombing Plage-de-Ste-Cécile had an escort of P-38s from the 370th Group, the P-47s of the 407th likewise covering 37 Marauders of the 397th Group on a mission to Varengeville without loss. A similar P-38 escort was provided by further elements of the 370th for the Fécamp force, which comprised 38 B-26s of the 387th Group. Lightning

escorts were provided for the other medium-bomber missions of the day, the 367th, 370th and 474th Fighter Groups doing the honours.

It was primarily a B-26 force that raided Beaumont and Cormeilles, the strength being drawn from the 386th, 391st, 344th and 322nd Groups, with the 416th additionally sending 35 A-20s to the latter target, where they unloaded their bombs at 19.50hrs.

Four PFF Marauders led in 30 B-26s from the 322nd and 32 from the 391st on the afternoon of 21 May, when the mission schedule selected Abbeville/Drucat airfield for substantial attack. In line with the policy of denying the Luftwaffe the use of all its front-line fighter airfields prior to D-Day, this operation was well protected by the Ninth Air Force's two Mustang

groups — the 354th (which put up 43 aircraft) and 363rd (18). Although the bombardiers had some difficulty with 9/10 cloud cover at the target, the force experienced no other mishaps and dropped 127 500lb GP bombs on the airfield as well as scattering leaflets. Having crossed into France between Cayeaux and Le Tréport, the B-26s exited over Pointe de St Quentin, a rough loop around the target with different ingress and egress points being standard operational procedure — there was no desire to give the coastal flak two cracks at the bombers on their way in and out.

There was a further attempt to reduce the flak batteries on 22 May, the 397th sending 34 Marauders to blast batteries at Ste-Marie-au-Bosc. There was considerable RAF fighter activity in the

Above: Prior to the sort of heavy landing that almost guaranteed a final trip to the graveyard, this A-20G of the 645th BS, 410th BG, appears to have flown through something unyeilding. Named 'Zombia', the aircraft had completed 101 missions. *Merle Olmsted collection*

form of Rangers and Ramrods in the area and no escort was provided to the bombers, which nevertheless came to no harm and achieved good results from their bombing. US fighter groups from the Eighth and Ninth Air Forces, as well as RAF mediums in the form of Mitchells and Bostons, maintained a huge traffic pattern over northern France during these weeks, the 22nd being no exception.

Three aerodromes — Beauvais, Cormeilles and Evreux — and two flak concentrations were bombed by the 344th and 386th Group in the afternoon, the Marauders being escorted by the Thunderbolts of the 358th Group.

Evreux was the secondary target for a Havoc force of 68 aircraft from the 409th and 410th Groups, both of which were unmolested courtesy of the escort provided by the P-47s of the 362nd Group. In the event, this force bombed the primary at Cormeilles and the result was officially rated as 'excellent'. This was not a day to be anywhere near that particular airfield, for all the B-26 strikes were rated from 'excellent' to 'good', with the 344th's boxes being particularly outstanding.

On the other side of the coin was a poor rating for two other boxes (34 aircraft) of 344th Marauders which hauled their bombs to Beauvais. The worst score of the day was laid at the door of the 386th, which was humbled by a 'gross' rating when a misread waypoint by the formation

leader resulted in the 18 Marauders going right off-course and missing the objective by some 15 miles. The innocent woodlands of the Bois de l'Annette received an unexpected deluge of American high-explosive.

That there was really nothing wrong with the 386th's bombing was demonstrated by a second box of 19 aircraft which unloaded on Beauvais with good results. At the end of a day's operations best described as uneven, the 'poor' credit for the 387th's anti-flak bombing at Barfleur and the 'fair' for the 323rd at St-Pierre-du-Mont meant that both gun batteries would probably have to be revisited.

Complying with FO 327, the Ninth readied a strong force of B-26s and A-20s, plus escorting fighters, for a series of airfield attacks on 24 May. Again, the mix would have been familiar to the bomber crews, for at briefing the names of three airfields — Achiet, Beauvais/Tille and Beaumont — would hardly have come as much of a surprise. Of the two flak batteries that the bombers would also attack, one was at Barfleur, which had not been knocked out the day beforehand, and the other at Ste-Marie-au-Bosc, which had also been visited previously.

The 322nd and 344th Groups drew Achiet aerodrome, and boxes from both groups achieved 'excellent' to 'good' bombing results. On withdrawal in the vicinity of Lille, the bombers' escort, provided that day by the P-47s of the 373rd Group, was attacked by FW190s. No bombers were hit, but the escort lost a P-47 in return for one enemy fighter downed.

The 386th and 391st Groups hit Beauvais under escort from the 406th Fighter Group, while all three A-20 units contributed to the total of 118 aircraft that bombed Beaumont, with only 'poor' results. Not much better was the performance of the 397th and 323rd Groups in attempting to place their bombs on the flak emplacements at Ste-Marie. All results were rated from 'fair' to 'poor'.

Cloud partially obscured the ground at Barfleur below the B-26s of the 387th and 394th, but pathfinder guidance enabled the lead box from the 387th to place enough bombs accurately for a 'good' rating. Deteriorating weather brought the following boxes' performance down to 'fair', other bombing not being rated as the results could no longer be observed with any clarity.

Above: The first B-26B to complete 100 missions from England was 41-31819 of the 322nd. Named after a popular British drink, it was signed by air and ground crews before going home to the States for a 'show the flag' war-bond sales tour. *S. Piet collection*

The evening of the 24th brought a further massive effort by the Ninth Air Force to render Abbeville, Cambrai and Beaumont aerodromes untenable, and the force of A-20s and B-26s also made repeat visits to port facilities at Dieppe, the Plage-de-Ste-Cécile flak batteries and a 'Noball' site at Behen.

Once more, all three Havoc groups contributed to the force sent against Abbeville, three aircraft out of the 416th's contribution of 42 aircraft dropping 'Window' to confuse enemy gun-laying radar. The results were excellent for two of the group's three boxes of A-20s, although the second box over the target did not do as well, managing only a 'poor' rating. It was not a good day for the 410th at the same target; the crews' efforts were described only as 'fair', while those of the 409th made bombing runs that translated into 'good', 'fair' and 'poor' concentrations right across the airfield.

As can easily be seen from the foregoing, the multiple-box formations adopted by the

Above: Close-up of the starboard side of 'Mild and Bitter', with autographs applied with whatever writing implement that came to hand. *S. Piet collection*

medium bombers did not result in uniformly good, bad or indifferent results. The small time-lapse between boxes passing the IP and reaching their aiming points enabled corrections to be made if the bombing by the box in front had clearly been off-target. That said, it was not unusual for the lead box to do better than

those behind, particularly as the former crews had a clearer view of the ground. Smoke and detonations could easily obscure the APs from the bombardiers in the following aircraft. This happened to the Marauders at Beaumont. The 391st stormed over the airfield, and the lead box of 38 aircraft bombed accurately to gain an

Above: The crew that flew 'Mild and Bitter' on its 100th mission in May 1944. Someone calculated that this B-26 had by then carried 166 crewmen into battle and had flown about 58,000 miles!
Imperial War Museum

Above: 'Lil Porkchop' was one of the early 322nd Group Marauders that flew more than 100 missions — a feat achieved by dozens of B-26s in the ETO. This view of the 451st BS aircraft shows a more modest bomb log early in its career. *J. V. Crow*

Above:
Marauder nose art wasn't all girls and racy names. WAC Virginia Reynolds paints the 25th bomb symbol on a B-26 with the 'class' name of 'Stirling Hutchens & Company Flyin' Circus'. It was flown by Lt 'John Bull' Stirling.
Imperial War Museum

Left:
Much Marauder nose art was of a high standard, and many people undertook the work. WAC Barbara O'Brien does the honours for B-26 'Jolly Roger' of the 450th BS in December 1943.
Imperial War Museum

Above: Nose art on a 323rd BG Marauder flown by Lt William J. Kelley. The rider to the name was probably a mark of affection rather than ridicule! *J. V. Crow*

Right: Similarity of name might indicate that this is the replacement for the original 'Rose' in the 323rd. *J. V. Crow*

Right:
Not to be outdone by their B-26 opposite numbers, the A-20 crews decorated their aircraft in similar fashion. 'Maxine', a J model of the 410th BG, had Texas leanings, as the state map below the cockpit indicates. The ship was otherwise dedicated to 'Clarice' and 'Dottie Lee' — assumedly the sweethearts of the rest of the crew. *USAF*

Below:
Sentimental message on the nose of an A-20G/H. *USAF*

Very well-rendered artwork on the nose of B-26B (42-96074) of the 584th BS. The Indian name meant 'Sleepy Eye'. *J. V. Crow*

Above: A grim view of an A-20J (43-10129) of the 416th, captured by the camera of a formating aircraft moments before it plunged down after taking a fatal flak burst on 12 May 1944. *USAF*

'excellent' rating. Box two did not do so well and achieved only a 'poor' result.

As regards the bombing of the gun sites at Plage-de-Ste-Cécile, the 387th's efforts ranged from 'excellent' to 'gross'. Here, the second flight of six B-26s improved on the bombing of the first, with an 'excellent' pattern. The third flight was 'good'. The effort of the second box began with a series of total misses ('gross' rating) and improved marginally with two 'fair' ratings for the second and third flights. At the same target, the 323rd contingent began by putting down an 'excellent' concentration, but other crews bypassed the objective. When the second wave came in again, the first flight made an 'excellent' drop; 'fair' was the best that the succeeding flight could achieve.

At Dieppe the 397th's bombing of the port installations and industrial areas was accurate enough, to rate an overall 'good' score for the 37 participating crews. Three B-26s dropped 'Window', while others were obliged to execute violent evasive action to avoid the worst of the flak.

Bombing of the 'Noball' target that was the objective of the 394th began badly when the lead bombardier experienced an electrical equipment malfunction and dropped to the east of the IP. The second flight was obliged to 'go round again', while the third experienced much the same problem as the first crew and also bombed east of the target area. It was the second box's second flight that did the most damage, the aiming by the leader and his flock of five B-26s garnering an 'excellent' rating, improving on the first which achieved only 'fair' results. The third flight aborted; although one flight did hit the objective squarely, that translated into only six aircraft out of 39 doing any real damage. In terms of AAF damage-classification for 'Noball' sites, the results of this mission had to be marked as an imprecise 'C — possible A'. In such a case, it all depended on what the bombers actually hit and what state the V1 launching site was in at the time, because it

was not unknown for the Germans to abandon a site that may have looked completely intact from above.

Night loss

On the night of 23/24 May the 322nd Group experienced a loss of personnel and aircraft almost as serious as that of the ill-fated Ijmuiden raid the previous May. This one, mercifully cloaked from any adverse publicity at the time, was something of a 'guinea-pig' mission for the veteran Marauder unit, as it had been selected for something for which it had never really trained.

Well aware of the good use the Germans made of the hours of darkness, when the predominant Allied day bombers were absent from the battlefield, AAF commanders decided to deploy the B-26 in a night-attack rôle. This had been envisaged as a possible secondary rôle for the Marauder, although next to nothing had been done to modify the aircraft for it.

During May 1944 the medium-bomber attacks on French targets were enormously damaging to the German war effort. One of the B-26 groups involved in 33 separate attacks on airfields during the month was the 496th Squadron, part of the 344th Group — the 'Silver Streaks'. *Imperial War Museum*

Above: Slogging through a not untypical cloud of flak bursts, the 455th BS, 323rd Group, runs in to the target at Dieppe. Too close for comfort, the flak bursts killed the bombardier of the aircraft at far right, although it still dropped its bombs. *USAF*

And, operationally sound though it was to be in a position to deploy a 'round the clock' air force, *ad hoc* experiments rarely worked well. This, the crews thought, definitely came into that category. The requirement was for selected crews to bomb with pinpoint accuracy at night, from between 4,500 and 7,000ft, using flares and under pathfinder direction. Not totally daunting by wartime standards, it was not really a job for unmodified B-26s with their glaring, undampened exhausts, no radar, no visual aids to detect enemy fighters and so on. But, once they got used to the novelty of flying in the dark, the Marauder men found they could indeed form up at night with few problems. These, the cynics predicted, would immediately become apparent as soon as the aircraft got over enemy territory.

In some ways the pessimists were correct. On the first mission there were few positive results from the pathfiner-led force's foray to Beaumont-le-Roger aerodrome. Similarly, the second 322nd night mission yielded little in the way of results. The third such mission did not take place until just over a month after D-Day.

On some days the Ninth's tactical bombers operated under their own AAF field order and the RAF concurrently flew fighter-escort operations not indirectly in support of the US bombers, the mission numbering being combined. Thus 24 May saw FO 329/'Ramrod 922' taking place, largely against rail bridges in Belgium. Two aerodromes, those at Monchy-Breton and Lille/Nord in France, were also attacked by the US mediums. It was the Havocs of the 409th and 416th that had Monchy as their objective, 71 aircraft being escorted by 48 P-47s of the 406th FG. Once again, the bombing results were described as disappointing, although no aircraft were lost or damaged.

At Lille the B-26s of the 344th and A-20s of the 410th formed a joint force, but this attack had to be all but abandoned, as did the planned B-26/A-20 strike on the same target. In sum, the day's work turned out to be little more than a waste of fuel for many aircraft; not all the bombing by some boxes at the Liège/Renory rail bridge could be observed, and the notorious flak around the city claimed two B-26s of the 323rd. Otherwise, the results achieved were 'good' to 'excellent', the lead boxes of the 386th and 391st Groups returning, along with the 394th which attacked a bridge at Liège/Seraing, with the best bombing of

the mission. The other 'excellent' pattern was achieved by a single box of the 387th which had bombed a rail bridge spanning the Meuse at Kinkenpols, near Liège.

On 26 May the medium bombers attacked bridges at Poissy and Vernon, with similar targets appearing on the board for the following five days until the end of May. The intensity of bridge attacks that month was reflected in some figures. Of the 13 structures bombed, 12 were reckoned to have been destroyed and one damaged badly enough to make the passage of heavy military traffic dangerous. Bombing of this kind was no mean feat, considering that a bridge looks like a strand of hair from two miles up; even through the bombardier's telescopic sight, it appeared not much thicker than a pencil.

Amiens

The importance to the Germans of the marshalling yards at Amiens was well enough known to Allied air commanders; the centre controlled much of the traffic on the main lines serving Lille, Valenciennes and the Pas de Calais area as well as services south to Paris and Rouen. As a military target it was difficult in that the yard lay within the eastern suburbs of the city, making accurate aiming essential, but, some 500 yards to the north, the River Somme, flowing east-west and parallel to the rail tracks, provided a reliable aiming-point for the aircrews. Aiming-points were clearly defined for the bomber crews at briefings, and on the afternoon of 27 May the Ninth's A-20s prepared to attack the yard. All groups were involved, and the day was to be long remembered by both the aircrews and the inhabitants of Amiens.

Something of a maximum effort was laid on for the Havoc force, which was to break the tracks, wreck switching gear and generally disable the yard, taking the locomotive depot as its aiming-point. The attack was to be led by the 409th Group, the following boxes being composed of the 410th and 416th. Fighter-bombers were to operate at the same time on diversionary sweeps, and the A-20s would have an escort of P-47s. The formation of 38 409th aircraft would form into two boxes, comprising 34 A-20Gs and four J-model lead ships with bombardiers. A similar composition was despatched by the 410th, which comprised 43 aircraft in two boxes, with 38 G models and five A-20Js. Finally, there were 41 aircraft from the 416th, consisting of three A-20Js and 38 gun-nosed models, in two combat boxes.

Take-off time at group airfields was shortly after 12.00hrs, the 409th A-20s rendezvousing with the 358th Group's Thunderbolts shortly afterwards. Weak and inaccurate flak greeted the crews as they crossed into France. As they proceeded further into hostile territory, other barrages computed the height of the American bombers correctly, and the A-20G (43-9694/W5-H) flown by 2nd Lt Raymond L. Gregg of the 640th BS was hit and went down northwest of Forges-les-Eaux. There were no survivors. This loss disrupted the formation and caused the flight to take wild evasive action in the face of flak that resulted in a further loss, the aircraft of Capt Leland F. Norton (43-9446/W5-Z). The latter aircraft was an A-20J-5 lead ship, the loss of which would badly handicap the unit's bombing, and the 409th decided to abandon the mission. FW190s then intercepted the group, 1st Lt Leon Robinson's gunner trading fire with one of the fighters before the German pilot gave up the chase.

On withdrawal, the A-20J-5 flown by Capt Leslie B. Huff (43-9448/W5-T) was shot down by the notorious coastal flak

and ditched off Le Tréport. Two Spitfire pilots kept a close eye on proceedings as the American bomber settled, and an ASR Sea Otter puttered down to pluck Huff and one other crew member from their dinghy.

In the meantime the mission passed into the hands of the other two A-20 groups; of these, the 416th, which had a number of aircraft damaged by flak, was hampered by a navigational error that put the group near Poix, miles south of Amiens. As they circled around, with Clermont to their left and Beauvais to their right, the group lead, Maj M. W. Campbell, gave the order to abandon the mission. The formation passed out over the coast at St-Valery-en-Caux, most of the Havocs still with their bombs aboard.

The 410th's two element strike (comprising 43 and 27 aircraft) was scheduled to have been made at 15.10hrs. But the group apparently arrived over Amiens early (at around 13.40) and attempted to carry out the mission as briefed. Crossing the town, and with the marshalling yards in their sights, both boxes released their loads. Again, the lead box of the first wave dropped more or less in the right place, if a little short — but all the following boxes, in both attacks, scattered bombs not on the marshalling yard but across the built-up areas of Amiens, wrecking many houses and causing inevitable casualties. Few if any bombs from the following boxes fell where they were intended. One aircraft from the 647th BS, flown by Lt Richard K. Robinson (A-20G 43-9965/6Q-K) was shot down by flak.

Other missions on the 27th were carried out by the Ninth's Marauders, there also being numerous fighter sorties with the primary purpose of escorting the mediums, and RAF Ranger sorties as well as bomber operations took place during the course of the day. That evening, the A-20s made another attempt to finish what they had hardly begun earlier, by complying with FO 332 — target: Amiens marshalling yards. Again the briefing was precise as to the IP, direction of attack and aiming-points, and again all three A-20 groups took part. Take-off was at 19.00hrs for the 409th at Little Walden, 33 aircraft being scheduled to fly the mission. There was soon one less. As group lead Capt Roger D. Dunbar climbed out, nobody in his crew of four (which included the group photographer) apparently noticed another aircraft on a

collision course. With its wheels still down, the A-20 had its entire tail unit severed by a P-51, which shed a wing as it went down to crash. The Havoc crashed with one survivor, Sgt Angelo Mattei, who was pulled from the wreckage by a Mrs Everitt, who had seen the aircraft come down. Later, group personnel collected $3,000 to present to her as a mark of grateful thanks for her courage. The money was used to help educate her young son.

With an unfortunate start to the mission, the 409th carried on to the target, meeting intense barrage flak northeast of Formière. This hardly proved lethal to the bombers, unlike the 'wall of flak' 6,000ft wide by 2,000ft high that confronted the crews as they neared Amiens. Evasive action prevented any casualties, however, and the flights signalled 'bombs away' at 20.35hrs. Again the citizens of the town were subjected to the whistle and crump of exploding bombs, which this time fell on the Gare du Nord station and its immediate area. Stray bombs created more rubble in the surrounding streets, however, and the French awaited the next onslaught.

Led by three 'Window' ships, the Havocs of the 416th appeared over the city mere minutes after the 409th. The flak thundered as the bombardiers adjusted their sights prior to release, and 1st Lt Lucian J. Siracusa — who was, incidentally, Australian rather than American — suddenly had his work cut out to hold his A-20G (43-10203/5H-R) on an even keel. Hit in the right wing, the Havoc lurched out of formation, trailing smoke from a ruptured fuel tank. The bomber came to earth and burned east of Bertangles, all three members of the crew escaping with their lives to become PoWs.

The 416th's troubles were not yet over, as the intense flak claimed another victim, the A-20G flown by 2nd Lt Harry Earl Hewes Jr. With an uncontrollable engine fire, 43-9983/2A-J of the 669th BS fell in flames; although things looked bad for the crew, all three men managed to bail out and survived. The flak's toll of the 669th's Havocs increased as the group pulled off the target. A burst ignited a wing tank of A-20G 43-10206/2A-F1, flown by Allen W. Gullion Jr, who could not prevent the aircraft from making a long dive towards the ground. All three crewmen jumped out of the aircraft before it exploded in the Bois des Parisiens at Vignacourt.

As the 416th withdrew, with other aircraft in the formation having suffered flak damage, the townsfolk of Amiens emerged to count the cost of another American assault on the marshalling yards. Short bombing by the 416th, undoubtedly due to the heavy flak, had again resulted in demolition of and damage to dwellings well clear of the rail tracks. And the 410th was still on its way in for its bombing run.

By 21.05hrs two boxes of Havocs had poured more HE onto the Amiens rail network, the mission costing the group the aircraft flown by 2nd Lt Warren A. Thompson. Flying A-20G-35 43-10218/6Q-M of the 647th BS, Thompson had serious trouble as the flak made contact and fire took hold in the left engine nacelle. The Havoc dropped out of formation, but again the crew was lucky to abandon the aircraft in good order, all members coming down not far from a flak battery at Bray-sur-Somme.

As the rail centre at Amiens had not been disabled by the previous bomber sorties against it, FO 334 laid on a repeat mission on 28 May. This involved the B-26s of the 344th and 391st Groups, which were part of an ambitious day's operations that listed the targets as two V1 sites, two port targets and a German radio station at Bruges. After a late-afternoon take-off and form-up the formation headed into France, with the 28 B-26s of the 391st in the lead and 37 344th aircraft following. Their briefed route took the Marauders out across Beachy Head; over France they would make for Rouen and Amiens. Approaching the IP, which was northwest of Hornoy, the Marauders encountered flak, and one result was a curious incident witnessed by numerous crew members in accompanying aircraft.

A flak burst came too close to the B-26B (42-95943/T6-F) of the 573rd Squadron flown by 1st Lt Harry D. Porter. As co-pilot to the B-26 flown by Lt Clark in the second box of the high flight, 1st Lt George L. Parker saw a flak burst under the right wing of Porter's aircraft and what looked like oil coming out of the right engine. Clark's crew tried to contact the damaged B-26, but its crew showed no sign of having heard the radio call. Porter's Marauder then began to drop back before pulling up as if to regain position in the flight — but the bomber started to peel off right over Clark's ship, which was forced to drop out of formation to avoid a collision. Parker then observed the damaged Marauder level-out, apparently back under control while nevertheless losing altitude. It was seen crossing back under the flight, going down. By then the 391st was at the IP and the formation began a turn that would take it into Amiens. Porter's Marauder then made what looked to Parker to be a controlled final crossover below his flight before it was lost to sight in cloud. No parachutes were observed from the B-26, which had obviously suffered worse damage than the thin trail of smoke from the right engine indicated.

All seven of Harry Porter's crew were listed as MIA, which was standard practice, as news of the exact fate of downed crews took time to be transmitted to the bases in England, if it came at all. In this case, six parachutes were apparently observed by watchers on the ground.

Meanwhile, the group scored 'gross' to 'good' bombing ratings at Amiens, the bombs overshooting and undershooting the railway tracks. The 'gross' score was by one of the flights in the second box, which placed every one of its bombs in open fields beyond the town.

Although some of the May 1944 medium-bomber sorties to French targets appeared little short of disastrous and to negate any positive results of Gen Sam Anderson's earlier purge to weed out the unskilled or badly-trained and make bombing as precise as he could possibly make it, there had been some progress. Bombing errors were never entirely eliminated, but the ruthless clamp-down on inefficiency had seen bombardiers transferred and pilots replaced if they were not up to the job. Anderson's dilemma was that it was a waste of resources — and an unnecessary risk to the crews — if bombs were simply hauled across the Channel only to miss their intended targets. The débâcle at Amiens spoke volumes as to what could so easily go wrong on otherwise intricately-planned missions.

Anderson told pilots that they had to work more closely with their bombardiers to achieve results, and went so far as to demote or replace squadron or group commanders if he believed that they were not equal to the task. Nobody escaped scrutiny. The personal files on each individual member of a crew — those that followed a man everywhere he went during his military career — usually told Anderson everything he needed to know.

Wing Headquarters also probed into the physiological aspects of the kind of air war the Ninth was fighting. Personal motivation was checked and double-checked so that the 1,001 factors that bore on an individual's ability to be a useful member of a bomber crew were examined for any flaws. Fear, preoccupation, nerves, false pride, lack of practice — all these things came into the equation. Some errors could be traced back to insufficient training, and ignorance of the need to maintain awareness of what could go wrong on a typical mission.

Errors in bombing were due to numerous seemingly-minor mistakes and often a degree of ignorance about aircraft performance. It was drummed into pilots, for example, that the B-26 required 45 seconds of straight and level flight if the bombardier was to make a proper run into the target. That seemed like a lifetime to many flyers, but it had to be held. Anderson's investigation found that many crews had been taking far less time than that, and, more often than not, the bombs had missed. Equally, there was a need for pilots to know that, if they made a 30° turn and held it for 15 to 18 seconds, the aircraft would be a mile off-course — and it would require that much correction to bring it back onto the original heading. Some of it was basic flying procedure, but there were enough men who displayed scant knowledge of such things for Anderson to make changes. Some might have seemed harsh at the time — but the Ninth's bombing record, not to mention the commanding general's reputation, was at stake.

6 Crescendo in Normandy

June '44

Delivering high-explosive on targets from the Cherbourg Peninsula to the Belgian frontier, the air operations on 1 June foreshadowed a five-day crescendo of fire as the final preparations for D-Day were completed. By contributing about 1,100 sorties, the pre-invasion effort by the Ninth's B-26s and A-20s reached something of a peak — the scale of effort that had long been possible whenever the weather held.

On 3 June, crews of the 410th Bomb Group lifted their Havocs off the runway for the 32nd group mission of the war. They soon became part of a vast phalanx of Allied aircraft more than 250-strong which was to attack airfields, coastal gun batteries and road bridges in northern France.

One A-20 from the 410th's 644th Squadron, whose primary target was Chartres aerodome, was hit by flak. With its centre fuselage wrapped in flames, the onlookers could only stare in horror as Lt Benjamin D. Randolph struggled to keep the A-20 in the air. His efforts were to no avail and the aircraft fell away, taking Randolph and his crew, S/Sgts David A. Sagag and Frank Desanno, to their deaths. A fine pilot, popular with everyone, Ben Randolph had been an original member of the squadron during its training days in the US. His loss was deeply felt.

The increase in tempo in recent weeks had not fooled the crews. There was a widespread feeling that something big was about to break. And the time for it to happen was coming closer.

The groundcrews at the medium-bomber and fighter bases were among the first AAF personnel to realise that the invasion was imminent when, on 5 June, they were asked to paint black and white stripes around the fuselages and wings of every operational tactical aircraft on the bases in England. This huge task had to be completed with feverish haste, with sprayguns and brushes if these were available, but at some bases the job was done with makeshift applicators such as brooms and paint-soaked rags. In some cases the stipulated masking-out of code letters and national insignia was not done 'by the book', and some decidedly scruffy aircraft resulted. The reason for this new marking was, as with most such practices, to improve recognition by other aircraft and, particularly, 'friendly' gunners on the ground and on ships.

Being confined to base was the final indication that most personnel needed that the great moment had come. There were grumbles on this point, particularly from pilots who had recently completed their scheduled 50 missions and were about to go home. There was no way that their experience could be spared at so important a time, so they were obliged to remain until the invasion was a reality.

Varying weather conditions continued to give the Allied high command many anxious hours during 4 and 5 June. One postponement had to be made, but the available margin was only a matter of hours if the tides at the French beaches were to be utilised to the full. Any further enforced delay and all the preparations could be put in jeopardy. The unseasonal weather still made the undertaking a huge gamble even when a final decision was taken.

During the night of 5/6 June, four F-3-configured A-20s of the 155th NPS took off from Chalgrove and climbed to their mission altitude of 8,000ft. These Havocs — three of which carried flash bombs and the fourth the Edgerton Lamp — employed 'Gee' to locate their target area. This was found to be covered by a heavy overcast, but Lt Edward Lentscher's crew switched on the powerful light to illuminate roads at Villedieu and Coutances. When the photographs were developed, the roads were seen to be empty — clear enough evidence that the Germans were about to be taken by surprise. If that had not been the case, these and other roads into the beach-head area would have then been carrying heavy military traffic.

Then, in the early hours of 6 June, the invasion was on.

'Overlord'

At first light on 6 June the Ninth Air Force launched its B-26s to hit three coastal batteries in group strength. Among the first American airmen to witness the incredible armada of ships with their disgorging landing craft were the crews of the 56 344th Group Marauders, which took off at dawn to be over the target at precisely 06.09 — 21 minutes before the first landing-craft grounded on the beaches. Roaring off behind formation leader Maj Jens A. Norgaard (flying Marauder 'Mary Jo', named after his wife), the 'Silver Streaks' set course for Cherbourg. Their objective was the gun batteries at Beau Guillot, La Madelaine and St Martin de Varreville — one gun emplacement to each box of bombers.

On the target approach, flak claimed the B-26B (42-95902) flown by 2nd Lt James B. McKamey; hit in the right engine and with a fire in its full bomb bay, the aircraft was pulled out of formation and turned to head back across the Channel. The pilot's aim was clearly to ditch and give his crew the chance of being picked up, but fate took a hand and the B-26 exploded in mid-air. Despite this, three 'chutes were reported before the Marauder's sudden, violent demise, as the rest of the group turned for home, taking a course between the islands of Guernsey and Alderney. As they did so, the most amazing sight most of the airmen would ever see began to unfold on the sea below. Landing-craft ploughed toward the shore, which was soon being pounded by naval shellfire.

Hard on the heels of the 344th came the B-26s of Col Coiner's 397th from Rivenhall. Briefed to release its bombs at 06.21hrs, the formation dropped to 3,500ft to try to see the objective through the murky dawn off Utah Beach. When the seven German positions came into view, the group lost no time and bombed at the set time, nine minutes before the first troops waded ashore. Thanks largely to the almost total Allied domination of the

Above: Dawn, 6 June 1944. Every operational medium bomber on every base in England had black and white identification stripes applied for the invasion. It was a massive task, completed only shortly before the first sorties in the early hours. This scene was on one of the 386th Group's dispersals at Great Dunmow.
Imperial War Museum

airspace above them, only 12 men were killed during the landings. Six Marauders took flak damage.

In planning the medium-bomber contribution to support the landings, Sam Anderson had already had to order numerous changes, not all of which were popular. Now there were a few more: insofar as the regular mission composition was concerned, he reduced the size of a B-26 combat box from eight to six, primarily in consideration to the safety of Allied troops. Split-second timing was essential. A B-26 flying at 250mph covered ground at 399ft per second, and it had to be stressed to the crews that any missed approaches had to be aborted — there was too great a danger of hitting friendly troops, and there would be no time to make corrections.

Against the objectives nearest to friendly troops, the B-26s used 100lb bombs with instantaneous fusing. Larger bombs might have made deep craters that would impede men and vehicles. The target approach had also to be parallel to the beach rather than perpendicular, as this too could unnerve and perhaps endanger the men wading ashore below. Each B-26 box would bomb on a signal from the leader; the smaller-size boxes were an insurance against any HE that did happen to miss, reducing the devastation that might have ensued if 18 aircraft had bombed 'long' or 'short' of the target. The smaller boxes in very tight formation gave the crews a few

headaches, as they marginally increased the risk of collision, but the paramount consideration by air commanders had to be the safety of the invading troops.

Nothing had been left to chance. The Marauder groups had previously carried out a pre-D-Day exercise in which they released 100-pounders onto the beaches surrounding the inlet of the North Sea known as The Wash. Ground observers measured the craters made and pronounced them deep enough to have exploded any land-mines but shallow enough to allow a vehicle to pass over without getting stuck. Practice runs were also made with the co-operation of ground

Above: Among the stark images of the cost of the air war to the Allied air forces put out by the press agencies was a sequence of 1944 photos of a B-26 of the 453rd Squadron as it began a fatal roll to the left with its entire left engine shot away. The target was Wittlich. *Imperial War Museum*

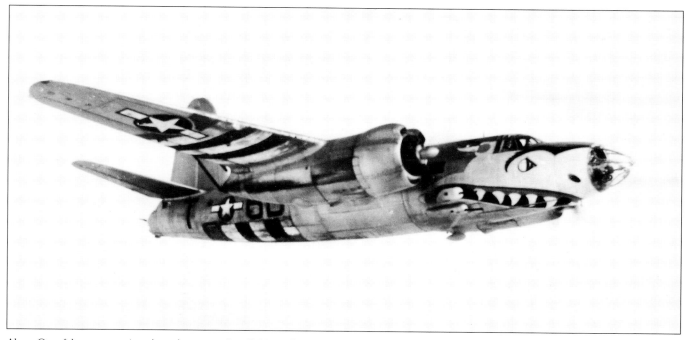

Above: One of the most attractive colour schemes worn by a B-26 was the yellow 'face' design of this ship (B-26B 42-96165) from the 599th BS, 397th Group. It became even more colourful later, when it was transferred to the 387th and acquired a 'tiger tail' stripe. *J. Hamlin*

Above: Even if the mission had to be scrubbed *en route*, bombing-up still had to take place. Muscle power gets 1,000-pounders ready for loading into B-26B 41-31755. *Imperial War Museum*

Above: Over the Matching runway threshold, the pilot of B-26C 42-107610 of the 391st Group prepares for another characteristically-fast landing. *J. Hamlin*

troops jumping out of landing craft, realistically rehearsing for the real thing.

As D-Day unfolded, the weather remained far from ideal. Brereton and Anderson had wanted a minimum ceiling of 4,000ft to bomb the selected targets visually. It was not there, so it was agreed to let the bombers go in considerably lower, but high enough for them to get safely clear of the bombs when they exploded. For this they needed at least 1,200ft, and even that height was looking doubtful as the 04.30hrs take-off time approached on 6 June. The crews scheduled for the later strikes had been shown sand-tray models of the beaches they were to hit, and, even though other aircraft had preceded them, the early wake-up time of 02.00hrs made everyone realise that the great day had arrived.

As the crews boarded their aircraft it was raining, and the cloud base hung stubbornly at 1,500ft. Each group had been ordered to have 54 bombers ready for take-off. These would form boxes of 18, three flights of six, to bomb at half-minute intervals. They would bomb five minutes before the first troops hit the beaches.

With 400 aircraft somehow formed up — individual commanders could hardly believe they had managed that in the dark,

damp conditions — the armada set course for Normandy. It was so cold that some Marauders even iced up. Such conditions cried out for blind bombing, and some of the heavies indeed dropped on inland targets using 'Oboe'. Not the mediums: they were visual all the way. Some crews went in at 2,000ft, some at 4,000 — it all depended on what the weather was doing when they actually arrived over Normandy at their briefed time.

The Marauders made their runs, turned for England, landed, rearmed and flew back cross the Channel. With the troops firmly ashore on Utah, the bombers gradually returned to business as usual, flying a little further inland to hit road junctions, bridges and targets of opportunity. Some groups bombed well to the east of Normandy to foster the myth that a second prong of the invasion would strike in the Pas de Calais, as many Germans still believed it would.

To men witnessing the naval bombardment, the roar of defending guns and the whistle of bombs left no doubt that this was 'it'. Impressive as the might of the invasion looked (and sounded) to men struggling through the surf from the landing-craft, some were in for a shock, for

many of the huge gun emplacements remained intact despite all the explosive rained on them in previous weeks. The AAF itself was under no illusion as to the relative ineffectiveness of conventional bombs against concrete pillboxes and bunkers several feet thick. As fire swept the new occupants of Omaha Beach, not everyone believed that this operation was going to be a walkover. It was said with a certain cynical emphasis that, on D-Day itself, almost nothing went entirely according to plan, and the Omaha Beach *débâcle* was one of the first and most damning examples of the truism that if anything can go wrong it will do so.

As the amphibious part of the invasion proceeded, the air above the Normandy coast was alive with Allied aircraft; there was virtually no challenge from the Luftwaffe, the first German machines in the area only putting in an appearance in the afternoon. No fewer than 3,342 tactical sorties were launched by the Ninth Air Force during the day, these including 823 by Marauders and A-20s. Fighters and reconnaissance units made up the balance, and from their bases in England they established a 'race track' pattern of operations that continued for days on end.

Above: A single 410th BG A-20J or K over the kind of overcast that was very familiar on European combat missions. *USAF*

With D-Day a reality, the intensity of missions for the Ninth's medium and light bombers spiralled. This fine formation view shows a typical mix of solid-nosed A-20Gs led by an A-20K bombardier ship. The unit is the 416th. *Imperial War Museum*

Bridges, marshalling yards, junctions, field artillery, gun emplacements and roads in and around Normandy were devastated by tight-formation boxes of medium bombers, all now with their distinctive Allied Expeditionary Air Force stripes standing out sharply against camouflage paint.

In the afternoon of the 6th, 36 A-20s of the 416th Group flew their second mission of the day. They soon hit overcast, which separated the second box as well as three aircraft from the lead box, leaving 14 aircraft to hit the primary target — a German strongpoint threatening the beach-head. At the head of this group was deputy lead Capt Richard K. Bills. Despite reaction from the flak, the group made its run into the objective at 12,000ft, the briefing having stated that, if the conditions were very bad, the attack was to be made from as low as 2,000ft — a dangerous height for the A-20. (In fact, crews reckoned that anywhere between 1,000 and 5,000ft was little short of suicidal for the aircraft in the ETO.) Shortly after take-off, the leader's radio had gone out and Bills took over, his task being to guide the second box of bombers and follow the first into the target — which was fine if the first box could be seen! Bills and his aircraft headed off to try to catch up.

As the Havocs crossed the Channel, the ceiling relentlessly lowered, driving the formation dangerously low as it crossed over the enemy coast at 4,000ft. Circling once to give the other pilots a chance to re-group, Bills then made his target run-in with visibility down to less than a mile.

Weaving to avoid the worst of the light and heavy flak, the 416th's aircraft approached the IP. Bills' crew were pleased to see the first box of A-20s approaching the target; their navigation had been spot-on. Throwing up a vicious box barrage, the German gunners hit three A-20s immediately; committed to the bombing run, Bills waited for the bombardier to utter the magic words. When 'bombs gone!' came at last, the pilot wrenched the A-20 into a steep-diving left turn. Behind it, the flak was going wild, with hundreds of rounds bursting. Bills' turret gunner, S/Sgt William A. Meldrum, blazed away at the ground guns.

The indifferent weather caused some of the Havocs to experience icing on the return leg. Having had his radio destroyed, Bills doggedly headed for home with another A-20 sticking close to his ship. Gingerly he made the let-down to Wethersfield, worrying that the flak damage the aircraft had taken would now

manifest itself in the most dangerous way. A flat tyre gave some anxious moments but the A-20 ran true, stopping just in front of a steep embankment.

For D-Day support missions, it had previously been decided that, unlike the Ninth's fighter groups, which were placed under tactical air commands to directly support specific army formations, the medium bombers would remain an 'independent' force. They would fly ground-support missions right across the front, using their superior range to switch from sector to sector, as required. In addition, they would continue to work down an established list of tactical targets in occupied Europe.

Despite the huge concentration of airpower fanning out over the amphibious landings, the enemy, unconvinced that the Allies would have picked the relatively difficult (and distant) Normandy coast for the main invasion, hesitated fatally; the German generals and their Führer awaited what they believed to be the main landing area in the Pas de Calais, and held back tank forces that could have put heavy pressure on the Allied armies. When the Germans finally realised the true facts, the beach-head had been established. With the Normandy terrain

Above: Partially retaining its old olive drab camouflage, B-26C 42-107695/ER-V of the 450th BS flies above Channel shipping during the invasion. *Imperial War Museum*

Above: Complying well with regulation application of AEAF stripes which decreed that fuselage code letters should not be obscured, B-26B 41-31832/U-RU of the 554th BS, 386th Group, sets out on a mission, *circa* June 1944. *Imperial War Museum*

militating against a major, broad-front counter-attack, the enemy armour and troop concentrations were picked off piecemeal by far-ranging fighter-bombers, mediums and heavies. It was when the Allied troops began to push inland that they came up against many small pockets of enemy troops, well dug-in. The notorious bocage country enabled field after field to become a strongpoint, the tough hedges and drainage ditches making progress slow until each enemy position had been eliminated. Fortunately the British and US tactical air commands had planned for just such an eventuality, and relays of P-47s, P-38s, Spitfires, Typhoons and Mustangs were kept busy bombing and strafing in front of the Allied positions.

Numerous small-scale actions developed, and the Germans rarely gave ground without a bitter fight, but by deploying airpower so effectively the USAAF (relying primarily on bombs carried by P-47s and P-38s, for the first few weeks) and RAF fighter-bombers (bombs, and rockets fired by Typhoons) systematically broke any cohesive attempt to hold up the Allied drive inland. Not all the invasion beaches were secured easily; pinned down on Omaha, US troops took murderous casualties from well-dug-in enemy positions.

To exploit the initial advantage gained by the armies, the Allied air forces cut a swathe of destruction inland to block off all approaches to the coastal areas. This often took place well behind the front line in the case of the medium bombers, and on 7 June the 387th Group was handed the task of making life difficult for the 17th Panzer Division, which was reported moving north into the beach-head by rail. To deny the enemy tanks their target, the B-26s attempted to bomb the railway junction at Rennes. The weather foiled this operation, although the group managed to hit a rail line west of Vire and also attacked a vehicle choke-point discovered at St Lô.

On the 8th, nearly 400 B-26s ranged across France, once again blasting sidings, fuel and ammunition dumps, railways, bridges and troop concentrations. The 387th Group's contribution included a successful morning mission that hit the rail junction at Pontabault. Capt Robert E. Will's flight carried out the best bombing, his bombardier, Lt Rudolf Tell, placing the bombs exactly on target. In the afternoon, Capt Rollin D. Childress was briefed to lead 18 Marauders to knock out a fuel dump in the Forêt de Grimbosq. Take-off was at 19.58hrs, and, although the ceiling was at 900ft, the formation assembled without difficulty. *En route* and climbing through the overcast, the B-26s became dispersed, and 11 returned to base. One had to crash-land at Gravesend in Kent, and a second crashed while landing at Friston, Suffolk.

Childress, meanwhile, gathered up three aircraft and pressed on. The flight dropped to deck level at times, the pilots trying to pick up landmarks in terrible visibility, which was down to a quarter of a mile in places. Finally picking up the target, Childress made his run and bombed from 6,000ft, guided by his bombardier, 1st Lt Wilson J. Cushing. As the Marauders turned away, buffeted from the resulting explosions, the crews knew that the dump had been destroyed. Then the flak retaliated. Moderate at first, it turned into heavy fire with alarming accuracy — enough to nail the B-26 flown by Capt Charles W. Shrober. The Marauder exploded in mid-air, and no 'chutes were seen to emerge from the stricken aircraft.

Heading for home, the three B-26s plunged through the weather to make a landfall over England. They put down at base at 22.30hrs. Group CO Thomas Seymour offered his congratulations on the tenacity displayed by Childress — a view endorsed by the 98th Wing commander, Col Millard Lewis. Later a telegram arrived from the army, stating that the bombing had destroyed enough fuel for an entire Panzer division.

This kind of rapid communiqué from the front, plus other sources of data, enabled IX BC headquarters to maintain an up-to-the-minute picture of the situation as it developed in France. To keep abreast of events on the ground, the bomber units also required a constant flow of reconnaissance photographs, these being provided mainly by the Ninth's own F-5s and F-6s. In the meantime, an enormous effort was made to establish emergency airstrips in France. Primarily required for transport aircraft to evacuate the wounded, the early availability of these landing grounds had been given top priority during the planning of the invasion. Air Service Command engineers were among the first troops to land and push forward to prepare for the arrival of their graders and shovels to flatten surfaces, on which were laid steel-plate runways. These strips were the vanguard of a network of bases that would eventually accommodate the bulk of the Ninth Air Force. After transports, fighters naturally had priority, for it was these that could hit the smallest target with deadly accuracy, be it a group of enemy tanks, a roadblock or a fortified building, only a few miles from the advancing troops.

In what had already been a notoriously poor year in terms of spring and summer weather, mid-1944 brought rain and low cloud very soon after the invasion had started. Less-than-ideal flying conditions prevailed for some time, which occasionally forced the heavies to abandon their intended targets in Germany for a further heavyweight deluge of tactical targets in Normandy.

Many targets were of necessity categorised as of the 'opportunity' type during this period, and the Ninth's tactical bombers would often fly against a set of specific objectives — such as the bridges over a particular river — and hit other locations, either at the same time (with a split force) or in separate missions. Many hundreds of B-26s and A-20s were invariably involved in most operations during June.

Clamping down firmly on 16 June, the weather succeeded in keeping all of IX Bomber Command on the ground, but 2,265 sorties were possible on the following day, the majority of these being in support of the Normandy beach-head.

'Noball' sites were attacked on the 20th, following another day when no medium-bomber sorties could be flown. Among the participating Marauder groups was the 391st, racking up its 100th mission since the start of operations. The milestone was celebrated in traditional style later that day, the revellers including the Group Chaplain, John A. Moore. Having flown the century mission in a B-26 named 'Rationed Passion', he was presented with a 'medal' in a mock ceremony enjoyed by all.

V-weapons sites were the main targets selected for the mediums on the 21st, but something different was outlined at the briefings on 22 June. As part of a constant series of sorties flown throughout the daylight hours, the B-26s and A-20s would lay down a 55-minute 'rolling bomb carpet' designed to clear the ground in front of the US First Army's VII Corps, which was handed the task of capturing the port of Cherbourg. Split-second timing and pinpoint accuracy on the part of the bombardiers were required to prevent any

Above: To get some action pictures, Ninth Air Force PR photographer Capt Robert Adleman flew as the tunnel-gunner/observer in an A-20 lead ship during a post-D-Day mission to Rouen. After taking this view of the Havoc immediately behind, he kept the camera rolling to record its demise when flak blew off its entire tail. *Imperial War Museum*

Above: Total write-off for B-26 42-96078 of the 599th BS, 397th Group, on 17 June 1944. The aircraft carried the unfortunately-prophetic name 'Slightly Dangerous'. *Author's collection*

Above: Excellent view of 'Irene', an A-20J of the 410th Group, on 22 June 1944. *USAF*

Above: After D-Day the Ninth's bombers generally deleted upper-wing AEAF stripes, usually by painting them over. A pair of 454th BS aircraft demonstrate how they tended to look from above. *Imperial War Museum*

Above:
A formation of 397th Group B-26s, with D-Day markings still very much in evidence on a variety of finishes. The group flew numerous aircraft without any upper-surface camouflage. *USAF*

Left:
A poor-quality but interesting photograph of B-26B-55 42-96074/K5-Q 'Ish-Tak-Ha-Ba' in post-D-Day markings. *F. Christ*

Above: The first A-26s in the Ninth Air Force were evaluated by the 386th BG. There were a few accidents arising from a weakness in the nosewheel oleo, but overall the aircraft was well received by the combat crews. *F. F. Smith collection*

Allied casualties as the troops moved forward. One aircraft was lost from the day's operations, which also took in a range of tactical targets.

Having been grounded on the morning of the 23rd, 175 B-26s and A-20s got off during the afternoon to give seven V-weapons sites a going over. Accompanied across the Channel by 630 Ninth Fighter Command P-47s and P-38s, the bomber crews were assured of close escort, the fighters also carrying out strafing attacks on communications centres.

Three more days of 'maximum effort' by the mediums were followed by another stand-down on 26 June, the day that Cherbourg fell to US troops. The poor conditions that prevailed until the end of the month did not prevent the movement of the first Ninth Air Force fighter-bombers to bases in France — a process that began on the 29th.

First Invaders

On the other side of the Atlantic, an event had taken place on 23 April that would have some significance in the future history of the Ninth Air Force. Lifting off to fly the Atlantic that day was the first Douglas

A-26 Invader for the AAF in the ETO. This was A-26B-10 (41-39132), which was followed over on 28 June by three A-26B-15s, with more being despatched during July and August. These machines and 14 others would form a squadron-sized in-theatre evaluation force in the 386th Bomb Group, pending the Invader's future deployment with the Ninth.

July '44

Command changes in the Havoc groups early in July saw Col Ralph Rhudy taking over the 410th Group at Gosfield on the 2nd, while Col Thomas R. Ford was the new CO of the 409th at Little Walden from the 4th.

July had begun with more disappointing weather conditions, the result being that no medium-bomber missions could be mounted until the 4th, and even then the effort was a fraction of what the command was able to send across to the Continent, given a clear day. Radar assisted the 95 B-26 and A-20 sorties to locate and bomb German positions near Abbeville and a

rail bridge at Oissel. Better conditions on the 5th allowed IX BC to despatch nearly 180 mediums to bomb rail targets around Caen as well as buildings identified as German headquarters associated with the V-weapons programme.

A month on from D-Day, the medium-bomber crews provided a continuing service of ground support to the troops, the Ninth's fighters in turn flying their own sweeps and providing escort to the bombers.

On the 7th, more than 100 B-26s and A-20s attacked rail bridges near Tours and targets around Beauzeville and Lisieux, 280 sorties by these two aircraft types carrying out a further bombing of a V-weapons headquarters the following day, the latter being located at Château de Ribeaucourt. The bombers also hit German army strongpoints around Caen, fuel dumps and road and rail bridges.

During the month the first of the 18 A-26Bs and Cs assembled at Great Dunmow for the initial combat evaluation by the 553rd Bomb Squadron. This event came as a surprise to squadron operations officer Capt Lee R. Meyers and Group operations officer Lt-Col Harry G. 'Tad' Hankey, who was then due to go home. Neither had any advance warning of the requirement to take charge of a group of crews who had trained on the Invader in the US. According to the 386th Group unit history, the first A-26 simply arrived and was parked in the 533rd Squadron area. In the cockpit, Meyers found the 'Dash One' technical orders and a note from the ferry pilot that said simply: 'Have fun.' According to 553rd Squadron pilot Skip Young, he and Meyers checked the aircraft over before the latter 'cranked it up' and took-off. The only problem he experienced was when he attempted to test the A-26's single-engine performance, whereupon the propeller refused to unfeather and Meyers had to land on one engine. Reading the technical orders for the type that night, Meyers flew the A-26 the following day, which went much better. He was to take the aircraft up six more times before flying it on a combat mission on 19 September. Young flew it before rotating home, and noted that it had 'all kinds of problems' that demanded the attention of a modification centre.

Hankey recalled that Gen Anderson himself briefed him to the effect that he should take charge of a group of crews bringing Invaders in from the States. He would lead the first five missions on the new type — then he could go home. Hankey was amazed that the colonel in charge of the group from the US was convinced that the A-26 could win the war on its own by bombing at medium altitude and then going down to strafe. To the Marauder veterans, the latter was questionable practice, to say the least, and some heated arguments ensued.

As the 386th was definitely slated to convert to the A-26, Hankey gave the assignment his best shot. The aircraft subsequently arrived over Great Dunmow, having flown in via Prestwick. Overcast and rain made it far from the best of days to land a new aircraft with inexperienced crews who had trouble even locating the Essex aerodrome. When they did so, the first Invader touched down 'long', the pilot applied the brakes too hard and the aircraft slid off the end of the runway, swung sideways across the perimeter track and ended up in the adjacent mud. Another pilot managed to complete his landing but stalled halfway down the runway, the aircraft coming to rest at right-angles to it, with its nose sticking out just a little too far. In came another A-26 ace, who hit the stalled one with his left wing and ended about 70ft away, also in the mud. Hankey remembers the landing hut at the end of the runway firing so many red flares 'it looked like the Fourth of July'. But all warnings were ignored and in they came. Some aircraft did land without incident, but there was damage to six, three of which were glass-nosed A-26Cs.

Hankey promptly grounded all the Invader pilots. He allowed those who had made a good landing to check out as pilots in the 553rd, while the rest were given a spell on B-26s as co-pilots. And Hankey's five combat missions? Weather put paid to four of them and only one — to attack German strongpoints at Brest — was attempted, on 6 September, before he went home.

Hankey's comments about the Invader were positive: in a report he prepared for Gen Anderson he stated that flight crews with B-26 experience would find it easy enough to get used to, and that flying it in combat would be no problem, provided that similar medium-altitude missions were

Above: A very hard landing in an A-26 could wrench engines out of their mountings, giving the groundcrews days of remedial work. It is assumed that this deranged engine was the result of combat damage. *J. Bivens*

Above: Low-loaders came in useful to haul stricken aircraft to a maintenance area. This early-model A-26B (41-39343) of the 386th Bomb Group had clearly had to make a belly landing. *J. Bivens*

Above: An A-26B Invader with the yellow tail stripe of the 386th Group. Groundcrews appreciated the quick-release engine-cowling panels, one of which is seen on the ground under the nose of this 553rd BS aircraft. *J. Bivens*

to be undertaken. There were in fact eight A-26 missions during the evaluation by the 553rd Squadron, flown between 6 and 19 September. Thereafter the Invaders were 'returned to depots' with a list of modifications that would delay full deployment by the 386th Group until 1945.

The group was unable to return all the Invaders it had received for the initial evaluation, as two wrecks were left behind at Dunmow when the unit began moving to France on 26 September. One A-26B (41-39158) had crashed fatally in August during a brief demonstation flight for the benefit of 2 Group RAF, there then being a fair chance that the Invader would enter British service to replace the Boston and possibly the Mitchell. The crash at Dunmow, while unfortunate, had little influence on the decision not to request the type under Lend-Lease.

Checking out these early-production Invaders and preparing them for combat

Above: The forward-hinged cockpit canopy on early Invaders was criticised for its restrictive framework in other war theatres, although the Ninth found few problems with it. This A-26C has had its two nose-gun ports plated over. *J. Bivens*

bove: This well-adorned A-26B of the 416th Group has the early-style canopy; most units operated a mix of Invaders with both types. *Merle Olmstead collection*

Left: Fitted with the revised 'clamshell' canopy this A-26 clearly perpetuates one of the preoccupations in the Ninth! *J. Bivens*

Below: Like the A-20 before it, the Invader came with 'strafer' and glazed-nose sections. One of the former A-26Bs is seen here with 15 missions chalked up. *J. Bivens*

Left: 'Solid' noses were just made for fangs and fierce-beast faces, as this Invader crew realised. Both aircraft here are from the 386th Group. *J. Bivens*

Below: Someone took time to paint this elaborate piece of nose art on an A-26C. Artists could make dollars or stock their foot lockers with liquor for work like this. *J. Bivens*

Detail view of an A-26B's wing-mounted package guns, which gave the Invader a total forward firepower of 16 guns if the top turret was locked to fire forward. *J. Bivens*

Above: Pilot's side view from the Invader's improved canopy, complete with push out panel, on A-26B-15 43-22373. *J. Bivens*

took several weeks. They appear to have all been fitted with the early design of cockpit canopy which was flush with the fuselage and had heavy framing that restricted lateral vision — as, of course, did the long engine nacelles. A forward-opening canopy-roof section allowed crew access to the flightdeck. Ninth Air Force crews did not apparently find the vision from the A-26's cockpit as much of a restriction as their opposite numbers in the Pacific, who felt this feature to be quite prohibitive during low-altitude attack missions.

There were some reservations from gunners over the practicality of using the remotely-controlled gun barbettes in combat, notwithstanding the fact that in essence it was an efficient enough system. Groundcrews particularly appreciated the Douglas design approach to engine maintenance, which allowed complete access, with the removal of cowling panels using quick-release fasteners.

Most (if not all) the A-26s arriving in the UK for the Ninth Air Force were processed through Base Air Depot 2 at Warton in Lancashire. The first example, a B model (41-39203), arrived on

4 September, and four aircraft were cleared for service by the depot that month, with eight following in October — a month when 34 more were at the 'work in progress' stage. By November the delivery figure had risen to 115 aircraft, less two which collided and fell into the nearby Ribble river estuary. In total, Warton processed 711 Invaders up to 27 July 1945.

Night attack

If the summer days of 1944 were filled with action for the American medium-bomber crews, the nights were tranquil by comparison, at least for most of them. That changed a little for selected crews of the 322nd Group, which, as mentioned earlier, had formed a special night-attack flight. On 7/8 July the idea was put to the test, when the group attempted to strike a 'Noball' target. This was Château de Ribeaucourt, previously confirmed (and attacked during the day on 7 July) by the Maquis as the headquarters of Flak

Regiment 155 (W) and staffed by groups of officers and technicians who directed the V1 offensive. The *château* was apparently still habitable despite the earlier bombing, and the nocturnal mission was on. In clear moonlight, the group took-off and before long was picked up by searchlights; the flak opened up, and then someone yelled a warning: 'Night-fighters!'

Messerschmitt Bf110s of NJG 6 struck the 322nd with their characteristic efficiency when the Marauders were but 10 miles into enemy territory, and promptly blasted nine B-26s out of the sky. Bomber gunners reported 14 attacks on their formation within the space of a few minutes. The first 'kill' was recorded by the German crews at 22.10hrs, and, in total, 14 victims were claimed. The combat was not entirely one-sided, however, as two of the Bf110s apparently went down, one the victim of German flak.

A tenth Marauder limped home full of holes and put down at Tangmere in West Sussex, never to fly again. Another survivor

Above: Putting your feet through the hole to show how big it was became a regular stunt for the benefit of PR men. This B-26 had staggered home rent by cannon shells after attack by NJG 6's Bf110s on 7/8 July 1944. The night raid cost the 322nd nine Marauders. *USAF*

got home but was badly damaged when its landing gear collapsed on touchdown. All in all, it had been a disastrous night for the group but some lessons had been learned; the 322nd had managed to bomb on the pathfinders' signal but the *château* was missed. For the time being, night missions by B-26s would continue.

The German night-fighter crews might themselves have been rather mystified as to the identity of their victims during the night's work, successful as they had undoubtedly been. Their combat reports identified all the kills as 'Wellingtons', which might have been understandable had the RAF not withdrawn this type some time previously. It can be speculated that the Nachtjagd indeed recognised their opponents for what they were but nobody felt confident enough to claim American bombers, which, as

everyone knew, flew mostly in daylight.

In typical fashion, Ninth Air Force public relations did not hush up the epic night action; instead, surviving B-26 crews were persuaded to pose in and on their shell-torn Marauders, the storyline being that the gunners had successfully warded off the Germans in a large-scale running air battle.

To develop the night pathfinder mission, other B-26 groups had begun training in compliance with a plan that all of them fly a rota of nocturnal sorties for one month at a time. The 323rd Group was then training selected crews, and would fly its first such operational mission in August.

For several days IX BC was able to return to its now-normal effort by flying multiple sorties, although there were a number of early returns — harbingers of further days of inactivity such as 10 July, when only the fighters managed to take-off.

Missions were on again on the 11th, with 'Noballs', bridges and fuel dumps as the bombers' targets. The pounding continued on the 12th, although the conditions prevailing over England on the 13th again grounded the entire medium-bomber force. It was to position the B-26 groups of the 98th CBW a little nearer to targets in western France that its four component units moved south to occupy airfields in Hampshire. Personnel of the 323rd began packing up on 11 July to leave Earls Colne and move down to Beaulieu. This move was completed by the 21st, 60 Marauders having found dispersal space on the airfield situated on the fringe of the New Forest. Likewise, the 394th packed its bags and headed for Holmsley South, the 397th went to Hurn and the 387th occupied Stoney Cross.

On the 14th, bad weather still curtailed the air effort, although 62 sorties were possible; on the 15th, only four B-26s out of a force of 96 managed to locate a rail bridge at L'Aigle.

Back up to 375 sorties on 16 July, the command was able to support the fighting around St Lô, to bomb bridges likely to be of use by the Germans in the area, and to hit an enemy fuel dump at Rennes. Further depletion of German fuel stocks was also the object of some medium-bomber sorties on the 17th — a day which otherwise recorded attacks on marshalling yards. More rail bridges were struck by the command's aircraft on the 18th and 19th, but the conditions remained far from ideal for visual bomb-aiming.

In an effort to break the deadlock at Caen, where Gen Bernard Montgomery's British Second Army had been repulsed in its attempt to secure the town, the 323rd flew its first mission from Beaulieu on the 18th. Thirty-six aircraft bombed the defended area around Démouville. That bald statement belies the fact that the Marauders were but part of a series of massive air attacks that delivered an enormous weight of high-explosive on and around the unfortunate town. Before it was taken, Caen was pulverised not only by aerial bombs but also by artillery and naval gunfire.

On 20 July heavy rain prevented take-off at UK bases until the afternoon, when the bombers' targets included fuel dumps, guns and rail traffic. A total stand-down occurred over the following two days; then all 11 B-26 and A-20 groups participated in a 330-aircraft-strong force for missions on 23 July. The targets, many of which could be found only by pathfinder aircraft, included bridges and fuel dumps.

Above: Damaged nose of a 322nd Bomb Group B-26 that survived the fighter attack on the night of 7/8 July 1944. *Imperial War Museum*

'Cobra' tragedy

Operation 'Cobra' — an all-out aerial effort to break the deadlock at St Lô, which was a vital pre-requisite for the US First Army to advance deep into France — was delayed by bad weather on the 24th, and that part of IX BC scheduled to participate was instead diverted to blast ammunition and fuel dumps. 'Cobra' got going the following day, when, after sweeps by fighter-bombers and bombing by B-17s and B-24s, the mediums swept in at 12.23hrs to saturate designated target areas with 260lb fragmentation and 500lb HE bombs.

Friendly troops were moving out as early as 11.00hrs, thanks to the massive air attacks; the mediums had at the finish dropped 4,000 tons of bombs into an area occupied by just one German Army division. Such precise targets in and around a fluid front line were almost bound to be open to error, and on the 25th the worst happened — a 42-ship raid by B-26s fell short and the resulting detonations killed 102 men and wounded 380 more.

This tragic bombing error led to a heated inter-service debate over the merits of such support, the distance friendly troops needed to be from the impact point, and the precise direction taken by the bombers making their run-in to the target area. Errors by both medium and heavy bombers against tiny tactical targets made higher command chary about using medium bombers in such confined areas so near to friendly forces; henceforth this kind of job was given almost exclusively to fighter-bombers. Carpet bombing was, however, terrifyingly effective in terms of *matériel* destruction and its effect on enemy morale, and it was deployed subsequently.

The unfortunate events of 25 July tended to obscure the outstanding success of 'Cobra'. The bombing all but wiped out Lt-Gen Fritz Bayerlein's Panzer-Lehr Division by causing grievous personnel casualties and critical losses in vehicles. Overlapping bomb explosions utterly wrecked communications by destroying most of the command posts, and thoroughly demoralised the surviving troops holding positions barring the way to Maj-Gen J. Lawton Collins' VII Corps. The bombing enabled part of the 2nd Armoured Division to advance in company with the stoic 30th Infantry Division (which had suffered the AAF bombing) which rallied, and thrusting aside the Germans, embarked on the long drive to liberate France.

If the bombing of their own lines had been a grim experience for the Americans, the Germans who were on the receiving end of the deluge of high-explosive were utterly shattered. Field Marshal Hans von Kluge, who had replaced von Runstedt to become the new C-in-C of German forces in Normandy, summed up the effects it had had:

'Whole armoured units ... were attacked by terrific numbers of aircraft dropping carpets of bombs, so that they emerged from the churned-up earth with the greatest difficulty, sometimes only with the aid of tractors. The pyschological effect on the fighting forces, especially the infantry, of such a mass of bombs raining down on them with all the force of elemental nature, is a factor that must be given serious consideration. It is not in the least important whether such a carpet of bombs is dropped on good or bad troops. They are more or less annihilated by it, and above all their equipment is ruined. It only needs this to happen a few times and the power of resistance of these troops is put to the severest test. It becomes paralysed, dies; what is left is not equal to the demands of the situation ... the troops have the impression that they are battling against an enemy who carries all before him.'

The American view of the 'Cobra' incident was sanguine: in the circumstances, it had to be. Eisenhower himself, while acknowledging the tragedy, knew that medium bombers had certainly proven their value against small targets, due mainly to the superior concentration they could achieve compared to that of Fortresses and Liberators, but their bombardiers could hardly be expected to predict exactly where every bomb would fall. It was often difficult (if not impossible) to observe details of terrain with the required clarity from 12,000ft. Although exact timings were emphasised and a system of radio control was organised from the ground — backed up by the use of coloured smoke, fabric panels attached to vehicles, and sky markers which were highly visible from above — precision bombing by formations of twin- or four-engined bombers retained an element of risk. It took only one or two aircraft to drift off inadvertently to one side of the formation box for the bombs to fall hundreds of yards wide of where they were supposed to. That said, some remarkable feats of bombing were achieved by both mediums and heavies during the Allied drive across Europe, but in many cases tactical targets were very small, so the desire to improve the bombing was always present.

Bridges and dumps were among the targets that occupied the AAF mediums for the next few days of July, a number of sorties being undertaken at the direct request of First Army ground controllers, who passed directions to the aircraft by radio. More missions were aborted and yet more weather-related stand-downs imposed on the medium-bomber groups as the month ended. By this time, the American First Army could at last move on Mortain and Avranches, and Bradley could order Patton to turn east towards Paris. Amid much acrimony, Montgomery's 'holding action' at Caen was seen to have paid off. There now began a race to trap the bulk of the German Seventh Army in front of the Seine.

Above: Flexing as *per* the design of its very efficient wing, an A-26C of the 386th formates on a second Invader. *N. Franklin*

Above: Echelon formation of 386th Group Invaders, probably on a mission in 1945. The A-26 force built up quickly in France during the last months of the war, four groups becoming fully operational on the type. *N. Franklin*

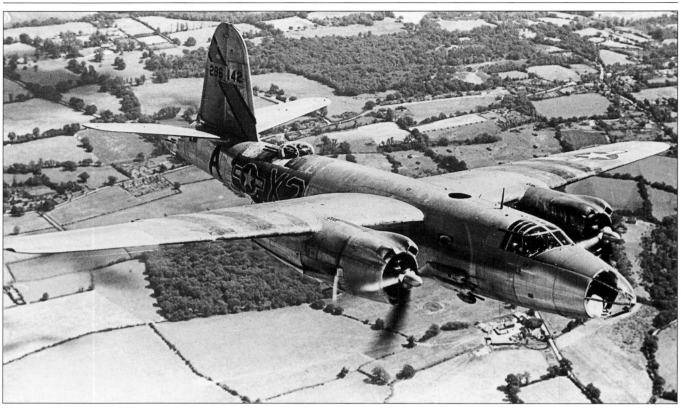

Above: A much-photographed ETO Marauder was B-26B 42-96142 of the 596th BS, 397th Group, seen here over the English countryside. *Author's collection*

Above: The 410th Group's 647th Squadron had the code '6Q' highly visible on this otherwise-battle-worn A-20G/H. *USAF*

7 Bridge-busting

August '44

Able to send 250 sorties off on 1 August, IX Bomber Command attacked eight rail bridges including those at Mézières-sur-Seine, Maintenon, Les Ponts-de-Cé and Bourth. George Patton's Third Army meanwhile began a race south to the Loire, whereupon his VIII Corps thrust westwards to liberate Brittany and the ports of Brest, Lorient and St Nazaire.

The Loire bridge missions were repeated on the 2nd, although the Third Army soon requested that these be suspended unless bombing was specifically required. It was counter-productive to wreck bridges that could be useful to Allied operations in Brittany, especially as Patton, charging ahead in what became his characteristic style, was not awaiting his own fuel supplies but using captured fuel stocks to save him time. Above his tanks winged the tactical air forces, which continued their sorties to wear down the Germans still further.

On 4/5 August the 322nd Bomb Group flew its fourth night mission. Much more successful than the one attempted previously, this resulted in the bombs going down on stockpiled fuel and ammunition in the Forêt de Fille. In moonlit conditions, the bombers evaded the single enemy night-fighter that appeared on the scene, two bombers being damaged when they encountered heavy flak.

During the daylight hours the early-August period was marked by widespread destruction of French bridges by the AAF — so much so that, by the 6th, the Germans were cut off at Falaise. Having scraped together the remnants of four Panzer divisions, von Kluge tried desperately to mount the counter-attack ordered by Hitler. It was doomed from the start. Only one bridge across the Oissel offered a possible escape route, and that was the target of the A-20s of the 416th on that same day. In the afternoon the group lined up on the bridge in the face of intense flak, which claimed three A-20s including that flown by the deputy group CO, Lt-Col Farmer. In return for destroying the bridge the group paid dearly, for five more Havocs failed to

return. For its gallant effort at Oissel the 416th won the first of two wartime Distinguished Unit Citations it was awarded. It would not have to wait long for the second.

Flying its first mission at night on 6/7 August, the 323rd Group went in on its gun-battery target at Ile de Cézembère at an altitude a little lower than that adopted previously by the 322nd. Obtaining permission to bomb at 2,300-3,000ft, the crews of the 41 aircraft that participated released individually on target indicators dropped by five pathfinder Marauders.

Bridges spanning the Loire and Seine, plus ammunition dumps, troop assembly areas and a marshalling yard at Compiègne, were bombed during the next few days, the latter target being attacked on the 5th of the month. A similar pattern of operations continued in a spell of reasonable weather that lasted for about two weeks, at the end of which time the Germans had been forced into a trap by the British 21st Army Group and Patton's Third Army, which had swung northwards, giving the German 7th Army nowhere to go. Bottled-up in front of bridges broken by Allied air attack, Wehrmacht troops awaited the inevitable as they watched the skies in vain for any sign of supply or indeed support from the Luftwaffe. In fact, this had been promised to von Kluge, and a force of fighters was indeed assembled on the airfields around Paris — but as soon as they took-off they were cut down by Allied fighters. Not one reached the Mortain-Avranches area. The army was on its own.

Night still brought the enemy a breathing-space, and, as noted earlier, the AAF had taken some practical steps to overcome this omission, but, even as the B-26 crews were 'getting their eye in', official enthusiasm for medium-bomber night missions — at least on a regular basis — was waning. Consequently, after the 323rd had flown one more, on 9/10 August, the programme was dropped. Few crews actually regretted the decision, as most viewed night missions as not worth the added risks, but B-26s continued to fly night pathfinder sorties. On the 12th, the Ninth carried out the

USAAF's final attack on a bridge over the Seine, and the fate of the German 7th Army was sealed.

Changes and honours

Effective 3 August, Col Harold Mace relinquished command of the 416th Group to take up leadership of the 98th Wing. Starting in the second week of that month, Mace's old group flew a hectic series of missions, for which it won a second DUC. The group was then led by Col Theodore R. Aylesworth, who was to remain in command until the end of the war.

Mace himself, promoted to Brigadier General, commented on two outstanding missions flown by the 394th Group to destroy a bridge at Compiègne on 9 August. In the cumulative attacks, the B-26s completely wrecked the bridge, prompting a teletype in which Mace described the bombing as 'beautiful'; on the AAF scale of accuracy, that clearly transcended 'superior'!

America's highest

One pilot who contributed to that fine performance on the afternoon mission was as determined as the rest of the pilots to get that bridge. Capt Darrell R. Lindsey, at the controls of B-26B 42-96101/4T-N of the 585th Squadron, was leading the 'Bridge Busters' for the 10th time. At the head of 33 Marauders, Lindsey approached the River Oise and the bridge at L'Isle Adam. He watched the flak bursts coming closer and definitely growing thicker. With his own aircraft hit and others in the formation holed, he was on the bomb run when the German gunners found their range. A direct hit on the starboard engine knocked the B-26 out of formation. Lindsey recovered and climbed back up into the lead position. Fire was taking hold of the engine but the pilot held the aircraft on course — he had come to this river to knock down a bridge, and he was not to be denied. Lindsey held the B-26 steady, released his bombs and waited until the formation released theirs before ordering his crew to bail out. All of them did so apart from the bombardier, who offered to lower the wheels so that Lindsey might have a chance of jumping.

Above: On 18 August 1944 the 344th Bomb Group was given a typical Continental military target grouped close to civilian dwellings. The difficulties of placing the bombs accurately can readily be appreciated. Note the medium green and olive-drab 'scallop' camouflage of the nearest B-26. *USAF*

For the pilot, abandoning a Marauder usually meant going through the opening created by the extended nosewheel doors, a few feet away from his seat. The snag was that the aircraft had ideally to be kept straight and level while the gear was lowered. Release the grip on the control wheel, and a damaged machine like Lindsey's would immediately fall off to right or left.

The Marauder was still on fire, and at any second the flames could have reached the wing fuel tank. Lindsey refused the bombardier's offer: putting the wheels down might have induced a spin from which the aircraft could never have recovered. Reluctantly the bombardier dropped through the hatch and, as he floated down under his parachute, he saw the Marauder falling away like a flaming torch as the fuel finally ignited.

For his unselfish act of bravery, Darrell Lindsey was awarded a posthumous Medal of Honor — his nation's highest decoration for courage under fire. It

reflected positively on all the aircrews who made the supreme sacrifice while flying medium bombers in the European theatre.

Right at the top of the Ninth Air Force chain of command, another change of leadership at this time saw Gen Hoyt S. Vandenburg take over the running of IX Bomber Command from Lewis Brereton, who had been instrumental in seeing an efficient intrument of war rise like the proverbial Phoenix from its traumatic beginnings with the Third Wing, Eighth Air Force. The command could hardly have had a more capable commander than Vandenburg, who was destined to reach even greater heights in the postwar air force.

The retreating German army was subjected to a systematic rain of fire from the skies as the Allies pressed their advantage at Falaise; on 13 August, IX

BC aircraft hit fuel caches and no fewer than 70 choke-points in the area.

Keeping up the pressure on the Germans now desperately attempting to get out of France, the AAF tactical bombers found a plethora of targets. On the fringes of the central Allied thrust, Operation 'Dragoon' saw thousands of US troops landing in the South of France on the 15th. They soon sealed off that part of the country and ejected the remaining Germans. The noose was being tightened.

Bombing of road and rail bridges, among other tactical targets, continued through to 18 August, the bombers being grounded by bad weather on the 19th. The following day, the Eighth Air Force was similarly affected, although the tactical force managed to send 61 sorties to the Seine, where German troops, having been denied all the bridges, were waiting to be ferried across. Many were killed as the mediums went in to destroy their river transport. Patton, meanwhile, had established a bridgehead on the far side of the Seine, at Mantes. The British and Canadians had by now reached the river, and began crossing six days later.

No bombers were able to fly between the 21st and 24th, although the 25th was brighter and a large force of B-26s and A-20s attacked German army positions in the Brest area, 278 aircraft out of 320 despatched finding their briefed targets. A great boost to the Allied cause that day was the German surrender of Paris, to a jubilant Free French Army.

As the tactical air forces raced to keep up with forward Allied armour spearheads, the liberation of the French capital gave the efficient (if unsung) signals and communications units a bonus: the Eiffel Tower provided a magnificent relay centre for the sending and receiving of radio signals, which were increasingly vital for the direction of air units. Although the mediums were less affected by the headlong advance of the ground armies, the fighter-bombers were in danger of being left behind by the US First Army (Hodges) and the US Third (Patton).

Throughout the remainder of August, the Ninth continued to be adversely affected by England's inclement weather, although numerous sorties were flown by the mediums. The 322nd's fifth nocturnal pathfinder mission took place on 28/29 August, and this too was successful. All but one of the 73 aircraft taking part bombed the target at Mont de Bolbec, guided in by flares dropped by the pathfinder ships. On the 28th, Bourges and Péronne aerodromes were bombed in direct support of US ground forces.

The sudden stab at a small target continued to keep the Germans off balance, as they rarely knew exactly where a formation of Allied bombers would strike. The Ninth's light-bomber groups became masters of this type of interdiction, and on 31 August the 410th Group flew its 100th mission of the war. It had carved out a generally good record in just four months of action, and the self-styled 'Beaty's Raiders' — named after group commander Lt-Col Sherman R. Beaty — could be justly proud.

There were those who reckoned that the high command selected an ammunition dump in the Forêt des Arques (about five miles south of Dieppe) especially for the

410th to cause a few fireworks to celebrate the century mission. In any event, it was important that the target be destroyed to deny the enemy stocks of artillery shells; Allied positions were coming under barrage fire, laid down by the German guns striving to protect Wehrmacht troops withdrawing to positions north of the Seine. If the dump could be destroyed, this would considerably ease the job of British and Canadian troops fighting in that particular sector.

If anything, the actual mission was an anti-climax. Led by Maj Robert C. Rawl, with Col Beaty on his wing, the A-20s swept in, not a single enemy gun firing as the bombs went down. More than 100,000lb of bombs dropped into the forest dump, which went up in spectacular sheets of flame and smoke. As intended, the bombing opened the way for the ground troops, and while the 410th's crews were enjoying a 100th mission celebration, complete with birthday cake, a 12-hour push began which carried them 40 miles, to about 15 miles short of Dieppe.

By July and August the 25th BG at Watton already had Mosquito XVIs and a B-25 for night photography of V1 sites in the Pas de Calais under the codename Project 'Dilly'. As a Marauder could carry 30 photo flash bombs, 10 more than the Mitchell, four B-26G Marauders were acquired to improve target illumination by the Group's 654th Bomb Squadron (R). The Eighth Air Force's photographic unit at Mount Farm installed two K-19B cameras below the radio operator's compartment forward of the bomb bay, accessible enough for the operator to change film cassettes in flight, if necessary. One of these gloss black-painted B-26Gs was transferred to the 7th PR Group to replace a B-25, the other three flying night PR missions beginning 10/11 August.

The original 654th BS B-26G flew 13 more night sorties before the ground forces captured the V1 sites, the B-26s then performing more special PR sorties over France, but in daylight. These were to photograph those railway lines and depots needing repair by the Allies to hasten the flow of supplies to Patton's Third Army.

September '44
Stubbornly-defended German fortified positions at Brest again occupied the Ninth's bombers on 1 September, similar operations being undertaken for several days until another weather-related grounding

order was signalled on the 8th. It should be borne in mind that targets such as Brest were likely to have been much reduced by the time the tactical bombers were able to take to the air again. In practically all operations in support of ground troops, fighter-bombers were active concurrently. Considerably less hampered by the weather than were the mediums, the P-47s, P-38s and P-51s hammered small-scale targets into submission on all sectors of the front line. Allied success on the ground during September became a heady mix of satisfaction and anticipation that the war might be over more quickly than anyone had hoped. First Army took Sedan on the 7th, Liège on the 9th and Luxembourg the following day, and Hodges had crossed the German frontier south of Aachen by breaking through parts of the Siegfried Line by the 14th. Third Army's famous 'end run' had carried it beyond Verdun to the Meuse, where it was obliged to pull back from a crossing at Pont-à-Mousson, but Patton had established a small bridgehead south of Metz by the 10th.

As related elsewhere, the Marauder-equipped 386th Bomb Group had two days previously embarked upon a combat evaluation of the A-26. With 18 of the new aircraft on hand, the group's 553rd Squadron completed a useful period in anticipation of full re-equipment, the 'field test' reducing any risk that a front-line combat group would re-equip with a sub-standard aircraft in the middle of a war. This was quite unlikely to happen in the case of the Invader, but certain things that show up in combat situations could not always be duplicated by slide-rule calculations or at remote experimental centres.

The A-26 passed with flying colours, with some of the previously-loyal Marauder men visibly wavering in their attitude to it by the end of the evaluation on 19 September. There were some reservations, but crew reaction was generally favourable. Armed with the results of the A-26 flying several real combat missions, the AAF and Douglas Aircraft were about ready to approve the aircraft as a widespread replacement in all the A-20 groups and the majority flying the B-26.

On 9 September IX BC sent some of its aircraft on a slightly different mission — that of dropping leaflets to inform the people of Belgium that liberation was at hand. The US Third Army was then in the act of holding previously secured positions at Arry, on the River Moselle, in the face of a German counter-attack. Air support to American forces was provided on the 10th, the mediums hitting a Moselle road bridge and a rail crossing at Custines.

German strongpoints in and around the town of Metz were bombed by the mediums on 11 September, 358 Marauders and Havocs taking part in the attack. British troops had meanwhile crossed the border into Belgium to liberate Brussels on the 4th and Antwerp on the 5th, the tactical bombers and fighters giving their usual close support to these and other ground operations. IX BC had primary targets in Nancy, where the bombers again pounded German army fortifications. These did not hold out for long, as the town was liberated on the 16th.

Further quantities of leaflets were dropped on coastal areas of Belgium by B-26s on 13 September. Twenty-four hours later it was back to 'business as usual', when 140 Marauders and Havocs hauled more tons of high-explosive to Brest, to help convince the German defenders that further resistance was useless and that they should abandon their fortified positions. They had already needed a good deal of persuasion.

Weather again grounded the bombers on the 15th — the day before a designation change turned IX Bomber Command into the 9th Bombardment Division, retroactively effective 30 August.

Move to France

There was no operational flying on the 17th or 18th, which gave the 410th Group's A-20s a chance to settle into Coulommiers in France from the latter date. The following day saw the Marauder crews of the 391st Group bidding *adieu* to Matching and setting course for Roye/Amy aerodrome, alias A-73. Personnel must have fervently hoped that their new home would allow better flying weather — at least the aircrews would no longer have to face the long haul across the Channel and part of France to reach their targets. The worst aspect of a move to the Continent for many tactical aircrew was that the accommodation was often primitive and more often than not in tents, just as winter was coming in. American inventiveness made the best of things, the tents invariably being quite warm and habitable once floors, stoves and all manner of liberated furniture had been installed.

Preventing the Germans from moving reinforcements into front-line areas was a key part of the work of the tactical bombers, a typical mission taking place on 19 September, when the marshalling yards at Düren were bombed. The Germans aimed at that time to hold on to Aachen and, to prevent essential supplies from reaching the enemy garrison, US bombers aimed to disrupt rail movement further up the line. Consequently, about 40 B-26s attacked the marshalling yards at Trier on 20 September. In addition, these same aircraft bombed German positions at Herbach.

On 21 September the 'White Tail' Marauders of the 323rd Bomb Group moved to Chartres (A-40) — one of many airfields occupied by the Ninth's tactical squadrons and which they had, more likely than not, bombed during the German occupation. In the coldest days of the winter months, many a frozen mechanic would curse the skill of the Ninth's own flyers in removing the roofs (and sometimes most of the walls as well) of the skeletal hangars in which they worked. The 9th's bomber units based in France were now surrounded by their own fighters, several groups of Thunderbolts, Lightnings and

Above: The 391st Group flew many B-26s without any upper-surface camouflage, including this example from the 572nd Squadron. *J. Hamlin*

Mustangs already being based on French soil. There too were the vital reconnaisance units, whose largely unsung war went on with hardly a break — without their efforts, the tactical groups would have been blind to the fluid situation on the ground.

A 23 September weather recall prevented medium-bomber sorties into Germany, with all aircraft remaining grounded the following day. On the 25th, the fortress at Brest finally fell to the Allies, the tactical bombing having materially assisted the ground forces in capturing it, to the tune of 1,573 sorties over a period of six days. On reflection, however, the view was officially expressed that this effort could have been better directed at the German army, then fleeing headlong out of Belgium and France; preventing more enemy troops from reaching Germany would have been more worthwhile than wresting a bypassed area from troops who were clearly trapped, with little hope of escape.

Havocs in France

Rather than the more usual, phased move by several groups over a period of days, it was decided on 27 September to transfer the entire 9th Air Force A-20 element to Continental airfields at the same time.

Accordingly, Bretigny (A-48) became the new base for the 409th Group, while the 410th hung its collective hat at Coulommiers (A-58) and the 416th went to Melun (A-55).

All groups then retained the standard mix of A-20s fitted with solid noses and those equipped to carry a bombardier. While all Havocs used by the Ninth were dimensionally similar (the clear-nosed Js and Ks being only slightly longer overall), it was not possible to interchange the nose sections. It soon became apparent that bombs (rather than guns) had the greater importance for A-20s in Europe, and, by utilising the external wing bomb racks, they were more effective in terms of ordnance load per aircraft.

Little time was lost in a potentially disruptive base move, as the A-20s joined forces with the B-26s and bombed fortified positions near Metz on the 28th. A further change of airfield took place on that same day when the Marauders of the 394th Group went to Bricy (A-50).

On the 29th, the original B-26 group in the ETO flew to Beauvais/Tille (A-61). The 322nd's Marauders, which had always been identifiable by their lack of any geometric tail markings, quickly settled into their new surroundings. Much the

same kind of activity took place at Cormeilles-en-Vexin (A-59) the following day, when the 344th's Marauders also made the move from East Anglia to France.

Five in a day

That a combat group's bad luck could be compressed into a single mission or one day had been demonstrated before, and on 29 September it was the turn of the 416th to ponder further the misfortunes of war. On a morning mission to German marshalling yards at Bitburg, north of Trier, the group lost two A-20s to flak as the attack was pressed home. In the afternoon, the Havocs flew to another yard at Jülich and encountered flak as they approached. Enemy fire struck the lead Havoc in a flight of three in the second box, which promptly blew up, the wreckage sheering the left wing off the second aircraft and severing the tail of the third. All three crashed just beyond the target area.

In total, the Ninth's medium-bomber effort for September amounted to 3,349 effective sorties, during which 5,591 tons of bombs were dropped for the loss of 12 aircraft; personnel casualties totalled 101 men.

Above: An A-26B of the 669th Bomb Squadron, 416th Group (almost certainly 43-8232/2A-A), at a Continental base. *Imperial War Museum*

October '44

On the 2nd, the Marauders of the 386th Group occupied Beaumont-sur-Oise (A-60), B-26s and A-20s each participating in three missions that day to pound what were identified as industrial targets at Übach. This operation turned out to be a near-fiasco, as most of the bombs missed their intended targets. Only two flights of aircraft put their ordnance down in the right place.

The next few days were quiet, as the weather again played its tricks. A gradual deterioration in visibility led to more than 330 Ninth Air Force bombers being recalled while *en route* to targets in the Netherlands on 5 October. The 397th BG was in France by 6 October, its aircraft using the airfield (A-72) at Péronne for the next few months.

Those Dutch targets identified as useful to the enemy and missed on 5 October did not remain immune from air attack for long: on the 6th, over 300 9th Air Force mediums went after a variety of them, including barracks, ammunition dumps and marshalling yards at Düren and Hengelo. Bridges at Arnhem and Aldenhoven were also bombed during the course of the day.

Rail tracks on the outskirts of Trier slid under the sights of the bombardiers of all three A-20 groups on 7 October, the targets including the city's marshalling yards and a number of warehouses containing military supplies. Six warehouses went up in smoke and four others suffered severe damage. In the meantime, the B-26s attacked a supply depot at Euskirchen as well as two bridges.

Another bridge at Euskirchen was bombed the next day by 30 aircraft and again on the 9th, but none of the target structures was confirmed as being wrecked.

Weather prevented any operations on the 10th. Neither could much be achieved on the 11th, as the weather 'fouled up' pathfinding equipment while the B-26s and A-20s were on their way to a German army base; once again, the recall order went out.

The bombers blasted two enemy-held rail bridges on the 12th. The next day, they followed this up with similar harassment of the Wehrmacht by attacking several bridges in the Netherlands, eastern France and western Germany known to be used for bringing up supplies to various points in the front line — which now stretched right across the continent of Europe.

Above: A 420th Group A-20J or K races the clouds *en route* to a target. *USAF*

Above: All but one of the Marauder groups adopted tail stripes and symbols to assist forming up prior to a mission. A yellow triangle identified the 391st Group, these B-26s being from both the 575th and 572nd Squadrons. *J. Hamlin*

Right: B-26 42-96313 of the 572nd Bomb Squadron, 391st Group, during a 1944 mission. *J. V. Crow*

Left: An A-26B (41-39265) of the 671st Bomb Squadron, 416th Bomb Group, parked next to a P-38. The group's black rudder stripe is clearly shown. *J. V. Crow*

There followed three days without missions as the weather closed in, the tactical bombers operating again on 17 October when 35 B-26s attacked a rail bridge at Euskirchen. Over at Melun, the personnel of the 416th anticipated a further spell of combat in the A-26. There was a temporary withdrawal from operations by each squadron (beginning with the 670th) as the crews familiarised themselves with the 20 or so aircraft flown into A-55 from England. The majority of these were apparently the same aircraft which the 386th Group had used for the initial A-26 evaluation in mid-1944. The group's Havocs were flown back to England as they were replaced by Invaders.

Familiarisation with the new attack bomber was to be completed in one month, although the group would not completely relinquish its Havocs. The majority of the early Invaders delivered to the Ninth Air Force were solid-nosed B models, and A-20Js and Ks continued to serve as lead ships, pending the delivery of adequate numbers of A-26Cs.

The 416th's accelerated conversion programme saw the 671st Squadron initiate a 'dawn to dark' schedule starting on 18 October, full conversion of 18 to 20 crews in the space of three to four days being the aim. Bad weather intervened to disrupt the training schedule to a significant degree. One pilot took-off from Melun on 22 October, within five minutes found local fog completely obscuring anything recognisable, and, employing what might be termed the 'homing pigeon' instinct, headed for England to find a place to land! Missing (presumed lost in an accident) for two days, he returned on the 24th. This kind of incident added to the worries of group commander Theodore Aylesworth; the foul weather had already resulted in the loss of one Invader on the 15th and damage to another on the 19th. The latter accident was attributable to the A-26's weak nosewheel oleo (a known problem that was being attended to), but it was clear that the 416th needed more time to complete the conversion, and in November there would be a slight change of plan in the group's schedule.

Five days of bad weather at least gave the 416th's groundcrews a chance to catch up on maintenance, some form of which was needed virtually all the time their parent groups flew combat missions. It goes without saying that this was true of all

the groups, irrespective of the type of aircraft operated. While the bombers remained on the ground, the goal for which many of their recent missions had been flown materialised in the Allied capture of Aachen on 21 October.

Any such enforced slackening in operations by the bombers was generally taken up by TAC fighter-bombers, which were very active over the battlefield. The Thunderbolts also took on more ambitious targets, among which was to breach the earth and masonry dam at Dieuze. The dam was destroyed on 20 October to prevent the Germans from doing the same thing when US troops were in the act of fording the Étang de Lindre river.

There was hardly any medium-bomber activity until 29 October, and, during the lull, the 9th Bomb Division took the chance (on the 28th) to relocate its headquarters to Reims. Unknown to the Allies, the reduced air activity as a result of the bad weather could not have been more timely for the Germans. The respite from air attack was broken on the 29th when the Ninth's bombers flew sorties against five Dutch and German rail bridges, about 170 aircraft taking part in the missions, which reduced further the enemy's vital rail links. The 29th was also something of a red-letter day for the 322nd, for the pioneer ETO Marauder group carried out its 300th combat mission; two days previously the unit had been awarded a DUC for its work since its combat debut on 14 May 1943 up to 24 July 1944, which, of course, took in the period supporting the D-Day landings.

November '44

Hopes that the war would be 'over by Christmas' looked increasingly slim as November began. Weather forecasts were not encouraging, and it looked highly unlikely that it would be practical to launch an all-out assault on the territory of Hitler's Reich until the conditions improved. As snow continued to fall, few of the combatants realised that what they were enduring was one of the worst winters the continent of Europe had experienced in decades. In the next few weeks the conditions all but brought the war to a standstill. Turning his back on a developing Russian offensive which would precipitate a massive, near-total military collapse of German forces on the Eastern Front, Hitler focused on the final preparations

for a counter-strike in the West.

Increasingly bad weather kept the Ninth's bombers on the ground on the first day of the month, although things moved into high gear the following day, when five railway bridges were bombed by a force of 147 aircraft. The bombers had a fighter escort, the 'little friends' making their contribution to the destruction on the ground as well as bringing home low-level photographs of the tactical situation.

More transportation targets in western Germany were attacked on 3 November, including a rail overpass at Kaiserslautern and bridges at Bad Münster, Neuwied-Irlich and Konz-Karthaus. Again, fighters covered their medium-bomber charges.

The 416th Group was taken off operations on the 3rd to allow it time for full conversion to the A-26, the pilots ferrying the A-20s back to England on the 4th. They returned two days later, having been held up by bad weather, with new A-26Bs. About 40 B models were in place at Melun by the 6th, there still being a lack of A-26Cs in the UK at that time. A three-day stand-down was imposed while the Invaders were thoroughly inspected.

Trier was revisited by the mediums on the 4th, 218 of them dropping bombs on depots and gun positions at Eschweiler. In the meantime the US XIX Corps had entered Aachen. Targets in and around Hamburg were attacked on the 5th, although the bombers were all back on the ground on the 6th due to bad weather — a situation that persisted for three days. It was the 9th before 74 aircraft (out of 514) could bomb arsenals, other military stores, artillery camps and so forth, designed to break the deadlock imposed by the German fortified positions north of Metz, which stretched some 10 miles from Thionville to the Moselle. Among other wretched manifestations of the bad weather, the knee-deep mud made a cohesive advance by infantry and vehicles impossible. Operation 'Madison' was a ground offensive designed to break the stalemate, and this was begun on 8 November, supported by fighter-bombers.

In all these missions there were incidents and accidents laced with *pathos* and humour. On 9 November the 322nd Group's 451st Squadron lost a B-26 when Lt John Corley became another victim of flak. As the Marauder went down, six 'chutes were seen, indicating that the entire crew had abandoned the doomed bomber. The subsequent report was not so encouraging, as only Corley was known to have survived the bail-out. The same squadron records for the 9th noted how expediency took over when Lt Thomas Mattax brought off another 'impossible' feat in a B-26 — he landed on a narrow, paved road in France with his tanks almost dry. Having encountered a storm when returning from a mission, Mattax had used up fuel trying in vain to find an airfield, and the road had to suffice.

It was intended that the bombers would fly a ground support mission on the 10th, but the elements had other ideas and, although they did manage (in most cases) to take-off, more than 150 aircraft were obliged to return to base. Despite being

denied some of their air cover, the army managed to cross the Seille river in three places on 8 November and to capture eight German villages.

More luck attended the operational plans for the 11th, when 190 medium bombers attacked a further variety of targets in numerous locations. On the 12th, the command was obliged to cancel all bomber missions once again. Little happened for 36 hours, until better weather came in on the 16th. Their crews getting wearily used to taking maximum advantage of any easing of the weather, 119 bombers lifted-off from their bases; 90 reported being able to attack defended positions at Echte, Luchem and Eschweiler in direct support of the US First and Ninth Armies, which were about to launch Operation 'Queen' — a further ground offensive.

With a large number of B-26s and A-20s at its disposal, IX Air Division was able to carry out attacks on numerous targets on a single mission. Such was the nature of the ground fighting that small positions — even single buildings — were made into strongpoints to hold up the advance of an Allied column, if only for a short time. Thus medium-bomber crews found themselves being used increasingly like fighter-bombers, including strafing with their formidable battery of guns, although this remained a highly-dangerous undertaking.

Invaders' 'first'

On 17 November the weather front conspired to prevent about 100 mediums from finding their targets, although 30 A-26s of the 416th Group did manage to

Above: A 322nd Bomb Group B-26 coming off the stricken Neuenburg railway bridge over the Rhine on 19 November 1944. Destruction of the bridge, which lay east of the Belfont Gap, assisted the US Seventh Army's offensive to drive the retreating German army out of France. *Imperial War Museum*

bomb a stores depot at Haguenau. This was the first full mission for the group with Invaders, which were led in by A-20s. As the bombers dropped to 8,000ft to locate the target accurately, the Germans reacted, although their ground fire proved too light to do any damage and the bombs went down squarely on the depot. Later it was learned that the 416th had been the only group to carry out its briefed mission that day — a gratifying endorsement for the A-26.

Formation flying for the Invader was a variation on the theme adopted by the B-26s and A-20s, but with fewer aircraft. The standard box was made up of six aircraft in two 'V' formations, with the wingmen on the same level or slightly above the leader. The second flight was positioned 150ft to the right and 250ft below the leading box, with the third flight 150ft to the left and 500ft below. It was found possible to deploy the A-26 in very close formations, with the nose of following aircraft just clear of the tail of the one in front of it. Even so, the formations were flexible enough to take advantage of the speed and manœuvrability of the type.

Laying on a large-scale mission on the 18th, the command assembled more than 340 B-26s and A-20s to continue whittling down German defences and to disrupt the flow of supplies in 13 different locations. Part of the attacking force was composed of the B-26s of the 394th Group, which had enjoyed a run of 133

missions since 20 April without the loss of a single aircraft or crew. The group's target was a supply depot at Gey, southeast of Aachen. As it made a second run the Marauder flown by Capt Charles J. DeRitis was bracketed by flak and suffered a direct hit in its right engine. With 4ft of right wing missing, the B-26 flipped over on its back and plunged down. Nine men, including the group operations officer, the squadron navigation officer and the squadron bombardier, perished.

On the 19th, the bombers formed up into an even stronger force of 450-plus machines, including 41 A-26s and eight A-20s from the 416th, which bombed targets in and around 10 German towns in northwestern areas of the country, well behind the front. Despite the loss of some of its most important officers the previous day, the 394th contributed 56 B-26s to destroy an ordnance depot at Merzig. Going in at a very low 5,000ft, the 394th penetrated the weak and inaccurate flak to achieve an 'excellent' bomb pattern. The 416th dropped from 6,000ft and also obtained 'good' results — so much so that Gen Vandenburg sent a congratulatory message to the effect that the bombing materially assisted the advance of the Third Army.

On the 20th, the weather, with its monotonous regularity, decreed that the bombers should once again remain on the ground. By then, however, one of the recent 'repeat' targets — the troublesome

fortifications around Metz — had all but been overrun by US troops.

The 21 November mission list contained mostly rail targets at Bergstein, Echte, Sinzig, Neuwied and Derichsweiler, all of which were duly bombed by the Ninth's mediums. The B-26 element had a fighter escort, which also dive-bombed targets of opportunity. No flying was possible on the 22nd, 23rd or 24th, but on the 25th an ordnance depot at Landau and ammunition dumps in Neustadt and Kaiserslautern were attacked. A similar mission, with similar targets, was flown on the 26th by 173 aircraft, but no missions were possible on the 27th.

There was a return to smaller-sized targets on the 28th, 29th and 30th, the largest of this series of raids taking place on the 29th when 301 aircraft aimed their bombs at barracks and depots at Wittlich, Mariaweiler, Pier and Elsdorf. In many instances the sheer weight of bombs dropped obliterated these small targets, which would otherwise have caused a temporary slowing-up of the 'broad front' nature of the Allied advance. On the last day of November, 288 mediums attacked four defended villages, a marshalling yard and rail tunnel, a military camp and a repair centre for armoured vehicles. With its poor flying weather, the month had not been one of the best in terms of tactical bombing, but all units had done their best under very rugged conditions.

Above: Later-production B-26s had improved arrangements for collecting the 'empties' from the tail guns, as evidenced by the fairing on 44-67822 of the 584th Squadron of the 394th Group. *J. V. Crow*

8 Slimming the Bulge

December '44

In action for the first two days of the month, flying 132 sorties on the 1st, the mediums attacked defences at Fraulautern, Ensdorf and Saarlautern, while elements of the US VII Corps penetrated Inden and Hurtgen Forest. The 8th Infantry Division was at the same time moving into Brandenburger Forest. Visiting much the same region on the 2nd, 210 aircraft of the 9th Bomb Division attacked defended areas in selected German towns in the face of still-deteriorating weather conditions. Under intense Allied pressure, enemy armoured formations appeared to intelligence to be pulling back into northwest Germany, presumably taking advantage of the bad weather to refit. The weather succeeded in grounding the division's aircraft on the 3rd and 4th, although fighters were able to mount a number of defensive patrols and armed reconnaissance sorties.

Returning to action on the 5th, the three bomber types flew 172 sorties, these continuing to pinpoint targets behind the front lines — marshalling yards, fuel storage, a road junction and a railway bridge — under fighter escort. Part of the fighters' task was to cover three US infantry divisions moving into the Luchem, Bergstein and Lucherberg areas. Much the same pattern of operations was repeated on the 6th, with 154 sorties, the bombers attacking defended positions at Münstereifel, Erkelenz, Nideggen and Daun, while ground forces occupied positions along the Saar river. Then, not entirely unexpectedly, the weather prevented any operations on 7 December.

A modestly-sized mission by 29 Invaders on the 8th was directed against a rail bridge at Sinzig, no other activity by the command being possible, again due to the weather.

For the first time in the month, the command was able to send out a sizeable force of 254 aircraft on 9 December to bomb barracks and marshalling yards located in western Germany, the numerous small targets now being regularly described

Above: What fighters could do, flak could do, sometimes with much worse results. This 391st B-26 was badly shot-up on a mission over the Saar region on or around 14 December 1944. 1st Lt Edmund P. Dunn was lucky to get it back to base in more-or-less one piece. *Imperial War Museum*

in Ninth Air Force reports and daily summaries as 'defended towns'. These could contain various types of target associated with the enemy war effort, including amunition dumps, fuel stores, barracks, and road and rail transport.

Similar targets in Birkesdorf and Huchem-Stammeln were hit on 10 December, about 130 B-26s participating in the day's operations. Two US armoured and four infantry divisions continued to push into Germany to probe the western bank of the Roer river.

Weather forced the briefed sorties by more than 200 aircraft to be abandoned *en route* to German targets on the 11th, but a single crew which failed to hear the recall pressed on to Reichenbach to bomb the stores depot. Whether or not they got away with this solo effort is unknown, although no bombers were reported as lost.

Scheduled missions for the 12th were probably more ambitious than the 90 mediums that actually flew against a variety

of target in nine defended towns and villages, including Gemünden, Harperscheid and Wollseiffen. Similar types of attack by 250 aircraft were carried out on 13 December, the primary objectives being a supply dump at Schleiden and marshalling yards at Euskirchen. With two American army corps on the River Blies and about to cross the 'Westwall' at the town of Kesternich, troops had also infiltrated the Dillingen-Saarlautern-Habkirchen area and had established positions on the surrounding high ground.

A futher day of inactivity for the tactical bombers followed on 14 December. On the 15th, the 409th Group completed its month-long transition training on the A-26 and was pronounced ready to return to combat; the 9th Air Division was meanwhile able to send out nearly 300 bombers to attack oil stores, an enemy encampment and six 'defended positions'.

The Germans strike

Another grounding order was reluctantly issued by IX Air Division on 16 December, which dawned slowly with a freezing ground fog. American ground units had reached the Ardennes Forest, sitting astride an Allied front that now stretched for about 80 miles. The same low-visibility conditions prevented elements of the Luftwaffe from executing a special operation in support of what was understood to be a major German counter-offensive; Operation 'Bodenplatte', a mass attack on Allied airfields, had to be postponed to await better weather. In the meantime, the fighters would fly close-support sorties for the German Panzer and infantry units which had opened their thrust against weak US positions in the Ardennes to begin Operation 'Watch on the Rhine'. The first phase of what became famous as the Battle of the Bulge had begun. Some Allied fighter sorties were possible on the 16th, and these pilots returned with the first, startling news of a German counter-attack. It was received by an incredulous Allied high command, bereft as it was (for a few hours) of the usually reliable early warning from Ultra code intercepts. The attack on the Westwall — a two-pronged pincer movement, designed to push the German army back to the Rhine — was abandoned. In the early hours of the 17th the Ultra decodes of enemy radio messages confirmed the rumours.

By fully exploiting the appalling weather, Gerd von Runstedt attempted a repeat of what the German armoured columns had achieved in the attack on France in 1940: a lightning thrust through the 'impenetrable' Ardennes Forest. Led by the 6th Panzer Division driving on St Vith, the Germans' intermediate objective was to seize crossing-points on the River Meuse at Namur and Liège, and ultimately to thrust into Antwerp, attack Allied forces poised to drive into Germany and capture the port. Initially von Runstedt committed 71,000 troops and 160 tanks to this over-ambitious (not to say highly-optimistic) operation, which relied so heavily on the bad weather preventing overwhelming enemy air attacks on his tanks and troops. He nevertheless gambled that he might get away with this, if only for a few, vital days. He really had no choice but to try to carry out Hitler's orders.

Unable to react by bringing to bear even a fraction of their air support, the Allied armies had little option but to pull back and give ground to the surprisingly strong tank force that the Germans had been able to put together in almost complete secrecy. Twenty divisions were moving forward to threaten a very thinly-stretched front line, held at some points by the minimum number of troops, many of whom were hardly equipped to stop Tiger tanks. The tactical air forces, ostensibly a few minutes' flying time from the front and easily capable of halting the offensive, were rendered powerless for days, as ice, snow and fog covered vast tracts of Europe, from England down to Italy.

One bright spot for the Allies came on 18 December, when two very courageous F-6 pilots spotted a key German Panzer column of 60 tanks *en route* to Stavelot, with the result that P-47 fighter-bomber pilots braved the arctic conditions to carry out attacks on them until darkness fell. The Thunderbolts managed to destroy or disable half the tanks and 56 out of a reported 200 trucks.

In the meantime, the 9th Air Division was able to send 165 medium bomber-sorties against five 'defended town' targets in western Germany, as well as 500 fighter sorties, but even this sizeable effort was much less than was needed. Nevertheless, the 274 tons dropped by the 386th's B-26s through cloud over Blumenthal and Hellenthal temporarily blocked the road to Schleiden, that town being bombed the following day. Subsequent attacks blocked the road again, holding up traffic pending a clearing of the rubble — a small but important bonus for the Allies, who, unlike their opposite numbers, had time on their side. Any hampering of the German advance over roads that could take vehicular traffic became increasingly important as the crisis deepened, for simply taking to the bordering fields was often a difficult (if not impossible) option for motor transport as well as tanks. Plunging blindly off a blocked route with ditches and low-lying fields was not to be recommended, however desperate the situation. This made things marginally easier for the attacking aircrews, particularly as the Germans had banned any civilian traffic from the roads around the Ardennes: only military vehicles would be seen through the gun- and bomb-sights of Allied aircraft.

Tactical air headquarters were pulled back from Maastricht to St Trond on the 19th, mainly as a precautionary measure; few Allied commanders could accurately gauge the strength of the enemy counter-thrust or what its objectives might be. Blind bombing by the Eighth Air Force's heavies was maintained during the period of greatest crisis, but it was the direct battlefield support that was so lacking, this being the type of operation most adversely affected by the appalling weather. Ice, snow and fog combined to keep the entire 9th Air Division on the ground on the 20th, 21st and 22nd, there being little or no aerial activity over the Ardennes salient for the three-day period.

'War's most beautiful sunrise'

Then on the 23rd, the weather changed for the first time in a week; on that morning the sun broke through and airmen awoke to find clear skies. Within hours the air war over the Western front was on again with a vengeance. The bulk of the available Allied aircraft able to reach the Ardennes region flew that day, including nearly 400 9th Bomb Division B-26s, A-20s and A-26s. Their targets were German communications and rail links directly in the rear of the advancing Wehrmacht columns, the 386th and 391st Groups being briefed to destroy a railway viaduct at Ahrweiler. Preoccupied with their own missions, the fighter groups could not offer immediate escort to all the tactical strikes, but the situation allowed for no delay — the bombers had to go.

The 391st led the attack on the viaduct, with 30 aircraft, including pathfinders. Having missed a planned rendezvous with a fighter escort they had been promised, the Marauder crews ploughed on, acutely aware of the importance of carrying out their mission. Heavy flak removed the PFF aircraft as the 391st lined up for the bomb run. As the bombardiers set their sights, the flak suddenly fired a red burst and then ceased abruptly at 11.55hrs. On this pre-arranged signal, enemy fighters bounced the second box of Marauders, while the first box, more-or-less clear of the intercept, could not see the target. Under heavy attack, the second box picked up the viaduct, carried on and dropped its bombs. Round went the first box, came in again, picked up the AP and released the bombs. Enemy fighters — the Focke-Wulf 190s and Messerschmitt Bf109s of JG 2, 3 and 11 — then proceeded to tear the 391st to pieces, to exact an eventual toll of 16 Marauders downed. For some of the

Above: The worst day for the B-26 force in WW2 was 23 December 1944, when the Luftwaffe fighter force supporting von Runstedt's winter offensive hit the bombers hard. This remarkable photo shows Marauders trying to evade an attack by FW190s that day. *J. Prien collection*

bomber gunners this was their first sight of enemy fighters, and few had experienced them being so aggressive. Well aware that friendly fighters were not in their immediate area, the Marauder crewmen gave the interceptors as hard a time as they could, their machine guns being highly capable of bringing their adversaries down if they ventured in close enough. For 23 minutes the fighter attack went on; gunners reported at least 69 clashes between bomber and fighter, their claims amounting to seven. Most of the participating Marauders were shot-up, some badly.

Whether or not a particular bomber formation fell foul of the German interceptors was often a matter of pure chance. Flying in the same area as the mauled 391st, the 386th encountered flak, but was otherwise unmolested by fighters and dropped its bombs without trouble, apart from some aircraft sustaining damage from shrapnel. The 322nd was assailed by 50 enemy fighters near Euskirchen and lost two Marauders. Eight was the grim toll exacted from the 397th, which came up against two dozen Focke-Wulfs and

Messerschmitts minutes after attacking the Eller bridges.

Better fortune attended the 344th, which was attacked after making its run on the Mayen bridge: the fighters were not able to bring any of the Marauders down. A second mission by the 386th to bomb Nideggen evaded the German fighters completely, and the group returned home without any casualties.

A rail bridge at Mayen had also been selected as the target for the 387th and 394th (with 40 and 33 B-26s respectively, plus a fighter escort). The first and second boxes of the 387th became separated, the second box finding itself without its escort as it swept into the target. Spotted by the pilots of 15 to 25 Bf109s, the Marauders were subjected to a swift, savage attack that chopped down four bombers from the low flight. As the Messerschmitts dived away, the two low-flight survivors maintained station and followed the first box into the flak bursts over the target.

By now very familiar with USAAF medium-bomber tactics, the flak crews peppered the sky in front of the formation, to claim a PFF aircraft and a flight leader's ship. Two other B-26s were in dire straits from the fighters and flak as the bombardiers were finally able to align their sighting crosshairs on the bridge. Five out of seven flights of the 387th salvoed their bombs to record four 'excellent' and one 'superior' bomb pattern, which put one bridgespan in the river and toppled a second. More damage was done by the bombs dropped by the 394th, which lost the use of its PFF equipment but released visually. The result was a timely break in the important rail link between Koblenz and the front line.

Few veterans of the groups involved will ever forget 23 December 1944; for the men of the 410th Group, the day was summed up in one word: Kyllburg. The marshalling yard there was the primary objective for the Havocs, 53 of which flew the mission to knock it out. Thirty-two aircraft found the target and dropped 175 500lb GPs on the sidings and main line, which was thus closed to through traffic. A communications centre at Lünebach was the secondary, and this was also attacked with 'good' results.

The December weather made the freezing interior of the A-20 an unenviable place to be. This dubious characteristic of the Douglas bomber was a drawback to which the crews were well accustomed, but on freezing winter days any altitude increased the draughts, making life very uncomfortable for the occupants, particularly the turret gunners. Cramped into their transparent cupolas with little room to move, they were unable to wear a standard AAF chest parachute pack during combat missions — there was simply no space for that and the gun controls.

During the afternoon of the 23rd, about 200 more medium bombers returned for another crack at several of the same targets. Unfortunately for some of the American crews, the Luftwaffe fighters that had reappeared in some strength over the Bulge for the first time in months had not all been driven off by hordes of 'little friends'. Some of the FW190s and Bf109s got among the mediums to cause further carnage. Diving recklessly through the fire put up by the bomber boxes, the Jagdflieger inflicted the highest daily loss in the history of the Ninth Air Force.

Bearing the brunt of the assault by the FW190s and Bf109s of JG 1 and JG 11 were the B-26s of the 397th Group, which had the important task of cutting the last remaining bridge across the Moselle at Eller, between the Ruhr and Dinant in Belgium. Heavily armed though they were (German pilots admitted later that the B-26 was the aircraft they least liked to attack, for that reason), the odds were too great for some elements to withstand.

One of the numerous first-hand accounts of the air combats of the 23rd was that of Capt Edward M. Jennsen, who led a box of Marauders behind a pathfinder ship, *en route* to rendezvous with the fighter escort. When no fighters appeared, the B-26 crews had no choice but to proceed to the target unescorted. Heavy flak came up, and Jennsen's bombardier missed his aiming point. Jennsen banked around for another try.

This time the B-26 was on target, just as enemy fighters attacked. They came in 'twelve abreast and four deep', according to eye-witnesses. The men in Jennsen's crew reported that the German fighters hacked down five other Marauders before setting their own aircraft on fire. Releasing his bombs as the gunners almost burned out their barrels, Jennsen received a message telling him that he might have to wait 15 minutes before any friendly fighters appeared. More B-26s spiralled down as German fighters and American bombers laced the sky with machine-gun bullets and cannon shells. Gunners on Jennsen's ship claimed three downed in a running battle lasting a very long 25 minutes. Finally they were over friendly territory, and the fighters flew off.

In total, 35 Ninth Air Force bombers were lost on 23 December, but the sorties flown had largely succeeded in wrecking the Moselle bridges, bottling up a significant part of the enemy's precious armour — which he was losing at too fast a rate to replace. The 397th was one of the hardest-hit bomb groups, for, as well as losing seven Marauders to enemy fighters, three went down as a result of flak damage sustained in the target area.

Fuel supply critical

With few reserves left, the Germans could ill-afford heavy battlefield losses in terms of vehicles destroyed or disabled — and, when they began to run short of fuel for the Panzers, the entire pointless operation was jeopardised. Time was not on von Runstedt's side to execute properly a plan that was far too ambitious to have any real chance of succeeding. The German counter-offensive was also hampered by the stubborn and unexpected resistance of US troops at Bastogne and St Vith, and, although these forces became isolated, aerial re-supply enabled them to hold out against strong enemy pressure. Whenever the weather clamped down again, the enemy could make progress, but there were sure signs that a solid, high-pressure front was developing to keep the skies clear for a few days. Tactical bombers flew to support the Allies' effort to rally and organise their own forces in sufficient strength to counter-attack and stop the German advance.

On Christmas Eve 1944 the weather front arrived to bring clear skies, and the AAF flew its largest single heavy-bomber strike of the war when 1,874 Eighth Air Force and 800 RAF Bomber Command sorties were sent to devastate lines of communication and airfields throughout western Germany. These sorties directly supported the fighting in the Ardennes, which saw the Allies gradually regaining the initiative.

For its part, the Ninth Air Force put up 376 aircraft to attack much the same type of target as the heavies. Putting up 50 A-20s to hit a communications centre in the town of Zülpich, the 410th Group received a congratulatory message from Gen Anderson. Of the six flights involved, four were credited with 'superior' results for their bombing, with two rated as 'excellent'. The group was also awarded one of five DUCs that went to Ninth AF units for the 23 December operations.

Missions on Christmas Day carried marginally less risk than before: the bomber crews now found the Luftwaffe fighter response — so aggressive on the 23rd — at virtually nil, thanks to the destruction wreaked at their bases. Flak, which, as ever, hotly defended the rail bridges at Konz-Karthaus (the target of the 386th Group), was not too accurate. Neither was it at Trier, which attracted bombs from the Marauders of the 394th. Otherwise, the mediums hit Grevenmacher, Zülpich and Nideggen.

Urgent calls for Luftwaffe fighter protection by the German ground forces went largely unheeded, and, in some sectors, the vulnerable transport columns also lost much of the cover provided by flak batteries. Terrified by the bomb carpets and the slashing low-level strafing and bombing runs by American 'Jabos' (as the Germans called them), the offensive began to falter. Every hour that brought clear skies over the Ardennes was a bonus for the Allied air forces, which rapidly made up for lost time. Few military commanders were willing to put their faith in weather forecasts, and for a time it had looked doubtful if 25 December would be marked by many sorties. But at midday the sun dissipated the morning fog, and most of the 9th Air Division was able to get airborne. No fewer than 629 Marauders, Havocs and Invaders had swept down on road and rail bridges and other targets, the defenders of which reacted quickly enough to cause the loss of three aircraft to flak. The attacks resulted in the bombers' dropping 1,237 tons, primarily on roads. At Konz-Karthaus, the 386th's B-26s had a 'class' escort in the shape of the P-51 of the 361st Fighter Group — one of two Eighth Fighter Command units that had been seconded to the Continent to assist the TAC units in the current crisis.

The 394th's B-26s drew Nonnweiler as their primary, along with a road bridge at Taben; Keuchingen was also attacked. Locations closer to the German salient, such as Bitburg, Irrel and Ahutte, were also bombed, the overall air effort adding significantly to the enemy's discomfort; Bitburg was virtually wiped off the map, with some bombs exploding in the craters made previously by US aircraft. The town was said to be '110%' destroyed. A moon-like landscape of overlapping bomb craters at other locations attested to the ferocity of the aerial campaign to restore the Allies to an offensive stance all along the front.

At St Vith, which had been a German stronghold, 70 B-26s of the 323rd and 387th Groups dropped 135 tons of bombs, which promptly led the defenders of the town to flee the area in panic. With von Runstedt's remaining tanks becoming stalled north of the River Maas, the Belgian skies witnessed an awesome display of airpower as the German links with the homeland were severed in numerous places

and Allied forces gradually restored the front line to more or less what it had been in early December. Now the gloves were off, the war had to be finished without delay. In the air, the AAF had freedom to roam anywhere in western Germany and eastern Belgium, where there were plentiful targets for the tactical bombers and fighters. But, as if to demonstrate how good flying weather had to be exploited to the full, the conditions deteriorated again on the 28th, causing the tactical bombers to ride out yet another day-long grounding order.

As one of the most momentous months of the war drew to a close, every effort was made to put enough support sorties into the air to harass the Germans and maintain the cover for friendly ground forces, but the weather made both tasks extremely difficult. The worry now was that, if a constant relay of aircraft could not be maintained over his armour, the enemy might re-group and strike again, but December's high drama ended on a muted note, with the bombers remaining on the

ground once again on the 31st.

The medium-bomber losses to enemy fighters at the end of 1944 had put the combat loss figure to all causes for the year to over 300 — still a low figure, considering the spiralling number of sorties the command was now sending out. Losses to flak continued at a more-or-less steady level, damage to a high proportion of aircraft (rather than loss) often being the main result.

With thousands of German prisoners, including flak crews, in Allied hands, some interesting interrogation reports and observations on the air-ground war found their way into print as intelligence reports. Commenting on the non-appearance of the Luftwaffe over many sectors of the Western front, one PoW from a flak unit summed up the attitude of many manning the batteries. His unit, he said, had three simple rules: (1) If an aircraft has a silvery look, it's American; (2) If it's dark in colour, it's British; (3) If it can't be seen at all, it's German!

Above: Diagonal tail markings denoted two of the Ninth's B-26 groups, the 397th using yellow as its group colour. These Marauders are from the 598th Squadron. *J. Hamlin*

January '45

That the Germans were down but not quite out was shown in the early hours of 1 January, when Operation 'Bodenplatte' was launched against Allied airfields in Holland and Belgium. Hardly affected, because their bases were not the main targets, the aircraft of what (a few hours into 1945) had become simply the 9th Air Division, were being readied for combat. Later that day, 190 9th Air Division mediums were out hitting more targets, including rail bridges, a road junction, lines of communication and enemy headquarters in Belgium and on the German border; 135 sorties were flown the next day, mainly against rail targets, and, although the number of aircraft was well down on previous efforts, this was more to do with the weather than any action by the Luftwaffe. No flying by the division was possible on the 3rd, as the weather had again turned bad.

Not until 5 January could the tactical bombers fly again, their target then being mainly rail bridges. Structures at Bullay, Simmern and Ahrweiler were attacked to ensure little or no use by the enemy. Only 26 sorties were possible on the 6th, the participating aircraft all attacking Prüm, before another period of stand-downs lasting several days. Meanwhile the Germans, who had been halted before the Meuse in late December, were now forced onto the defensive; as the Americans held firm at Bastogne, so too did their adversaries try their utmost to eliminate the salient. Snow continued to fall, making ground movement and airborne supply equally difficult. The conditions which had so well masked the German preparations for the Ardennes attack the previous December now — with a fair degree of irony — returned, this time to allow them to fall back in orderly retreat.

To divert Allied forces away from his main line of retreat, von Runstedt made a thrust in Alsace and raced towards Strasbourg. As the general predicted, Allied forces moved quicky to pinch off this new threat, thus preventing the withdrawal from being turned into a costly rout. Nevertheless, the Allies were not about to let the German army slip away unmolested, and the ground forces opened an offensive towards Houffalize to link up with advance elements of Patton's Third Army. It was the job of the tactical air forces to close as many rail and road links into Germany as the conditions allowed, effectively sealing off the Ardennes. Exploiting the inevitable bottlenecks created by previous destruction of transport links was often difficult in view of the weather.

In a typical mission on 9 January, only 15 B-26s managed to take-off, but these doggedly pressed home an attack on a

Below: Arctic conditions greeted many units during the winter of 1944/5, one of the worst for decades. These 410th Group A-20s belonged to the 647th Squadron. *Imperial War Museum*

Above: Engines needed attending to whatever the weather, whatever state the airfield was in. This B-26 had been in action in January 1945 to stem the German Ardennes counter-offensive, and was getting help to start in freezing conditions on a Continental airfield. *Imperial War Museum*

German rail bridge. Otherwise the front was very quiet. Fighters operated on the 10th, but the Ninth's bombers had another inactive day. There were some sorties on the 11th, but the familiar 'one day on, one (or two, or three) off' situation seemed to be almost a set pattern, to which the bomber crews had become resigned.

More sorties were possible on the 13th, and the 14th by comparison saw an explosion of action when over 280 bombers went out to smash the remnants of von Runstedt's army still holding out in the Ardennes. Not all the medium bombing could be carried out as briefed. One group of B-26s, which was supposed to be escorted by the P-38s of the 474th FG, missed the rendezvous over an area covered by ground haze. On the 15th, the air effort by the 9th Air Division was reduced to just 16 sorties against one bridge.

Twenty-four hours later, the air activity was back up to 311 sorties. Bridges, an MV repair centre and communications centres were included on the target list.

Again, the Lightnings of the 474th Group drew an escort mission to Marauders, which made the rendezvous but clearly missed their target. The critical view of the fighter pilots was that their own aircraft could have done better, had they been armed with bombs!

Among the groups that did what they had set out to do was the 386th, which damaged a rail bridge at Bullay, while the 323rd and 394th Groups went after the wooden road bridge over the Our river at Steinbeck. The latter group ran in to the target with 22 B-26s, but lost its lead ship to intense flak. The rest did the job, although 11 aircraft received flak damage. Other medium bombers attacked Ahrweiler, Rinnthal and the village of Rodt, the results being described only as 'mixed'.

When the Bullay bridge mission failed to drop the structure into the water, it elicited a tongue-in-cheek message from 'Opie'

Weyland to Sam Anderson, to the effect that he could call on the fighter-bombers for any jobs his mediums could not handle. Anderson's reply was that, without his bombers' having so weakened the bridge, the 'pea shooters' (popular AAF slang for fighters) would never have dropped a span, as they did on 10 February.

Almost inevitably (or so it seemed), the Ninth was grounded the following day. Little happened on the 18th, 19th or 20th, but on the 21st, 166 bombers took a crack at the marshalling yards at Mayen, as well as a bridge, rail junction and marshalling yard at Euskirchen.

With the German army now firmly in retreat, the Allied air forces determined as far as was possible to make sure it would never again be in a position to re-group in strength.

On 22 January, 304 medium bombers were able to strike effectively at the transport links between Belgium and Germany. Marauders of the 387th and 394th Groups, representing a combined force of 49 aircraft, succeeded in destroying the road bridge over the Our river at Dasburg, 16 miles south of St Vith. This river, which formed the border between Luxembourg and Germany, represented an ideal bottleneck if the crossing-point could be closed. Under direction of four B-26 pathfinders from Péronne using 'Oboe', the 387th's aircraft achieved 'excellent' to 'superior' results, with 108 1,000lb GP bombs which broke the bridge. Just to make sure, 22 Marauders of the 394th swept in at 12,000ft to drop another 41.5 tons. With the bridge down, a massive traffic jam, estimated to contain 1,500 vehicles, began to develop — a target ripe for destruction by air attack. This was duly delivered by fighter-bombers, which indulged in an orgy of destruction. The US Army's artillery was not left out, as air spotters passed co-ordinates to the gunners who pounded the hapless Wehrmacht transport. Half of the vehicles trapped in the 'pocket', which was even larger than that created at Falaise in 1944, were estimated to have been destroyed.

A further jam was created at Prüm by a similar number of vehicles belonging mainly to the 6th Panzer Army. Again, the fighter-bombers peeled off into their bombing and strafing runs to deny the enemy scores of vital tanks, AFVs, trucks and horse-drawn vehicles, few of which could be replaced, at least in similar numbers.

Low-level again

Officially, at least, the Ninth Air Force had not ordered any low-level attacks by medium bombers since the Ijmuiden raid in May 1943. But, on the 22nd, IX Air Division decided to unleash the bombers against the stalled German road traffic, using primarily the 416th's Invaders. Having been designed for just such a job as this, it was felt that the heavy firepower of the A-26 would be very effective. Unfortunately, it turned out to be a terrible experience for the group. Having located a target convoy at Dasburg, Lt Howard Nichols of the 15th TacR Squadron passed co-ordinates to five group Invaders, which dived on a convoy at noon. Very heavy return fire greeted the diving aircraft, and the one leading immediately lost an engine and had to put down, to be quickly joined by a second

which had also to crash-land. Neither crew was lost, as the A-26s came down in Allied territory.

Nichols then picked up six A-26s of the 671st Squadron over Luxembourg and led these back to Dasburg for another crack at the convoy. There were about 75 trucks below as the Invaders went in for their strafing and bombing runs. In a repeat of the earlier strike, the lead Invader received heavy flak and was set on fire. A second also went down and a third took heavy flak damage in the left wing. Nichols shepherded this aircraft out of the target area, and the other three Invaders, which were undamaged, also headed back to Luxembourg. Four down and one badly damaged was not a good result, and the day's work only highlighted the deadly effect of flak against low-flying bombers.

On 23 January the low-level rule was left to the discretion of the pilots, the day's targets including bridges and troop and vehicle concentrations noted by intelligence and PR flights at three different locations. Six A-26s of the 409th achieved little, only one aircraft managing to attack, and the 410th, which also sent out six Havocs, found a convoy at Blankenheim which it attacked from 1,500ft. Fifteen motor vehicles were claimed destroyed in return for damage to four A-20s from light flak.

Low-level missions were then cancelled by Anderson, who was appalled at the wastage. Despite this, the A-20s and A-26s continued to go in on targets below 10,000ft when the conditions, particularly the weather, merited it. Sometimes an approach from a lower-than-normal altitude made the difference between modest damage to the enemy and none at all.

Despite the low-level losses in January, crews rated the Invader as an effective ground-attack aircraft; it proved to have better single-engine performance than the A-20, and was clearly capable of meting out a devastating rain of fire from its closely-grouped nose guns. Marauders also got back to low flying to a limited extent, and the A-20 groups had been dropping down low after bombing their targets for some time beforehand. Tactically, a dive away after leaving some targets made for sound practice; the flak, often using shells fused for medium heights, could not always follow the aircraft quickly enough. That said, pilots could never be absolutely sure how much flak there was to protect a given target; it was a truism that, as the territory

available to the Germans shrank, so the flak guns were pulled into ever-tighter areas to defend that which remained.

Armed as they were with as much forward firepower as a P-47, Invader pilots, particularly, had wanted to find out how effective the aircraft was at strafing. The answer was often qualified by the degree of flak and the skill of the German gunners. Pilots could certainly destroy targets at low level, but they ran a high risk of being hit while doing so.

For the A-20 pilots, the greatest danger in hedge-hopping back to base — and more often than not opening fire on a choice target or two en route — was that the German 40mm, 37mm and 20mm cannon, designed specifically for anti-aircraft use in mobile mounts, were deadly. Used in quadruple, quick-reaction mounts, these guns were probably responsible for bringing down more Allied aircraft than almost any other ground weapon in the enemy's formidable arsenal.

More communications centres were attacked by 9th AD aircraft on 24 January, although the effort amounted to a modest 25 sorties. While bad weather pinned the Eighth Air Force to its English bases on the 25th, the mediums were able to put up 170 sorties to interdict rail lines, bridges and the by now familiar communications centres. Dasburg and Prüm were mopped up by the fighters in a final round of attacks on the German vehicle jams.

Twenty-six B-26s went out on the 26th, their target being a railway bridge and traffic at Euskirchen — an area served by lines running from Cologne and Bonn. A weather grounding was in force on the 27th, but 95 sorties were possible on the 28th, Mayen being included in the targets for the day, which otherwise took in familiar bridges and overpasses at Eller, Sinzig, Remagen and Kaiserslautern. A 'maximum effort' on the 29th saw 394 9th Air Division bombers attacking a variety of targets in western Germany, while the month was rounded off with a total grounding due to the weather on the 30th and 31st.

Despite the poor operating conditions, the Ninth's bombing claims for the week of 22-29 January reached a staggering 11,569 items of German heavy equipment. This figure comprised 53 locomotives, 2,871 items of rolling stock, 460 tanks and AFVs and no fewer than 8,185 motor vehicles.

Above: A B-26, almost certainly from the 344th Bomb Group, over the temporary steel railway bridge at Nonnweiler, 15 miles southeast of Trier, on 27 January 1945 — a month after Marauders had destroyed the original span during the Battle of the Bulge. *Imperial War Museum*

February '45

February opened with an attack by 146 medium bombers on German Army defensive positions and bridges between the Rhine and Moselle rivers during the first day, IX and XIX TAC fighters providing escort to mediums carrying out armed reconnaissance as well as bombing sorties. The latter included an attack on Euskirchen marshalling yards and the town of Arloff.

While the mediums were completing their daylight sorties, the 410th Group made ready to fly its first nocturnal mission that evening. The group, which had been pulled out of the line in January to re-train, sent off 25 A-20s at 20.50hrs, but 22 of them then received a recall message which was triggered by a not unusual report that bad weather was imminent. Three crews did not receive the call and flew on to bomb the target as briefed — a communications

building in the centre of Hillesheim. With the aid of 'Gee', the Havocs released their loads at 22.04hrs without the results being observed. All aircraft returned safely at 23.50hrs.

As the Ninth's only designated night-bomber unit, the 410th went out again on the night of 3/4 February, when 18 A-20s hit an MT depot at Mechernich, the primary target. Eight other aircraft dropped their loads on a rail junction designated as the secondary target. To assist the night forays, the 410th had been equipped with several A-26s and Marauders, which acted as markers and flareships for what became known unofficially as 'Blackout' missions, due to the fact that no lights were shown inside or outside the aircraft. On 3/4 February, the

26 A-20s were supported by eight B-26s and two Invaders.

Elsewhere on the 2nd, bridges east of the Rhine were bombed by over 350 mediums, other attacks being carried out on 'defended positions'. The Germans now enjoyed little respite from air attack when the weather permitted Allied aircraft to get airborne. It was only the elements that provided the Germans with some relief from the constant bombing and strafing, although the high-level, strategic bombers were often able to come in above the overcast and bomb through it by radar, so there was little peace for those on the ground actively opposing the Allies.

Among the targets definitely destroyed on 2 February was a fuel dump at Zell, the objective of 1st Tactical Air Force B-26s.

This combined force was a provisional one formed from USAAF B-26 groups and Armée de l'Air units also equipped with Marauders, plus fighter groups, to handle operations from the southern areas of the European theatre in support of the US Sixth Army Group. Closing fronts drew the 1st TacAF, Ninth and Twelfth Air Forces ever closer together.

The weather held on the 4th to allow attacks to be made on road and rail junctions, but there was no flying for the mediums on the 5th. An enemy-held village was bombed on the 6th, along with an ammunition dump and various targets of opportunity, 261 aircraft participating in the day's missions. Down went the effort again on the 7th, when just a dozen B-26s took-off to bomb rail sidings at Lippe. The figures were up to around 320 the following day, targets including the familiar rail junction, communications centre and marshalling yard; various opportunity targets were also attacked by part of the force.

On 9 February the 323rd Bomb Group made another base move, to A-83 Denain/Prouvy. More communications centres were attacked by 347 mediums during the day, a similar number of bombers flying against tactical targets on the 10th.

This phase of the war, as far as the 9th Air Division was concerned, was part of the lengthy Rhineland campaign which had begun as early as 15 September 1944; as the broad sweep of the name implies, this would actually last until 21 March 1945, although the Battle of the Bulge had introduced the Ardennes-Alsace campaign, which lasted from 16 December 1944 to 25 January 1945.

Targets of opportunity again figured at briefings for the 320 aircrews who flew on 10 February to bomb tactical positions, a rail bridge and a vehicle depot.

Marshalling yards at Bingen and Modrath were the targets for 97 sorties the next day, following which the 9th Air Division was again grounded due to bad weather — a situation recurring with monotonous regularity, but one which the flyers had little or no choice but to accept.

During the second week of February the A-26/A-20 groups moved base, the 409th going to A-70 Laon/Couvron, the 410th to A-68 Juvincourt and the 416th occupying A-69 Laon/Athies. This put them nearer their potential transportation targets, some of which were attacked on 13 February. During the day, the command put up an impressive 622 effective sorties, relays of bombers pounding rail targets, an ammunition dump and a vehicle park. The defences claimed 14 aircraft — statistically small, compared to the number of sorties, but the highest daily loss since December 1944.

Above: Taxying through an icefield on 4 February 1945, the 323rd Bomb Group heads once more for combat. In the foreground is 'Hades Lady', a battle-scarred veteran of the 456th Squadron. *Imperial War Museum*

Above: Two 2,000lb bombs falling from the bays of two 344th Group B-26s on the unit's 200th combat mission in 1945. *Imperial War Museum*

Right: B-26B 'Booby Trap III' was a Marauder that was fated to be destroyed in a mid-air collision over Cambrai, France, in February 1945. This photo was taken a short time before the event. *J. V. Crow*

Among the next day's targets for the 344th's Marauders was an afternoon run to a rail bridge near Koblenz, specifically the Kronprinz Wilhelm bridge at Engers. That particular St Valentine's Day was memorable for members of the 495th Squadron, which was briefed to destroy this particular Rhine crossing. It was the 344th's 201st mission. As usual, what preoccupied the 17 B-26 crews before take-off was the number of guns known to be defending that particular stretch of river: 112 along the route the bombers would normally have taken, with 35 more at the bridge itself.

One of the pilots, Capt J. W. Cotton, and his bombardier, 1st Lt Don Leigh, opted to forgo the usual evasive action, reasoning that the flak would be so dense that such manœuvres would not benefit the bombers. Better would be a 'straight in' approach that would give maximum sighting time and improve bombing accuracy.

In bright conditions, the force lined up for the bridge, the flak seeking them out. By holding the ship (named 'Rum Buggy II') steady on course, Cotton enabled Leigh to sight the target with almost leisurely ease, despite the shrapnel rattling along the Marauder's skin. The ruse worked and his bombs (part of

34 tons that went down) hit the bridge dead-centre, for an 'excellent' rating. A bonus shown on the strike photos was a train just about to cross — which may or may not have been able to stop in time. After the customary 'bombs away', Leigh (to his later embarrassment) gave out the Hollywood-style yell: 'Let's get the hell outa here!' What mattered to his crew was that the diving turn the pilot made achieved just that, and 'the Buggy' made it home. Five other group B-26s were not so lucky, including two from Cotton's own flight; all those that returned received heavy battle damage, Leigh counting 272 holes in his own. Also active on 13 February, part of the Marauder force flew about 90 sorties to the marshalling yards at Mayen.

A slight change in emphasis was revealed on 16 February, when the bombardiers were told that among their regular targets there would be a factory making jet engines. Not having been unduly troubled by the appearance of the Messerschmitt Me262, the B-26 crews nevertheless noted the importance of this plant before going out and bombing it. Other locations in the Ruhr — an area once notorious for its heavy flak defences — were also attacked during the day.

The bad weather returned on the 17th, and a reduced 31 sorties were made by B-26s to fell a railway bridge at Mayen. The 9th Air Division was then able to operate on six consecutive days, from 18 to 23 February, the mediums attacking rail bridges, ordnance and motor-vehicle depots and ground defences. All three types of division aircraft were invariably involved in these large-scale strikes, that on the 19th being typical. The targets included what was described as a prime-mover depot at Mechernich, rail bridges at Neuwied-Irlich, Pracht and Niederscheld, plus an ordnance depot at Wiesbaden.

In a week of unusually reliable weather for the time of year, the division sent 348 aircraft to bomb an oil depot, marshalling yards and bridges on the 21st. As well as the inevitable flak, which brought down one B-26, the mission was marked by the intervention of Luftwaffe fighters, which shot down a further three Marauders.

A huge, 450-strong air armada was launched by the Ninth on 22 February to work down an ambitious target list that was a catalogue of rail installations, including 46 bridges, 12 marshalling yards and 11 stations. This was Operation 'Clarion',

involving Allied air forces in the ETO and MTO and designed to paralyse all remaining German rail links. Some of the participating bombers made their run-in at a lower level than was usual — the first time that the pilots of a large force of mediums had been given a free hand to do so. Few were going to pass up the first real chance they had had of using the B-26's package guns for strafing. Two flights of the 322nd's 449th Squadron had as their target the Lang Gins rail bridge. Bombed as normal from 10,000ft, the bridge was hit well, after which the Marauders dived. In groups of three, the aircraft dropped down right to the deck to shoot up marshalling yards at Butzbach, a station at Friedberg and a factory situated at Bad Nauheim.

One of the attacking B-26s was 'Flak Bait' — the Ninth Air Force bombing record-holder in the 322nd Group. Ed Pakish was flying the ship that day, with Svenn A. Norstrom as co-pilot. The latter recalls that ground fire monotonously followed the bombers as they raced across their targets and that the veteran B-26 was by then growing a little tired. It could hardly keep up with the two other Marauders as the flight came off one target and, true to its name, it picked up some more metal splinters. No real harm was apparently done, but soon 'Flak Bait' was on her own. Racing across the Rhine at low level, the crew sought an airfield, as the aircraft was consuming 'gas' at a higher rate than normal due to the full-throttle, zero-feet flying.

Realising that Beauvais was a base too far that day, Pakish found an A-20 airfield, got permission to put down and prepared to land. There were some anxious moments when all aboard realised that the flak had hurt the B-26 more than was first thought, and the nosewheel refused to extend. Shaking it down did the trick, but, as ever in such a situation, the crew worried that it might not have locked. As things turned out, all was well; the gear lowered and the brakes worked — but 'Flak Bait' had taken it again that day. Hydraulic lines were found to be almost severed, the radio compass had been blown away, and even the emergency compressed-air lines had been cut by shrapnel. A large hole had also been torn in the leading edge of the fin, so battle-damage repairs were definitely needed before the aircraft could return to its home base.

Another pilot who flew the 22 February low-level mission was Ralph F. Jackson. His

recollection of the unusual sortie included watching the B-26's indicated air speed reach the absolute red-line limit of 352mph (as stated in the training manual) as it dropped to below 1,000ft to strafe the rail yards (presumably at Butzbach). After using his package guns, Jackson banked left to give his gunners a chance to fire at a string of railway wagons. By now flying just beyond the town, he was amazed to see what seemed like an appreciative audience cheering and waving from behind a fenced-off area. It was a PoW camp that the crews had not been briefed about, and everyone was glad that no bombs or bullets had gone astray. With a better turn of speed than 'Flak Bait', Jackson's ship got back to Beauvais, and was found to have taken a single bullet in the right wing and lost a rear fuselage hatch cover. The latter had probably been 'sucked out' by a combination of the low altitude and high speed, which happened to several other Marauders being flown on the limit, low down.

On the ground, Operation 'Grenade' had begun on the 23rd, as 'Clarion' continued; backing up the many heavy bombers flying tactical sorties, the 9th Air Division supported the US Army's crossing of the Roer by bombing targets to the east of the river. Behind the scenes, the policy of replacing the B-26 with the A-26 continued. On the 23rd the first Invader arrived for evaluation with the 391st Group at A-73. The aircraft began to be checked out by a number of crews prior to the arrival of sufficient aircraft to equip the group. The 394th was also to receive several Invaders, but, although the group went as far as applying its diagonal white tail stripe to some aircraft, in the event the group was to remain a Marauder unit until the end of the war.

The Allies were now going all-out to smash the remnants of the German war machine, and on 24 February about 500 medium-bomber sorties were flown against numerous tactical targets connected with rail transport. That night, 34 of the 410th's A-20s attacked the marshalling yards at Hillesheim. The Havocs were led in by A-26 and B-26 pathfinders, and the bombing results were reported as 'good'. But, just as they were getting used to flying combat missions at night, the 410th's crews were informed that the programme, such as it was, had been cancelled. The reason given was that the rapid progress of the ground war had all but removed the need for such operations. After flying a total of four night missions, the 410th's Havocs were returned to regular daylight sorties.

Further tactical targets, including four rail bridges, were bombed on the 25th, the mediums reporting little contact with enemy fighters, which were heavily engaged with fighter groups of both Eighth and Ninth Air Forces. As was almost guaranteed during the period, the Americans came off best in such engagements, pilots claiming 30 shot down during the morning missions. The fighters were adversely affected by bad weather on the 26th, although IX Air Division was able to despatch 235 aircraft against a wide variety of targets, two rail junctions being included. With February waning, the air commanders exploited a spell of reasonable flying weather to put up 700 sorties in a 48-hour period.

Among these late-February targets was Ahrweiler railway bridge, which had been the objective of the B-26 flown by MoH winner Darrell Lindsey the previous August. The bridge, presumably repaired since, attracted 118 sorties on the 27th, installations at Münstereifel and Monheim also being bombed that day. The last day

of the month was another substantial effort by 340-plus medium and light bombers which aimed to knock out ordnance depots at Pulheim, Rheinbach, Rommerskirchen and Stammeln. A rail bridge at Pracht was also attacked.

Repeat raids on important targets, particularly bridges, had long been an integral part of IX Air Division's operational brief. Reconnaissance was able to keep a close watch on repair work put in hand by the Germans across several hundred square miles of territory in a single day. Whenever rail links such as marshalling yards, crossing-points and bridges showed signs of being back in operation after repair, the location was added — or re-added — to the bombing target list. At those locations still in enemy hands, the whole cycle began again with another air attack.

Being able to call upon virtually unlimited numbers of volunteers as well as slave labourers, the Germans could effect repairs surprisingly quickly in some areas, depending on how much damage had been done by previous air raids. It was, however, to the advantage of Allied airmen that the

almost universal use of steam locomotives to haul trains in World War 2 could not be hidden for very long. Trains attracted air attack like few other forms of transportation, being systematically bombed and strafed across thousands of miles of track — but even with so many locomotives and pieces of rolling stock reduced to shattered hulks, the German trains managed somehow to keep running, not in certain critical sectors but behind the lines. One of the main reasons for the medium bombers to continue ranging out many miles from the front lines was to choke off the flow of supplies nearer to their source; the fighter-bombers could generally stem the flow nearer to their intended recipients.

Night photography came into its own during the short hours of daylight from November to February, and many targets otherwise hidden were exposed to the A-3s of the 155th PRS. Such sorties had added significantly to the Allies' 'round the clock' intelligence data during the critical winter of 1944/5, but the Germans continued to enjoy a small respite during the hours of darkness.

Above: A-26 Invader artwork with bomb log in 1945. The red stripe around the nose was a warning to keep clear of the propeller arcs. Forward of that was a taped-over breakpoint for the nosecone. *J. Bivens*

Right:
Another fine example of
Marauder nose art, this
time on a 584th
Squadron ship flown by
Col T. B. Hall. The
aircraft was B-26C-1
43-34203, the parent
unit the 394th Bomb
Group. *J. V. Crow*

Below:
This combat box of
Invaders belonged to the
670th Squadron of the
416th Bomb Group.
USAF

Above:
A Marauder of the 322nd Group's 450th Squadron on the Continent in 1945.
J. V. Crow

Left:
Yellow tail bands and wing guns on A-26s of the 386th Group in 1945. Both the 553rd and 554th Squadrons are represented.
F. F. Smith collection

10 End Run

March '45

The first three days of March saw the weather continuing to hold; the tactical bombers took full advantage and flew well over 500 sorties during the period. Once more, some of the targets had a familiar ring: Pulheim, Rheinbach, Rommerskirchen and Stommeln, which harboured communications centres, Giessen, where there was an ordnance depot, and a road bridge at Pracht, were all bombed during a 340-aircraft effort on the 1st.

Five bridges were among the objectives on 2 March, the attacks being designed to prevent the movement of enemy troops to reinforce positions being attacked by the US Third Army. Other targets continued to hinder movement behind the lines. Enemy storage facilities at Wiesbaden were among the locations revisited on the 3rd, the bombers also seeking out depots and communications centres at Giessen, Bergisch Born and Nahbollenbach. Rail bridges at Remagen and Simmern, plus the marshalling yard at Kirn, were among the day's transportation targets. The bombers were escorted by fighters, which carried out their important secondary duty of reconnaissance.

Bad weather then forced a much-reduced bombing effort on the 4th, although 180 aircraft did operate against rail and communications targets at Recklinghausen, Lenkerbeck and Herne, among other locations, before nightfall. Rather than clamp down completely as it had done so often before, the weather remained reasonable. US airmen rose in the early hours of the 5th to find the skies clear. The usual massive effort to fuel, arm and bomb-up multiple groups of medium bombers swung into efficient, well-rehearsed action, and at the appointed time 565 aircraft were on their way to bomb six marshalling yards and a variety of other targets. The primary objective at that time remained that of assisting the ground forces by preventing supplies and reinforcements from reaching the German troops being pushed back across the Rhine.

On 6 March the weather was more true to form, but it did not prevent the Ninth from sending off more than 260 sorties to marshalling yards at Recklinghausen, Siegburg and Opladen. Targets of opportunity were also attacked in the town of Bochum. The weather managed to keep two of the three Ninth tactical air commands on the ground, although some support sorties were flown to cover US troops driving to the Rhine in the Rheinburg area.

Above: Bombing communications centres was an ongoing task for the B-26, and on 15 March 1945 the 394th Group contributed to a force of 400 Marauders attacking roads and intersections to stop German traffic on the US Seventh Army front. Among the participating aircraft was 'Redlight Rosie', a B-26F-1 (42-96281/5W-V) of the 587th BS, adding one more to her eventual 108-mission record. *USAF*

By 7 March, although the bombers could not fly in the prevailing bad weather, the US First Army had established a bridgehead on the east bank of the Rhine below Cologne. Having found the bridge at Remagen intact, the American forces had fought tenaciously to take the bridge and prevent the Germans from demolishing it. In this they succeeded, and the bridge became a focal point for considerable land and air action, but by mid-month the Allies held positions along a 150-mile stretch of Germany's main river artery, from Koblenz to Wesel.

Two marshalling yards were bombed by the mediums on 8 March, as were additional tactical targets when the weather lifted sufficiently to allow 328 bombers to operate.

On the 9th there were over 600 medium-bomber sorties, with 382 taking place on the 10th, the targets on both days being many and various in the Koblenz-Braubach area. As on a number of occasions previously, the mediums were now bombing town and city suburbs, their aiming points being military targets in various districts. There were 696 sorties on the 11th and 450 on the 13th, the exact number operating on the 12th being unknown but surely similar, as the targets were many and varied. As this crescendo of destruction was clearly leading up to what everyone hoped would be the grand finale of the war, the 9th Air Division put up another 350 medium sorties on the 14th.

Decimated and demoralised, the enemy was demonstrably incapable even of holding tactically-vital Reich territory in the face of such overwhelming odds, and on 15 March the 9th Air Division rammed the message home by unleashing all its 11 bomber groups in support of Operation 'Undertone'. This was a far-reaching interdiction of communications centres at Neunkirchen and Pirmasens, marshalling yards at Turkismuhle and Erbach, and flak positions, the day's work being as usual aimed at giving the ground forces breaking through into southern Germany as safe a passage as possible. As well as bombs, the mediums showered Koblenz with leaflets advising that surrender was the best option for the town's inhabitants. Further leaflet raids were carried out by the mediums, as Allied commanders hoped thus to minimise civilian casualties in areas about to be captured.

If by the spring of 1945 the conventional Luftwaffe was all but a spent force, the brilliance of the German jet-fighter programme, most notably in the form of the Messerschmitt Me262, had also failed to live up to its potential — but what a potential it was. Quite capable of destroying every type of aircraft the Allies put over Germany, the Me262 had instead been hunted down and destroyed in the air and on the ground. The Luftwaffe had been unable to prevent the dire situation that resulted in insufficient time being devoted to jet conversion training, and had been powerless to circumvent the fuel shortage that plagued the new generation of combat aircraft. So bad had the situation become that the jet fighters, which had given the US and RAF high commands such a profound shock when they first appeared in combat, had been unable to turn a threat into reality. But the jets continued to be encountered in combat, and a Ninth Air Force fighter had shot down the first Me262 in October 1944. As of mid-March, the mediums had not been troubled by jet interceptors, and on the 16th, 17th and 18th the Ninth's bomber missions were directly in support of a thrust by the US Third, Seventh and Ninth Armies to place them securely on the far side of the Rhine. More than 1,500 sorties were completed against barracks, road and rail centres, defended towns, marshalling yards and ordnance depots. Five railway bridges were bombed on the 19th, as were communications centres; on the 20th over 360 sorties saw the mediums over a munitions plant, a rail bridge, targets of opportunity and what was described in mission reports as a 'town area'.

By despatching 848 sorties on 22 March, the Ninth reached a wartime peak; all three aircraft types participated, and 798 bombed their targets, for the loss of three aircraft, including a 322nd Group Marauder which received a direct flak hit and blew up. This happened in the morning, when 34 out of 36 of the unit's B-26s attacked Südlohn communications centre in the face of intense flak. In total, the defences inflicted various categories of damage on 126 aircraft. The 322nd returned to Südlohn that afternoon, and 12 B-26s all but obliterated the centre. Of the 36 aircraft flying the afternoon mission, 23 were able to go after secondary targets when the primary was reported to be well and truly down and out. Ten aircraft received damage from flak.

By deploying the A-26 in Europe the AAF experienced a change in the rôle of the attack bomber, which seemed to all intents and purposes to be approaching the twilight of its usefulness. This was not actually the case, as postwar events were to show, but the low-level-strafing element of the Invader's rôle had already been compromised by the degree of ground fire it had had to face in Europe. At safer, medium altitudes the aircraft excelled and, fitted as it was with a larger bomb bay than any other medium, it was effective enough. In the closing months of the war the AAF used numerous M-81 fragmentation bombs, 112 of which could be carried by the A-26.

That these massed formations of bombers could fly across Germany more or less with impunity was irrefutable proof that the Third Reich had lost the war, which now entered its final weeks. There were 804 tactical aircraft sorties on the 23rd of the month, the day's work including the pounding of a factory at Dinslaken. After the raid had passed and 158 tons of bombs had gone down, the factory's machine shops were totally destroyed in yet another demonstration of the awesome power of precision bombing. And then, on 24 March, Operation 'Plunder-Varsity' began — the airborne and land crossing of the Rhine at Wesel. More than 2,000 transports carried the British 6th and American 17th Airborne Divisions across Germany's great waterway while the British Second and US Ninth Armies crossed north and south of the town.

What began to appear in AAF records as 'clearing attacks' were the order of the day for the fighters, as the Allied parachute troops and gliders went in. The Ninth's bombers flew 688 effective sorties into the battle area on the first day, carpeting the drop-zones with fragmentation bombs, which immobilised numerous flak concentrations. Various objectives were smashed to ensure that advancing Allied troops were greeted with mute piles of rubble and a totally immobilised transport network, rather than defended strongpoints. Rail bridges, communications centres and other tactical targets were also hit, to prevent the area from being reinforced. As an indication of the scale of effort to enable the troops to deploy and secure their objectives, there were 641 sorties on the 25th and 300 on the 26th, before the weather began to

Above: Illustrating well the pleasing lines of late-production B-26s, this view shows a 586th Squadron G model (44-67835) doing what it was designed for on 25 March 1945. *Imperial War Museum*

deteriorate. As may well have been predicted, the conditions prevented any flying on 27 March.

As Allied troops continued to pour across the Rhine, the last V1 fell on English soil. Recognised as a failure, in that launchings never reached their planned peak number of firings, the flying-bomb offensive was terrifying to those on the receiving end and caused a not insubstantial lowering of civilian morale in London and its suburbs. In military terms a cheap and effective weapon *per se*, the V1 was a threat to which the Allied air forces had responded without delay and which they were instrumental in smashing.

The hundreds of sorties flown mainly but not exclusively by Marauders against the V-weapons sites contributed to one of the best bombing records returned by a single aircraft type during the war. Every group had several 'centenarians', and literally dozens of aircraft that had completed 50 missions — a situation speeded up by the short duration of 'Noball' sorties and their

frequency. It was natural enough that the long-serving Marauders would lead the field in the number of missions completed, but there were also many A-20s with high sortie rates, and several with over 100. The A-26s had not, of course, had as much time to pile up nearly as many missions as the others, but even they had a few score small black bomb silhouettes by the war's end.

Things improved to bring brighter weather on the 28th, enabling the Ninth to send out 215 bombers to attack an oil storage depot at Neuenheerse, among other targets. The entire Ninth remained on the ground on the 29th, before 337 bomber sorties took place over the front lines on the 30th. Among the targets was the repair depot at Bad Oeynhausen.

On 31 March the 322nd Bomb Group moved its Marauders into A-89 Le Culot, and the Ninth flew 550 combat sorties during the course of the day, visiting a marshalling yard, an oil-storage site at Erbach, and a 'defended town'. It is notable that, unlike some of the operations in 1944,

the mediums were attacking the majority of these targets only once. It was undoubtedly true that there were more aircraft involved than previously, but, if anything, the flak defences were heavier. Another reason was the improvement in bombing accuracy for which most commanders and crews strove to 'finish the job'.

There was an alternative feeling amongst the crews that some of the final missions — particularly the scale of some of them — were verging on the pointless. Near to total collapse, the Germans were offering little or no defence of some targets, which was another small but significant sign that continuing to attack them would incur needless casualties; it was crystal clear to US aircrew that their efforts would now make little difference. But the air war maintained its own momentum, and for the 9th Air Division it was the progress of the ground forces that had dictated its continuing deployment since June 1944. Until they stopped fighting, the Ninth would be there to provide support, however remote the actual battlefields may sometimes have seemed to the aircrews involved.

April '45

No flying was possible on 1 April, although the US First and Third Armies made further progress into the Ruhr region. On 3 April, 230 medium-bomber sorties were possible, with another 330 aircraft attacking an oil-storage depot, supplies and a marshalling yard on the 4th.

The 344th Bomb Group occupied A-78 Florennes/Juzaine on 5 April, the bad weather allowing a few extra hours free from combat flying for the group to settle in. No operations took place that day, but there were 99 sorties on the 6th as American troops began crossing the Weser. A further 268 medium-bomber sorties were flown on the 7th, when the targets were marshalling yards at Göttingen and Northeim in central Germany. Four aircraft were damaged in these operations.

There was a considerably larger effort the following day, when about 620 Marauders, Havocs and Invaders smashed at the three most important industries and services still operating in support of the German war effort — oil, communications and transport. The morning sorties saw the bombers release 843 tons for the loss of two aircraft and damage to no fewer than 44 from the flak, which was now highly concentrated around some of the more important targets in the 'shrinking perimeter' of German-held territory. The 323rd 'white tails' lost a single B-26 and had 14 others damaged for its part in the day's missions, which included an attack on Celle's marshalling yards by the 344th.

The afternoon mission of 8 April was to an oil refinery located at Nienhagen. The bombing brought spectacular results for a combined force of B-26s from the 387th, 394th and 397th Groups. Palls of smoke rose from the shattered oil-production centre, so much so that some bombardiers had trouble in locating their aiming-points. Other aircraft from this strong force of mediums bombed oil-storage depots at Münchenbernsdorf and a communications centre at Sondershausen, plus the Celle marshalling yards and various other targets located in urban areas of eight different cities.

The 386th Bomb Group's series of base changes brought it to A-92 St Trond, in Belgium, on 9 April, there being 700 effective sorties by Ninth tactical aircraft during the course of the day. Oil, rail and ordnance-dump targets were attacked by a force which was still composed mainly of Marauders but with an increasing number of A-26s. The tough Martin bomber carried out both of the 344th Group's missions to bomb a road bridge and marshalling yard at Saalfeld. The marshalling yards at Jena, as well as Saalfeld, oil storage at Bad Berka and Dedenhausen and ordnance depots at Naumburg and Amberg-Kummersbruck were the primaries, along with several targets of opportunity in those general areas. Much of the A-26 component of the force was in the hands of the 409th Group, which operated in company with the A-20s of the 410th to blitz the Saalfeld marshalling yards.

With the Invader winning its spurs over Europe, the Ninth was on the way to achieving standardisation on one medium and one attack bomber. The force would most likely have achieved complete replacement of the B-26 with Invaders, had the war lasted many more months. The A-20 remained in the hands of the 410th Group, as it would until the end, and the groups that had all but replaced it maintained a number of A-20Gs and Ks as bombardier lead ships. As related, it was the groups equipped with this type that were in most need of re-equipment — that, at least, was the view of the powers-that-be. Although some of the B-26 and A-20 crews disagreed quite vehemently at

Above: The first A-20 to complete 100 missions in the ETO was 'La France Libre' of the 416th Group. It was named and dedicated to the service of France at a ceremony at Le Bourget. *USAF*

Above: A-20J 43-9914 'Paula E', with well over 50 missions to her credit, disperses at one of the bases used by the 416th Bomb Group. *Merle Olmsted collection*

Below: A close-up of the name and scoreboard of A-20 'Paula E' reveals the second name 'Bootsie'. It was common for crews to paint the names of their loved-ones adjacent to their position in the aircraft. *Merle Olmsted collection*

Above: Good formation-flying was one of the keys to successful tactical bomber operations, as demonstrated by this Marauder box from the 597th Squadron, 397th BG. *Imperial War Museum*

first, the A-26 proved to be a more-than-suitable replacement for both types, considering how tactical operations had broadened to combine the basic rôles of both the older aircraft. Moves to have the Invader replace Marauders and Havocs quite late in the war engendered much discussion and 'shop talk' *vis à vis* the merits of the decision and of each aircraft that had equipped the Ninth. 'For' and 'against' views were freely aired and some opinions were changed with experience, but in general the crews approved of the modernisation of the Ninth's medium-bomber force.

Champion medium

Each combat group in the ETO believed it had its 'claims to fame', even if these were only modest and seemingly hardly relevant to outsiders. Some claims were more easy to prove, such as that of the aircraft that had

flown the most combat missions. All the B-26 groups had aircraft with individual bomb logs which reached impressive numbers, but the undisputed champion of all US bombers in Europe, including the heavies, was the battered old B-26 'Flak Bait'. Named all too appropriately, much to the consternation of its long-suffering but proud groundcrew, this B-26B seemed to attract flying steel on every sortie it flew, yet it completed no fewer than 202 missions with the 449th Squadron. There was no little irony in this tangible evidence of the faith placed in a potentially great aircraft by a few dedicated individuals, who refused to believe that a dog given a bad name had necessarily to be put down. The 'widow-maker' and hundreds of its kin had ensured that the most of the bereavement was on the other side.

Among the 423 tactical bomber sorties flown under fighter escort on 10 April was

the contribution made by the 391st Group, now fully converted to Invaders. Oil and ordnance depots at Leopoldshall, a rail bridge at Eger, a viaduct, marshalling yards and an 'industrial area' were included on the typically broad AAF target list for the spring of 1945. This was the first Invader mission for the 391st, and, in common with the other units that had made the transition, the crews appreciated that they had an excellent aircraft.

With 689 effective sorties on the 11th — the day the US Ninth Army reached the Elbe — the Ninth Air Force struck various targets at four locations, a truck plant and Aschersleben and Zwickau marshalling yards being included in the target list.

American servicemen around the world were saddened by the death of Franklin D. Roosevelt on 12 April. The President's clear-sighted support for Britain, for the judgements of his able field commanders and for the US war effort in general would ensure 'FDR' a place in history. Into his

Above: Ordnance depots in Germany were among the targets that absorbed many tons of bombs as the mediums went all-out to cripple the last pockets of resistance. This 597th Squadron B-26 was pounding a depot at Rudolstadt, 20 miles southeast of Erfurt, on 10 April 1945. *Imperial War Museum*

shoes stepped Harry S. Truman, the man whose name had been closely linked with the early trials and tribulations of the B-26. Whether the new President was informed that the bomber his committee had once tried to cancel was now one of the best in the Army Air Forces is not on record. It is almost certain that the new incumbent of the White House was not told that over 350 Marauders had completed 100 or more missions in the two European theatres of war. Rubbing in how misplaced the early criticism had proved to be was a B-26 irreverently named 'Truman Committee' belonging to the 322nd Group's 449th Squadron. Flying 189 missions in the conditions that prevailed in Europe was a fine accomplishment. Other crews were almost bound to latch onto the implied irony

of the senator's condemnation of 'their ship', and the 323rd Group had a B-26 that someone named 'Truman's Folly'.

The Third Army took Erfurt on the 12th and was just able to receive the air support it needed for that task; the mediums bombed ordnance storage at Kempten before a two-day 'bad weather' grounding order came into force. Flight operations were resumed on the 15th, 258 aircraft going to five marshalling yards and several targets of opportunity.

On 16 April the 391st Group's A-26s arrived at Y-29 Asch in Belgium, and the day's air operations included about 450 sorties against various types of target. Part of the German communications network was attacked at Zerbst, as was the marshalling yard at Wittenburg.

The 17th saw the mediums out in force again, this time over Magdeburg; the primary target was a marshalling yard at Tubingen, along with three ordnance depots. Such was the nature of the German defence during these last weeks of fighting that the mediums were in effect indulging in area bombing, albeit on a limited scale. Denying the enemy his carefully-hoarded but dwindling oil and fuel supplies was the intended end result of many heavy- and medium-bomber sorties during this stage of the war. Such locations — small storage areas and tank farms — were more modest than the big German refineries which had by then taken a huge pasting from the Eighth and Fifteenth Air Force heavy bombers.

Among the aircraft despatched on 17 April was the veteran 322nd Group Marauder that led all others in terms of missions flown, for the day marked the 200th mission for 'Flak Bait'.

On 18 April the tactical bombers flew nearly 600 sorties to destroy an oil-storage depot at Neuburg. In addition, two marshalling yards — one located at Jüterbog — and two rail junctions were hit. In the face of worsening weather on the 19th, the Ninth's tactical effort was a more modest 375 sorties. Primary targets were located in the city of Donauwörth, and part of this force also attacked three more marshalling yards as well as targets of opportunity.

For crews of the 387th Bomb Group, the 19 April sorties turned out to be their last, and it was clear that, with US ground troops in Leipzig and Halle, the war had but days to run. Flak emplacements were included in the tactical target list for 20 April, a force of 562 mediums additionally attacking two oil depots, two ordnance depots — including that at Straubing — and two more marshalling yards.

Jet combat

For the Ninth Air Division, the run to the marshalling yards at Memmingen on the 20th was to be memorable — for not quite the reasons the participating crews expected. Marauders of the 323rd, 394th and 397th Groups were involved in this part of the day's operations — a 'maximum effort', as decreed by the high command. Compliance with this order led to a train of events which resulted in losses for the 323rd Group, which, along with the others, was obliged to scrape up 'everything that could fly' to mount the mission. One pilot, 1st Lt James Vining of the 454th Squadron, was chagrined to have to fly a B-26F-1 (42-96256) named 'Ugly Duckling', borrowed from the 454th Squadron, which was in less than 'A1' condition. Still, there would be little to worry about — hadn't the briefing officer mentioned that the Russians were in Berlin and the Luftwaffe fighter force was finished?

After take-off, the group assembled for the run across the Rhine southwest of Stuttgart and into southern Germany. En route, the bombers were tracked by German radar which passed the co-ordinates to a control room at Feldkirchen, which in turn scrambled 15 Me262s of Jagdverbande 44 from München-Reim airfield.

As the 323rd's Marauders approached their IP, 12,000ft over Kempten, where some of the same group aircraft had blasted an ammunition depot four days

previously, the box formations spread out. This enabled single flights to bomb the target in trail.

With the last flight coming in low at around 4,000ft, the light 20mm and 40mm flak opened up. Trying to ignore it, the bombardiers settled into what would be a four-minute bomb run. Then someone yelled: 'Fighters coming in from the rear!'

The jets swept in, cannon blazing, and the B-26 gunners responded. But the long range of the 30mm guns in the Me262 could be devastating if the pilot had judged the high closing-speed correctly. At the controls of the B-26B-30 (41-31918/RJ-R) named 'Can't Get Started', 1st Lt Dale E. Sanders felt the thud of cannon shells moments before his left engine began smoking heavily. The Marauder started to fall out of formation but kept flying, and later there was an attempt by the crew to abandon it, although only one parachute was seen.

Meanwhile, in the pilot's seat of 'Ugly Duckling', James Vining braced for the collision he felt certain must come as three Me262s swept through his close formation, barely missing two Marauders as they went. One jet, piloted by Uffz Eduard Schallmoser, did make contact with the B-26G (44-68109/WT-M) flown by 1st Lt James M. Hansen of the 456th Squadron. The German Experte had struck the propellers of the lead B-26, and his aircraft spun away, shedding pieces of its rudder and pursued by enthusiastic machine-gun fire from Vining's ship and other B-26s. Vining himself fired a burst from his package guns which, he was amazed to see, actually hit the falling jet. Schallmoser managed to bail out, to land by no small coincidence in the grounds of his parents' house!

Better fortune attended the aircraft Schallmoser had rammed. Despite the German pilot's belief that he had shot it down, Hansen was able to fly the B-26 home to Denain, experiencing little adverse effect from the damage which, unbeknownst to the crew, was restricted to the tips of the propeller blade on the starboard engine. These had been bent back so uniformly that the engine revolutions were hardly affected.

An aircraft such as the Me262 really needed what came to be known later as 'stand off' weapons when attacking bombers flying at half its speed. Lacking a true air-to-air missile, it had the unguided R4M rocket as a useful substitute, and

Uffz 'Johnny' Müller proceeded to demonstrate how effective this weapon could be. Catching up with the same 323rd B-26 formation over Kempten some time after Schallmoser, he fired his R4Ms into the formation. Two Marauders fell away.

Having wounded among the crew, including Vining himself, the damaged 'Duckling' headed for home. Later, another group of Me262 pilots spotted the aircraft and, sensing an easy kill, made a pass. But this was no defenceless cripple: blazing away at the jets, the Marauder's gunners were determined to sell their lives dearly — an aggressive stance that paid off. The jets sheered off, chased now by P-51s, which had come upon the scene at just the right moment. Staggering away from the scene of battle the 'Duckling' later cracked up in a crash-landing, with, sadly, one fatal casualty.

Some USAAF groups were then already in the process of winding down their combat operations as the number of worthwhile targets dwindled away. But for other groups the war went on. On 21 April the Ninth Air Division sent 121 A-26s and A-20s to drop 239 tons of bombs on the marshalling yard at Attnang-Puchheim — an action which effectively closed the line between Vienna and southern Germany. On the ropes though the enemy was, the Allies dared not relax their guard totally, as there were rumours that the southern area harboured Hitler's redoubt. A heavily-fortified and fanatically-defended 'last ditch' bastion of the Reich would have been quite in keeping with the Nazi creed, and, although it turned out to be a myth (much to the relief of Allied commanders), this was unknown at the time. Only when the threat failed to materialise was it realised that the rumours had no foundation.

A more tangible threat to bomber crews was the remaining elements of the Luftwaffe's jet interceptor force which — under the dire circumstances of reduced fuel supply, a shortage of well-trained pilots, and operational airfields that were constantly blasted by heavy and medium bombers and strafed by American 'Jabos' — still posed a threat.

The area that the jets were pledged to defend had become squeezed between Bavaria and the southernmost parts of eastern Europe. From the AAF's perspective, that area had shrunk to the point where, in terms of bomber targets,

Above: Adopting a black instead of white rudder stripe, due to their natural metal finish, the A-26s of the 416th group did sterling work in the last months of the war. This machine, 43-22385, named 'Bula', hailed from the 668th BS. *Author's collection*

the previously separate MTO and ETO theatres had all but merged. Twelfth Air Force and 1st Tactical Air Force medium-bomber groups were now being briefed to attack targets in the same general areas as those allocated to the Ninth's bombers.

The Ninth was grounded by bad weather on 22 and 23 April, but, on the 24th, 172 tactical bombers attacked an oil depot at Schrobenhausen, as well as Landau aerodrome. The 386th, 409th and 416th Groups sent a strong force of A-26s, while the 322nd, 344th and 391st contributed their Marauders and the 410th its A-20s. Four pathfinder Marauders accompanied the force, as did 'Window' ships. Landau had recently been vacated by the Me262s of II./KG 51 — a fact known to US intelligence. There was an attempt at interception by Me262s but this was inconclusive, there being no losses from the day's American bomber sorties. The mission itself, hampered somewhat by

Above: At the point of 'bombs away' on 20 April 1945, an A-26 from a second 386th BG box wades through light flak over the target. *USAF*

Above: Out to grass in their hundreds, the B-26s were quickly disposed of once the shooting war had stopped. These 387th Group aircraft were at Beek (Maastricht) early in 1945 and outlasted many of their kin. J V. Crow

10/10 cloud cover, was a mediocre effort, the 280 tons of bombs dropped in 164 effective sorties doing little further damage, according to subsequent reports.

Only the 323rd and 344th Groups could really claim to have gone out with a bang, following their clash with Me262s. Other Marauder formations from the Twelfth Air Force had clashed with the jets of JV 44, led by the redoubtable Gen-Lt Adolf Galland, who was himself shot down.

On the 25th, the 344th attacked Erding aerodrome in company with the 323rd, the bombing by 96 Marauders (48 from each unit) being described as 'excellent'. For a change, there was no flak, but the 323rd crews did experience a German response in the form of an attempted Me262 interception. Most eye-witnesses saw only the one jet, fitted with a 50mm MK 214 nose cannon. This bizarre adaptation of a tank gun for aerial use was intended (perhaps optimistically) to bring down bombers with very few rounds. It looked to the American crews like a 'flying telephone pole', and the bomber gunners opened up with everything they had to deter it. This ruse was successful and the strange aircraft stayed out of range and was not seen to open fire. The Marauders carried out their aerodrome attack, few of the crews realising that this was the last time they would be called upon to earn their pay in this fashion. Erding disappeared under a

cauldron of bomb-bursts, and the crews claimed to have destroyed seven aircraft and several buildings, as well as thoroughly cratering the runway.

To ram home the fact that Germany was now all but defeated, one of the major factors in bringing about that situation had also completed its task by 25 April. That was the day that the Eighth Air Force was also stood down.

Those who cared to dwell on the implications of the final jet encounters realised that the future had, at the eleventh hour, caught up and overtaken events. Their existence all but rendered conventional bombers, powered by piston engines, obsolete. It hardly mattered that the promise of the warplane powered by one or more turbojets was never really fufilled in operational terms by the Germans. Ingenious though their scientists were, their efforts tended to be dissipated across too wide a range of projects. And, as is well known, politics and poor strategy probably militated more against the correct deployment of German's advanced weapons than did the Allies. But none of those things detracted from the fundamental strides made in aerodynamics, various forms of jet and rocket propulsion, and new systems such as ejector seats and air-to-air missiles. All these and more had now made the wartime bomber fleets — the 'old guard' — fit only to be expended as drones,

hacks and transports. It was a shock and, to many, really quite sad — but progress cares little for sentiment.

With US forces having crossed the Danube at Regensburg by 26 April, the air war continued to wind down; the remaining medium-bomber groups on combat duty went to Plattling, the 391st, 409th and 416th fielding a 125-strong force of Marauders and Invaders to plaster the aerodrome as part of the plan to neutralise as many German jet fighters on the ground. Once again, no flak came up as the bombers passed over.

A four-day weather-induced grounding brought the calendar around to one of the final acts of the war — the suicide of Adolf Hitler, on 30 April. The day before that momentous event, the 387th Group took its B-26s into Y-44 Maastricht (Beek) aerodrome, but no more missions went on the board for the 'tiger tail' group.

May '45

On 1 May, clearer weather allowed the Ninth to return to action, A-26s attacking a munitions factory at Stod in Czechoslovakia. The weather caused another grounding on 2 May — to the very last, the elements remained one of the most effective antidotes to tactical air operations.

On 3 May it really was the end of the war as far as the 9th Air Division was concerned. Fittingly perhaps, the oldest and newest bombers in the command flew the final sorties, the mission being a return visit to Stod. Eight B-26 pathfinders of the 1st PS led in 130 A-26s from the 391st, 409th and 416th Groups, the 391st's contribution being 30 Invaders, including two equipped with 'Shoran' to determine the precise point of bomb-release for the entire formation. The unopposed mission, like several preceding it, was something of an anti-climax, as the final bombs to fall from tactical bombers onto an enemy target in the ETO dropped away at 12.02hrs. There were no American crew casualties, and there was no aircraft damage, and little in the way of drama.

On 4 May 1945 the 9th Air Division was ordered to stand down, mere hours before the surrender of all German forces in the West was agreed, effective 08.00hrs on the 5th. For eight medium- and three light-bombardment groups, the job they had come halfway round the world to do was complete.

Above: The most famous B-26 of them all, 'Flak Bait' formates with a B-26G from the 449th Bomb Squadron. *Imperial War Museum*

Right: With the big red bomb saying more than words ever could, the champion Marauder of the ETO is pictured in Belgium in May 1945. Considering how apt the name proved to be, it was a miracle that the aircraft survived — and even more amazing that it was preserved for posterity. *J. V. Crow*

Above: Not as lucky as 'Flak Bait' and other B-26 centenarians, 'Bar Fly' went home only to crash during a Stateside flight. *J. Bivens*

Above: The nose of the aircraft was severed forward of the wing, while the fuselage snapped just aft of it. *J. Bivens*

Reflections

With peace, there was time to compile the facts and figures of the enormous air effort that had been necessary to secure the final, unconditional surrender of Nazi Germany. Such compilations were not merely public-relations exercises but important analytical data that would go towards planning the requirements for the strength of postwar air forces. Little did the personnel who put such material together realise that an air war on the scale of that between the years 1939 and 1945 would soon appear to be all but impossible.

As the enormous task of clearing up and rebuilding began in Europe, the war with Japan was still raging, and 'low time' ETO crews anticipated a possible transfer to the Pacific. Just three months after Germany surrendered, the awesome destructive power of the atomic bomb suddenly indicated that the outcome of any future conflict might very well be decided by just a few dozen bombers (probably less), rather than the thousands that had been necessary to win the recent air war. This new age did not detract from that achievement, and, as (in many respects) tactical airpower was to be the sole survivor of all the bombing policies executed in WW2, the figures on medium bombing were worthy of close scrutiny.

When the United States Strategic Bombing Survey had completed its deliberations on the conduct of the air war, there were a number of criticisms of the European campaigns: some important targets were not attacked early enough in the conflict, while others, such as bridges, V-weapons sites and forts, absorbed a disproportionate tonnage of bombs before being completely destroyed. With hindsight, many of the criticisms were probably valid. It had, however, been almost impossible for tactical commanders to evaluate thoroughly every call on close-support bombing during the war, particularly with an operational schedule as demanding as that faced by the Ninth Air Force from the day it began operations. It became standard procedure to call in the bombers if other methods of clearing obstacles had failed, despite the fact that broken buildings and piles of rubble occasionally offered superior defensive positions when the smoke and dust had settled. This was a known drawback, but one that was viewed as acceptable if it helped maintain the momentum of an offensive and enabled the ground forces to gain territory with fewer casualties.

Mission records

As far as the Ninth Air Force was concerned, it was natural that a number of groups would emerge as the 'top scorers' in the mission stakes, and it came as no surprise that the four original B-26 Marauder groups which had joined the Eighth Air Force prior to transfer to the Ninth had flown the most. In first place was the original group to arrive in England, the 322nd, which had completed 428. Joint second place was shared by the 323rd and 386th, with 409 each, followed by the 387th, which had flown 393. Fewer missions had understandably been undertaken by the trio of A-20 light-bomber groups, which had been in action for a shorter period of time. But, by coming in during the hectic spring of 1944, the Havoc crews were able to complete a high number of missions in an extremely short period of time. Of these, the 410th (the longest user of the A-20) completed 262 missions before the end of hostilities, by which time the group was in the process of converting to the A-26.

Throughout their combat period in the ETO, all groups had been hampered by the weather, and it is undoubtedly true that

Below: The 386th Group's 'Rat Poison' was one of many Marauders that triumphed over the flak more than 100 times, it and many others confounding the critics who thought the B-26 should be withdrawn from USAAF service. *Imperial War Museum*

Above: Showing off their elegant lines, A-26s of the 416th Group's 669th Squadron head out to a target in 1945. Interestingly, although the Invader entered service months after D-Day, two aircraft in this flight have lower-fuselage 'invasion stripes', probably to dissuade friendly gunners from opening fire on them. *USAF*

every unit would have had higher figures had operating conditions been more favourable. Of the three aircraft used, the Martin B-26 had gained an immortal place in aviation's 'hall of fame' as one of the best bombers of all time. Arguably just conceding first place in the all-round versatility stakes to the B-25 Mitchell, the Marauder did its basic job as well as any other aircraft in its class, and better than most. And, on the highly subjective topic of aesthetics, few other military aircraft ever looked as good as Martin's finest.

The A-20 was another excellent aircraft, but one that found its rôle somewhat compromised by the nature of the air war in Europe — indeed, the entire attack-bomber concept was perforce modified by conditions in the theatre. The type did very well to meet the challenge effectively.

The Invader turned in an exemplary record in the short time it had been in action in Europe. Statistics on the air war included the fact that Invaders had suffered a very low rate of loss per sortie. Though it was a latecomer, the A-26 more than returned the investment made in it. And with WW2 experience behind it, the Douglas twin went on to win even greater glory in postwar conflicts as the last piston-engined medium/attack bomber deployed by the United States.

In Europe, the tactical bombers had flown the following sorties:

TABLE 2

Aircraft	sorties	bombs (tons)	combat losses	enemy aircraft 'kills' (claimed)
B-26 Marauder	129,943	169,382	911	402
A-20 Havoc	39,492	31,856	265	11
A-26 Invader	11,567	18,054	67	0
Totals	181,002	219,292	1,243	413

NB: It is assumed that the above listing includes both IX and XII Air Force figures for the mediums.

(Source: Wagner, Ray: *American Combat Planes*. Macdonald, London, 1960)

A further source puts the total figure for Ninth Air Force bomber losses between 1943 and 1945 at 805; the huge effort to conclude the Central Europe Campaign (25 March to 8 May 1945) required 9,409 bomber sorties for the loss of 44 aircraft. During that period the command claimed widespread destruction of and damage to all forms of transport as well as fixed targets. In the 'destroyed' category were 725 tanks and AFVs, 180 dumps, 1,606 locomotives and 8,906 items of rolling stock. In addition, 656 rail cuts were made. It is emphasised that the above effort was achieved by both bombers and fighters, but the figures give an indication

of the intensity of the fighting. Also significant are the bomber gunners' claims for enemy aircraft — just three confirmed, with two 'damaged' and four 'probables'.

To determine accuracy of bombing, the Operational Research Section of the Ninth Air Division diligently maintained records and statistics which showed what each of the 11 groups achieved. Although the personnel in each unit reckoned to belong to 'the best damn' bomb group in the world', these charts often qualified such a statement. For May 1944 to March 1945, the division's average percentage of bombs falling within 500ft of the aiming point worked out at 30.6%. Of all the groups, the 410th came out best (with just over 40%), with the 391st second (34%) and the 416th third (32%). In fourth place was the 394th (31%), all the others being just on or below the average mark of 30% for the 10-month period.

The gradual improvement in bomb-aiming was shown by a further statistical summary for March 1945. The monthly average had by then risen to 37.3%, and, of all the groups, the 410th was way ahead, with over 50%. The 322nd, 387th, and 394th achieved an accuracy rate in the mid-forties range, with the 322nd and 387th tying for second place. No other groups were able to reach 40%. If at first glance these figures look a little disappointing, it should be remembered that overall bombing averages could be adversely affected by a few rough missions — the figures certainly did not mean that the groups that failed to make the top five places regularly returned worse results than those that did.

Gen Anderson was fulsome in his praise for the 410th Group, which achieved the best-ever bombing in April 1945. A total of 65 'superior' or 'excellent' bombing ratings were attained, which was impressive by any

Although it enjoyed a very low attrition rate, the A-26 was as vulnerable to a direct flak hit as any other aircraft. This 642nd Squadron aircraft is unlikely to have pulled out of a dive with half of one wing blasted away. *Imperial War Museum*

Above: Why anyone would name an A-20 'The Feather' is a mystery known only to the pilot or groundcrewman who chose it. The aircraft, an A-20G (43-9221), clearly served the 416th well, judging by the lengthy bomb log. A thin sharkmouth is also painted on the nose. *Merle Olmsted collection*

standard. Commenting on the reliability of the A-20s the 410th flew, the commanding general stated that in 9,648 sorties the group had had to contend with only 185 mechanical failures.

Occupation duty

With no further calls on their ability to cause destruction, personnel of the USAAF medium- and light-bomber groups prepared to return home. Most would leave their unwanted aircraft behind to be scrapped in Germany, because there were now far too many of them, and relatively few examples of the older piston-engined bombers would be required in the future. In the early months of peace, a massive rationalisation of the US armed forces began, resulting in a mass cull of unwanted B-26s and A-20s, which were scrapped in large numbers in Germany. Only the A-26 was given a place in the attack/ light-bomber units that remained.

Some of the 9th Air Division groups remained in existence for a short period to maintain a presence in Germany, where the AAF earmarked certain units for occupational duty. The 387th was not part of that set-up for long; having flown no

Below: It was relatively rare for B-26s to include aircraft kills in their scoreboards, as there were few clashes with enemy fighters, but 'Sneezy' has one. *J. V. Crow*

missions from Maastricht, the group flew its B-26s back to France on 28 May to set up home at B-87 Rosières-en-Santerre, near Amiens. Educational courses were introduced and a relaxed schedule of training begun. No-one knew for sure whether the 387th was bound for service as a reserve unit in the US or as a combat group in the Pacific. A routine was established, despite the continual loss of personnel as options to return to the States were taken up by individuals who had completed their tours.

Fortunately, at Rosières, unlike some of the other bases, there was little in the way of repairs to be done: the base's previous French and German occupants had left the runways and taxiways — as well as the living quarters — in good shape.

As one of the few remaining groups still operating Marauders, the 387th began to inherit some aircraft made surplus by other groups which were being deactivated or were re-equipping with the A-26. Some interesting markings combinations appeared on these Marauders when the group painted

Above: Peaceful flying over Germany was enjoyed by many air and ground crews while the AAF groups remained in Europe on occupation duty. One such flight was undertaken in August 1945 by the 344th Group's 'Little Eve'. *J. V. Crow*

Above: Another sightseeing flight was being enjoyed by the crew of an A-26C (43-22486) of the 495th BS, 344th Bomb Group, in August or September 1945. The group re-equipped with Invaders after the war. *J. V. Crow*

Above: Only on the point of converting to the A-26 from the A-20 when the war finished, the 410th took its Invaders home. This example, an A-26B-45 from the 646th Squadron, was at Pittsburgh on 10 December 1945. *R. Francillon*

Below: Many early-model B-26s undertook numerous second-line duties after the war, this example being at Gosselies/Charleroi, Belgium, in 1945. It appears to have the fuselage code 'Z-118', and retains AEAF stripes around the wings and fuselage. *J. V. Crow*

Above: Although it has 'Flak Bait' in storage, the USAF Museum at Dayton, Ohio, acquired an ex-French Air Force B-26G for public display. Some years ago it was painted in the colours of the 387th Bomb Group as a tribute to all those who served in B-26 units in Europe. *Air Force Museum*

its black and yellow 'tiger stripe' band over the symbols that had formerly identified other groups of the Ninth. Some B-26s also came from the groups that had once been based further afield, as the Twelfth Air Force had stood down its medium-bomber groups at much the same time. But, as mentioned, the two fronts had virtually become one as the Germans were squeezed into an ever-smaller area of Europe.

Personnel rotations home by thousands of individuals who had accumulated the required number of 'points' stripped many groups of almost all their experienced crews. Some units ceased to exist shortly

after the cessation of hostilities, and there were some seemingly-strange decisions made at the top. The 391st Group's 574th Squadron was uprooted in its entirety and changed for another complete squadron (the 643rd from the 409th Group) which was given the B-26 unit's old number. Its personnel were consequently alien to any 'old hands' from the group's other constituent squadrons, although the purpose was sound in that the

newcomers were crews fully trained to use 'Shoran', which was an official AAF requirement at the time. Selected groups which had been part of the Ninth Air Force remained in Germany for some months on occupation duty. Those remaining in Europe after the end of 1945 became part of a different command structure, as the Ninth was officially deactivated in December.

Appendices

Appendix One

Operational debut dates for units of the 3rd Bomb Wing, Eighth Air Force; IX Bomber Command; 9th Bombardment Division; 9th Air Division

15th Bomb Sqn (Light) (Boston)	29 June 1942 to 2 Oct 1942 (Molesworth/Podington); to 12th AAF, 13 Nov 1942
322nd Bomb Group (B-26)	14 May 1943 (Bury St Edmunds/Andrews Field/Earls Colne)
323rd Bomb Group (B–26)	16 July 1943 (Earls Colne/Beaulieu)
386th Bomb Group (B-26/A-26)	29 July 1943 (Boxted/Great Dunmow)
387th Bomb Group (B-26)	15 Aug 1943 (Chipping Ongar/Stoney Cross)
391st Bomb Group (B-26/A-26)	16 Feb 1944 (Matching)
1st Pathfinder Sqn (Provisional) (B-26)	21 Feb 1944 (Andrews Field)
416th Bomb Group (L) (A-20/A-26)	3 Mar 1944 (Wethersfield)
344th Bomb Group (B-26)	6 Mar 1944 (Stansted Mountfitchet)
394th Bomb Group (B-26)	23 Mar 1944 (Boreham/Holmsley South)
409th Bomb Group (L) (A-20/A-26)	13 Apr 1944 (Little Walden)
397th Bomb Group (B-26)	20 Apr 1944 (Rivenhall)
410th Bomb Group (L) (A-20)	1 May 1944 (Gosfield/Rivenhall/Hurn)
155th Night Photo Squadron (F-3A/A-20)	20 May 1944 (Chalgrove)
25th Bomb Group (R) (B-26) 654th BS only	10/11 Aug 1944 (Watton)

Identifying Code Letters and Nicknames for Ninth Air Force Bomb Groups

1st Pathfinder Sqn (P): – IH

322nd Bomb Group ('Nye's Annihilators'):
449th BS – PN
450th BS – ER
451st BS – SS
452nd BS – DR

323rd Bomb Group ('White Tails'):
453rd BS – VT
454th BS – RJ
455th BS – YU
456th BS – WT

344th Bomb Group ('Silver Streaks'):
494th BS – K9
495th BS – Y5
496th BS – N3
497th BS – 7I

386th Bomb Group ('Crusaders'):
552nd BS – RG
553rd BS – AN
554th BS – RU
555th BS – YA

387th Bomb Group ('Tiger Stripe'):
556th BS – FW
557th BS – KS
558th BS – KX
559th BS – TQ

391st Bomb Group ('Black Death'):
572nd BS – P2
573rd BS – T6
574th BS – 4L
575th BS – O8

394th Bomb Group ('Bridge Busters'*):
584th BS – K5
585th BS – 4T
586th BS – H9
587th BS – 5W

397th Bomb Group ('Bridge Busters'*):
596th BS – X2
597th BS – 9F
598th BS – U2
599th BS – 6B

409th Bomb Group (Light):
640th BS – W5
641st BS – 7G
642nd BS – D6
643rd BS – 5I

410th Bomb Group (L) ('Beaty's Raiders'):
644th BS – 5D
645th BS – 7X
646th BS – 8U
647th BS – 6Q

416th Bomb Group (L):
668th BS – 5H
669th BS – 2A
670th BS – F6
671st BS – 5C

* A number of groups either claimed this title or had it bestowed upon them by the press, and, although all groups had a legitimate claim to it, those listed appeared to identify with it more than the others. Common usage of such nicknames during the war varied to a considerable degree.

Continental Bases (in order of Group Movement)

(B)	Belgium
(F)	France
(G)	Germany
(H)	Netherlands (Holland)

387th BG to A-15 Cherbourg/Maupertius (F), 22 Aug 1944;
to A-39 Châteaudun (F), 18 Sept 1944;
to A-71 Clastres (F), 30 Oct 1944;
to Y-44 Maastrict/Beek (H), 4 May 1945;
to A-98 Rosières-en-Santerre (F), 30 May 1945;
to USA, Nov 1945; deactivated 17 Nov 1945

394th BG to A-13 Tour-en-Bessin (F), 25 Aug 1944;
to A-50 Orléans/Bricy (F), 28 Sept 1944;
to A-74 Cambrai/Niergnies (F), 8 Oct 1944;
to Y-55 Venlo (H), 2 May 1945;
to R-6 Kitzingen (G), Oct 1945;
to USA, Dec 1945; deactivated 31 Mar 1946

323rd BG to A-20 Lessy (F), 26 Aug 1944;
to A-40 Chartres (F), 21 Sept 1944;
to A-69 Laon/Athies (F), 13 Oct 1944;
to A-83 Denain/Prouvy (F), 9 Feb 1945;
to R-77 Gablingen (G), 15 May 1945;
to R-78 Landsberg (G), 16 July 1945;
to A-71 Clastres (F), Oct 1945;
to USA, Dec 1945; deactivated 12 Dec 1945

397th BG to A-26 Gorges (F), 28 Aug 1944;
to A-41 Dreux (F), 11 Sept 1944;
to A-72 Péronne (F), 6 Oct 1944;
to Y-55 Venlo (H), 25 Apr 1945;
to A-72 Péronne (F), 30 May 1945;
to USA, Dec 1945; deactivated 6 Jan 1946

409th BG to A-48 Bretigny (F), 18 Sept 1944;
to A-70 Laon/Couvron (F), 12 Feb 1945;
to USA, 25 April 1945; deactivated 7 Nov 1945

391st BG to A-73 Roye/Amy (F), 19 Sept 1944;
to Y-29 Asch (B), 20 Apr 1945;
to B-50 Vitry-en-Artois (F), 1 June 1945;
to USA, 25 Oct 1945; deactivated 25 Nov 1945

416th BG to A-55 Melun/Villaroche (F), 21 Sept 1944;
to A-69 Laon/Athies (F), 10 Feb 1945;
to A-59 Cormeilles-en-Vexin (F), 25 May 1945;
to A-69 Laon/Athies (F), 27 July 1945;
to USA, 13 Sept 1945; deactivated 24 Oct 1945

410th BG to A-58 Coulommiers/Voisins (F), 27 Sept 1944;
to A-68 Juvincourt (F), 9 Feb 1945;
to A-60 Beaumont-sur-Oise (F), 22 May 1945;
to USA, 25 June 1945; deactivated 7 Nov 1945

322nd BG to A-61 Beauvais/Tille (F), 29 Sept 1944;
to A-89 Le Culot (B), 30 Mar 1944;
to Y-86 Fritzlar (G), June 1945;
to A-71 Clastres (F), Oct 1945;
to USA, Nov 1945; deactivated 15 Dec 1945

344th BG to A-59 Cormeilles-en-Vexin (F), 30 Sept 1944;
to A-78 Florennes/Juzaine (B), 5 Apr 1945;
to R-75 Schleißheim (G), 15 Sept 1945;
to USA, Dec 1945; deactivated 15 Feb 1946

386th BG to A-60 Beaumont-sur-Oise (F), 2 Oct 1944;
to A-92 St Trond (B), 9 Apr 1945;
to USA, 27 July 1945; deactivated 7 Nov 1945

155th NPS to Rennes (F), c10 Aug 1944, thereafter operating from Châteaudun (F), Le Culot (B) and Maastricht (H) to Apr 1945; to Kassel, Darmstadt, Fürth and Furstenfeldbruck (all G) to 25 Mar 1949, when deactivated

1st PF Sqn (P) to A-61 Beauvais/Tille (F), 24 Sept 1944;
to A-72 Péronne (F), c1 Jan 1945;
to Y-55 Venlo (H), spring (?) 1945; deactivated in theatre, Apr 1945

NB:
'To USA' could mean movement of a complete unit, personnel without aircraft, or deactivation in theatre.

The coded classification of continental airfields was as follows:

A primarily used by USAAF units
B usually used by British units
R usually captured bases used by Allied air forces in Germany
Y new sequence for continental airfields when 'A series' had reached 99

Bibliography

Austin, Lambert D.: *344th Bomb Group (M) 'Silver Streaks'*; Southern Heritage Press, St Petersburg, Florida, 1996

Birdsall, Steve: *B-26 Marauder in Action*; Squadron/Signal Publications, Carrollton, Texas, 1981

Breihan, John R.; Piet, Stan, and Mason, Roger S.: *Martin Aircraft 1909-1960*; Narkiewicz/Thompson, Santa Ana, California, 1995

Destiche, Robert J.: *The History of the 559th Bomb Squadron, 387th Group (M) in World War II*; Insty Prints, Shreveport, Louisiana, 2000

Ducellier, Jean-Pierre: *La Guerre Aérienne dans le Nord de la France*, (March to August 1944 – five volumes); Abbeville 1994-1999

Freeman, Roger A.: *B-26 Marauder at War*; Ian Allan, Shepperton, Surrey, 1978

Freeman, Roger A : *Mighty Eighth War Diary*; Jane's, London, 1981

Freeman, Roger A : *The Ninth Air Force in Colour*; Arms and Armour Press, London, 1995

Francis, Devon: *Flak Bait: The Story of the Men Who Flew the Martin Marauders*; Duell, Sloan & Pearce, 1948

Havenener, J. K.: *The Martin B-26 Marauder*; TAB Books Inc, Blue Ridge Summit, Philadelphia, 1988

Hamelin, John F.: *Support and Strike!*; GMS Enterprises, Peterborough, 1991

Ivie, Tom: *Aerial Reconnaissance — The 10th Photo Recon Group in WWII*; Aero Publishers, California, 1981

Lipkis, Leon G.: *451st Bombardment Squadron*; privately published, USA

Maurer, Maurer: *Air Force Combat Units of World War II*; Franklin Watts, New York. 1963

Maurer, Maurer: *Combat Squadrons of the Air Force*; USAF Historical Division, Washington, 1969

Mesko, Jim: *A-20 Havoc in Action*; Squadron/Signal Publications, Carrollton, Texas, 1983 and 1994

Mesko, Jim: *A-26 Invader in Action*; Squadron/Signal Publications, Carrollton, Texas, 1980 and 1993

Moench, John O.: *Marauder Men*; Malia Enterprises, Inc, Longwood, Florida, 1989

Scutts, Jerry: *B-26 Marauder Units of the 8th and 9th Air Forces*; Osprey Publishing, London, 1997

Stovall, Jack D., Jr: *Tales of the Marauders, vol II*; Wings of Courage Press, Cordova, Tennessee, 1994

Traynor, Thomas A.: *The 410th Bombardment Group in World War II*; Avery Color Studios, AuTrain, Michigan, 1987

Walker, Hugh, and Newman, Richard: *391st Bombardment Group History, WWII*; 391st Bomb Group Reunion Committee, USA, 1974

Young, Barnett B.: *The Story of the Crusaders*; 386th Bomb Group Association, Fort Myers, Florida, 1988

Ziegler, J. Guy: Bridge Busters: *The Story of the 394th Bomb Group*; Ganis and Harris, New York, 1993

Index